Praise for the Carey Brothers and Home Remodeling For Dummies

"If you are in the mood to remodel, before you hire a contractor, hire Jim and Morris Carey. This book is easy to understand, puts you way ahead of the curve, and your friends will never say you're just a bubble left to plum."

— Chuck Woolery, television personality

"For anyone just thinking about remodeling a home in any way, STOP everything and go directly to your nearest bookstore where you will find this extraordinarily informative book that covers every question anyone might have — the directness and simplicity of the writing makes it a joy to read!"

— Cristina Ferrare, model

"The Carey Brothers are no strangers to this field. James and Morris Carey are 3rd generation contractors and specialists in residential remodeling. This book should be required for homeowners on a budget."

— Stan Kohler, Associated Press Graphics

"James and Morris Carey are two of the most down-to-earth, credible individuals I have ever worked with. They made the task of working around the house simple and understandable. Their book is perfect for the anti-handyman who has a fear of hammers and saws."

— Bob Agnew, Operations Manager, Program Director KNBR Radio

"*Home Remodeling For Dummies* not only helps do-it-yourselfers, but it benefits people like me who are hire-it-outers. After reading James' and Morris Carey's book, I know how to plan, stay within a budget, find sensible financing, and obtain bids on a project. I have a 50-year-old home, so I know I will use this book as a guide for my future remodeling needs."

— Eugenia Chapman, author of *Clean Your House and Everything In It* and *Find Your House and Everything In It*

"*Home Remodeling For Dummies* is a must-read for anyone who buys a fixer-upper. The Carey Brothers explain exactly how to turn a dump into your dream home."

— Ray Brown, co-author of *Home Buying For Dummies* and *House Selling For Dummies*

 ™

References for the Rest of Us!™

BESTSELLING BOOK SERIES

Do you find that traditional reference books are overloaded with technical details and advice you'll never use? Do you postpone important life decisions because you just don't want to deal with them? Then our *...For Dummies*® business and general reference book series is for you.

...For Dummies business and general reference books are written for those frustrated and hard-working souls who know they aren't dumb, but find that the myriad of personal and business issues and the accompanying horror stories make them feel helpless. *...For Dummies* books use a lighthearted approach, a down-to-earth style, and even cartoons and humorous icons to dispel fears and build confidence. Lighthearted but not lightweight, these books are perfect survival guides to solve your everyday personal and business problems.

> *"More than a publishing phenomenon, 'Dummies' is a sign of the times."*
>
> — *The New York Times*

> *"A world of detailed and authoritative information is packed into them..."*
>
> — *U.S. News and World Report*

> *"...you won't go wrong buying them."*
>
> — *Walter Mossberg, Wall Street Journal, on IDG Books' ...For Dummies books*

Already, millions of satisfied readers agree. They have made *...For Dummies* the #1 introductory level computer book series and a best-selling business book series. They have written asking for more. So, if you're looking for the best and easiest way to learn about business and other general reference topics, look to *...For Dummies* to give you a helping hand.

1/99

Home Maintenance FOR DUMMIES®

by **James Carey and Morris Carey**

Foreword by Dom DeLuise

IDG BOOKS WORLDWIDE

IDG Books Worldwide, Inc.
An International Data Group Company

Foster City, CA ◆ Chicago, IL ◆ Indianapolis, IN ◆ New York, NY

Home Maintenance For Dummies®

Published by
IDG Books Worldwide, Inc.
An International Data Group Company
919 E. Hillsdale Blvd.
Suite 400
Foster City, CA 94404
www.idgbooks.com (IDG Books Worldwide Web site)
www.dummies.com (Dummies Press Web site)

Library of Congress Catalog Card No.: 99-69705

ISBN: 0-7645-5215-5

Printed in the United States of America

10 9 8 7 6 5 4 3 2

1O/QY/SZ/QQ/IN

Distributed in the United States by IDG Books Worldwide, Inc.

Distributed by CDG Books Canada Inc. for Canada; by Transworld Publishers Limited in the United Kingdom; by IDG Norge Books for Norway; by IDG Sweden Books for Sweden; by IDG Books Australia Publishing Corporation Pty. Ltd. for Australia and New Zealand; by TransQuest Publishers Pte Ltd. for Singapore, Malaysia, Thailand, Indonesia, and Hong Kong; by Gotop Information Inc. for Taiwan; by ICG Muse, Inc. for Japan; by Intersoft for South Africa; by Eyrolles for France; by International Thomson Publishing for Germany, Austria and Switzerland; by Distribuidora Cuspide for Argentina; by LR International for Brazil; by Galileo Libros for Chile; by Ediciones ZETA S.C.R. Ltda. for Peru; by WS Computer Publishing Corporation, Inc., for the Philippines; by Contemporanea de Ediciones for Venezuela; by Express Computer Distributors for the Caribbean and West Indies; by Micronesia Media Distributor, Inc. for Micronesia; by Chips Computadoras S.A. de C.V. for Mexico; by Editorial Norma de Panama S.A. for Panama; by American Bookshops for Finland.

For general information on IDG Books Worldwide's books in the U.S., please call our Consumer Customer Service department at 800-762-2974. For reseller information, including discounts and premium sales, please call our Reseller Customer Service department at 800-434-3422.

For information on where to purchase IDG Books Worldwide's books outside the U.S., please contact our International Sales department at 317-572-3993 or fax 317-572-4002.

For consumer information on foreign language translations, please contact our Customer Service department at 1-800-434-3422, fax 317-572-4002, or e-mail rights@idgbooks.com.

For information on licensing foreign or domestic rights, please phone +1-650-653-7098.

For sales inquiries and special prices for bulk quantities, please contact our Order Services department at 800-434-3422 or write to the address above.

For information on using IDG Books Worldwide's books in the classroom or for ordering examination copies, please contact our Educational Sales department at 800-434-2086 or fax 317-572-4005.

For press review copies, author interviews, or other publicity information, please contact our Public Relations department at 650-653-7000 or fax 650-653-7500.

For authorization to photocopy items for corporate, personal, or educational use, please contact Copyright Clearance Center, 222 Rosewood Drive, Danvers, MA 01923, or fax 978-750-4470.

is a registered trademark under exclusive license to IDG Books Worldwide, Inc. from International Data Group, Inc.

About the Authors

James and **Morris Carey,** known as the Carey Brothers, are nationally-recognized experts on home building and renovation. They share their 20-plus years of experience as award-winning, licensed contractors with millions nationwide through a weekly radio program, daily radio vignette, syndicated newspaper column, and comprehensive Web site (onthehouse.com), all titled *On The House.*

These third-generation contractors hold 14-year broadcast careers in radio and television. They deliver user-friendly, hands-on advice in their radio program, which is carried coast-to-coast weekly, via satellite, to a rapidly growing network of more than 170 stations. The program also is broadcast via live remote from home and building expos nationwide and on the Internet.

With a long career in television, the Careys have most recently appeared as the home improvement contributors on CBS Television's *CBS News Saturday Morning.* Prior to that, the brothers were regulars on the Family Channel's *Home and Family* show, hosted by Cristina Ferrare and Michael Burger. They have also appeared as guests on national and local television programs, including *Vicki!* and ABC-TV's *Home Show, Caryl & Marilyn,* and *Home Matters,* among others.

Recognized for their efforts in answering immediate and constant structural concerns by the public in the hours and days following the devastating October 1989 earthquake, the Carey Brothers and KCBS radio in San Francisco received the George Foster Peabody Award, broadcasting's most prestigious honor, for their outstanding contributions towards "comprehensive, intelligent, and useful coverage."

Morris and James continue to own and operate a successful home remodeling and construction firm, Carey Bros., and have been named to *Remodeling* magazine's Hall of Fame "Big 50," which recognizes top achievers in the industry. They have also been honored as one of the nation's top 500 companies by *Qualified Remodeler* magazine.

The Carey Brothers are the authors of *Home Remodeling For Dummies,* published by IDG Books Worldwide, Inc., and *Cost-Effective Home Upgrades,* published by Ortho Books.

Homeowners can receive answers to their specific home renovation and repair questions by calling the Carey Brothers' toll-free number, 1-800-REPAIR-IT (737-2474), during their radio program, Saturday from 9:00 a.m. to 1:00 p.m. Eastern Standard Time, via e-mail at careybro@onthehouse.com, fax at 1-888-44-CAREY (442-2739), and on the Web at www.onthehouse.com.

Dedication

Summer vacation had ended. It was my first day back to school and my first day as a sophomore. The morning air was warm, and I perspired as I anxiously rushed to chemistry class. I was excited and scared all at the same time. I shot into the room and made a beeline for a seat near the back wall. I figured it was safer there because I felt that the teacher wouldn't be able to see me. I slouched back in my seat in an attempt to appear relaxed. I wasn't. Not even a little bit.

As I glanced up toward the front of the room, I caught a glimpse of her for the very first time. Suddenly, the anxiety began to disappear. She had taken the first seat in my row. The desks between us were still empty. I couldn't see her face. Naturally, her back was toward me. But, I saw her nonetheless. She was wearing a tight, gray-wool, calf-length skirt and a satiny white blouse. Her hair was sandy colored and she wore it short. She was tall and slender. I hadn't even seen her face, yet suddenly I knew that I had fallen in love. That was nearly 40 years ago.

We grew up, and she became my best friend. She became a woman of character and ambition. Even when she was a girl, she was wise and mature beyond her years. Yet, she has always been easy going and fun to talk to. She is passionate about everything she does, and everything she does is tendered with great compassion. Our moments together are priceless pearls of happiness filled with mutual admiration and endearing love. In the morning, her smiling eyes get me going. In the evening, her calming voice puts me at ease. She is a loving mother, a sexy grandmother, and my partner in life. She is my wife Carol.

Without her strength this book would not have been possible. "Yo, Adrianne, Rocky loves ya baby!"

— Morris Carey

To Carol, Chris, Jamie, and Chase; thank you for the freedom, encouragement, and support to do my life's work. I am so blessed to be your husband and father.

To Geno; thank you for giving me your daughter and for being a great father-in-law, grandfather, and a very special friend.

— James Carey

Acknowledgments

There are many people who contributed both directly and indirectly to the success of this book. While there are too many to list, we would be remiss without naming a few.

This book would literally have taken forever — certainly longer than IDG Books would allow — had it not been for some very valuable writing assistance that we received from Don Logay, Tim Green, and Bob Gould. Thanks for picking up the slack and helping us stay in good grace with IDG Books.

We wish also to thank Marie Dirkin, Wet & Warm Home Center, Antioch, California; Otto "Butch" Gross, The Appliance MD, Middletown, Maryland; Brian Hansen, Aloha Pools & Spas, Plymouth, Minnesota; Rite Hardware & Rental, Maple Grove, Minnesota; Phil Deatsch, California Pool Covers; Stuart Dennis, Culligan Water Conditioning; and the "home pros" at www. Homewarehouse.com for their technical expertise.

At IDG Books, we want to thank Kathy Welton and Holly McGuire for making this book happen and for giving us a second opportunity to share the better part of our lives' work with you. A special thanks goes to our Project Editor, Mary Goodwin. From day one and throughout this entire project, Mary forever had a smile on her face (even when providing a much-needed nudge). She offered constant encouragement and constructive feedback and helped shape this work to best meet the readers' needs. Mary challenged us, brought out our best, and, more than anything, made the project fun.

Aside from the subject matter, the most significant difference between this book and our previous IDG Book, *Home Remodeling For Dummies,* is the vast number of illustrations contained in this book. Hard as we might have tried, all the words in the world could not have simplified many of the tasks contained in this book, as do the creative illustrations by Shawn Wallace.

At On The House Syndication (our media company), many thanks to Lori Martin, our niece Marilyn Grillo, and to Santina Siemer and Jennifer Villegas for their encouragement and support, and for "minding the store" during this project.

At Carey Bros. Remodeling Company, special thanks to Carol Carey (Morris's wife), Morris D. Carey, III (Morris's son), Tracy Di Piero, and the entire staff of our remodeling company for doing such a super job while our attention was focused on this book.

And last but not least, our heartfelt thanks to Steve Youlios, Jeff Firestone, and Nancy Gross, NetCom Sales Strategies, Inc., the firm that represents our media work, for their unwavering support and devotion and for helping us realize our true potential.

ABOUT IDG BOOKS WORLDWIDE

Welcome to the world of IDG Books Worldwide.

IDG Books Worldwide, Inc., is a subsidiary of International Data Group, the world's largest publisher of computer-related information and the leading global provider of information services on information technology. IDG was founded more than 30 years ago by Patrick J. McGovern and now employs more than 9,000 people worldwide. IDG publishes more than 290 computer publications in over 75 countries. More than 90 million people read one or more IDG publications each month.

Launched in 1990, IDG Books Worldwide is today the #1 publisher of best-selling computer books in the United States. We are proud to have received eight awards from the Computer Press Association in recognition of editorial excellence and three from Computer Currents' First Annual Readers' Choice Awards. Our best-selling ...*For Dummies*® series has more than 50 million copies in print with translations in 31 languages. IDG Books Worldwide, through a joint venture with IDG's Hi-Tech Beijing, became the first U.S. publisher to publish a computer book in the People's Republic of China. In record time, IDG Books Worldwide has become the first choice for millions of readers around the world who want to learn how to better manage their businesses.

Our mission is simple: Every one of our books is designed to bring extra value and skill-building instructions to the reader. Our books are written by experts who understand and care about our readers. The knowledge base of our editorial staff comes from years of experience in publishing, education, and journalism — experience we use to produce books to carry us into the new millennium. In short, we care about books, so we attract the best people. We devote special attention to details such as audience, interior design, use of icons, and illustrations. And because we use an efficient process of authoring, editing, and desktop publishing our books electronically, we can spend more time ensuring superior content and less time on the technicalities of making books.

You can count on our commitment to deliver high-quality books at competitive prices on topics you want to read about. At IDG Books Worldwide, we continue in the IDG tradition of delivering quality for more than 30 years. You'll find no better book on a subject than one from IDG Books Worldwide.

John J. Kilcullen

John Kilcullen
Chairman and CEO
IDG Books Worldwide, Inc.

**Eighth Annual
Computer Press
Awards 1992**

**Ninth Annual
Computer Press
Awards 1993**

**Tenth Annual
Computer Press
Awards 1994**

**Eleventh Annual
Computer Press
Awards 1995**

IDG is the world's leading IT media, research and exposition company. Founded in 1964, IDG had 1997 revenues of $2.05 billion and has more than 9,000 employees worldwide. IDG offers the widest range of media options that reach IT buyers in 75 countries representing 95% of worldwide IT spending. IDG's diverse product and services portfolio spans six key areas including print publishing, online publishing, expositions and conferences, market research, education and training, and global marketing services. More than 90 million people read one or more of IDG's 290 magazines and newspapers, including IDG's leading global brands — Computerworld, PC World, Network World, Macworld and the Channel World family of publications. IDG Books Worldwide is one of the fastest-growing computer book publishers in the world, with more than 700 titles in 36 languages. The "...For Dummies®" series alone has more than 50 million copies in print. IDG offers online users the largest network of technology-specific Web sites around the world through IDG.net (http://www.idg.net), which comprises more than 225 targeted Web sites in 55 countries worldwide. International Data Corporation (IDC) is the world's largest provider of information technology data, analysis and consulting, with research centers in over 41 countries and more than 400 research analysts worldwide. IDG World Expo is a leading producer of more than 168 globally branded conferences and expositions in 35 countries including E3 (Electronic Entertainment Expo), Macworld Expo, ComNet, Windows World Expo, ICE (Internet Commerce Expo), Agenda, DEMO, and Spotlight. IDG's training subsidiary, ExecuTrain, is the world's largest computer training company, with more than 230 locations worldwide and 785 training courses. IDG Marketing Services helps industry-leading IT companies build international brand recognition by developing global integrated marketing programs via IDG's print, online and exposition products worldwide. Further information about the company can be found at www.idg.com.   1/26/00

Publisher's Acknowledgments

We're proud of this book; please register your comments through our IDG Books Worldwide Online Registration Form located at http://my2cents.dummies.com.

Some of the people who helped bring this book to market include the following:

Acquisitions, Editorial, and Media Development

Project Editor: Mary Goodwin

Acquisitions Editor: Holly McGuire

Technical Editor: Thomas Krautler

Illustrator: Shawn Wallace

Acquisitions Coordinator: Jill Alexander

Editorial Manager: Kristin Cocks

Editorial Assistant: Michelle Vukas

Production

Project Coordinator: Maridee V. Ennis

Layout and Graphics: Joe Bucki, Clint Lahnen, Barry Offringa, Tracy K. Oliver, Brent Savage, Jacque Schneider, Dan Whetstine, Erin Zeltner

Proofreaders: Corey Bowen, Mildred Rosenzweig, Charles Spencer, Robert Springer

Indexer: Steve Rath

Special Help: Amanda Foxworth

General and Administrative

IDG Books Worldwide, Inc.: John Kilcullen, CEO

IDG Books Technology Publishing Group: Richard Swadley, Senior Vice President and Publisher; Walter Bruce III, Vice President and Associate Publisher; Joseph Wikert, Associate Publisher; Mary Bednarek, Branded Product Development Director; Mary Corder, Editorial Director; Barry Pruett, Publishing Manager; Michelle Baxter, Publishing Manager

IDG Books Consumer Publishing Group: Roland Elgey, Senior Vice President and Publisher; Kathleen A. Welton, Vice President and Publisher; Kevin Thornton, Acquisitions Manager; Kristin A. Cocks, Editorial Director

IDG Books Internet Publishing Group: Brenda McLaughlin, Senior Vice President and Publisher; Diane Graves Steele, Vice President and Associate Publisher; Sofia Marchant, Online Marketing Manager

IDG Books Production for Dummies Press: Debbie Stailey, Associate Director of Production; Cindy L. Phipps, Manager of Project Coordination, Production Proofreading, and Indexing; Tony Augsburger, Manager of Prepress, Reprints, and Systems; Laura Carpenter, Production Control Manager; Shelley Lea, Supervisor of Graphics and Design; Debbie J. Gates, Production Systems Specialist; Robert Springer, Supervisor of Proofreading; Kathie Schutte, Production Supervisor

Dummies Packaging and Book Design: Patty Page, Manager, Promotions Marketing

◆

The publisher would like to give special thanks to Patrick J. McGovern, without whom this book would not have been possible.

◆

Contents at a Glance

Cartoons at a Glance

By Rich Tennant

page 5

page 27

page 167

page 311

page 335

page 343

Fax: 978-546-7747
E-mail: richtennant@the5thwave.com
World Wide Web: www.the5thwave.com

Table of Contents

Foreword

. . . .

*A*s I was reading *Home Maintenance For Dummies*, the Carey Brothers' fantastic, helpful, amazingly clear book, I realized that the table I was using was wobbling. I put the book under the shortest leg, and the table was instantly stable. There is no end to the things you can do with *Home Maintenance For Dummies*.

— Dom DeLuise

Introduction

● ●

*I*n our last *For Dummies* project — *Home Remodeling For Dummies* — we ventured with our readers down the sometimes rocky road of remodeling a home. Our goal was to prepare readers for the many steps and potential pitfalls involved in planning and executing a home-remodeling project, regardless of its size or complexity. Throughout that book the words "plan, plan, plan" became our mantra.

For this, our most recent offering, we have adopted an old cliché as our credo. In fact, had this not been a part of the best-selling *For Dummies* series, a more apt title may have been *An Ounce of Prevention Is Worth a Pound of Cure.* On the other hand, *Home Maintenance For Dummies* does have a nice ring to it! What's more, chances are good that by the time you've had a chance to sink your teeth into this book, you'll be anything but a dummy when it comes to maintaining your home.

For most of us, our homes are the largest investment that we will make in a lifetime. Thus, it makes good sense to do everything that we can to protect that investment from deterioration from the forces of nature, wood-eating pests, and good, old-fashioned wear and tear. As you will soon read, in addition to protecting the structural integrity of your home, regular maintenance will make it more comfortable, safer, and more energy efficient. And don't forget that a well cared for home stands out in the neighborhood, and that's worth something — a bigger price tag when it comes time to sell, or simply the satisfaction of knowing that you are in charge of your home rather than the reverse.

Few undertakings offer the pride and personal satisfaction that a home-maintenance job well done can. *Home Maintenance For Dummies* is so full of information on how to care for your home, we guarantee that your cup of pride and personal satisfaction will forever runneth over.

Finally, if we have met our objective, your reading will be peppered with lots of laughter. Enjoy!

How To Use This Book

Like most *For Dummies* books, *Home Maintenance For Dummies* is a reference, meaning that it was written with the expectation that you would not read it from cover to cover over a couple of sittings. Instead, we think that you will consider it as one of the most importance tools in your home maintenance arsenal — like your prized hammer or wrench that you pick up and use whenever necessary.

You will find that the Index is thorough, as is the Table of Contents. So, if you have a home-maintenance task in mind, simply let your fingers do the walking to the appropriate section of this book and let the games begin. This book makes for great armor — just don't get it wet.

Who Needs This Book

Everyone — unless you are independently wealthy and have no intention of lifting a finger to care for your home. Even then, this book could prove to be valuable. Who knows — you might just find it handy in rescuing one of your loyal servants. Seriously, if your home is an apartment, condo, single-family, flat, co-op, cave, or hut; if you rent, own, or borrow; if your habitat is old, new, or somewhere in between, this book is for you.

What We Assume about You

You know what they say about the word "assume." In any event, we do assume that you care about the appearance and condition of your home, and hence its value. We don't have this vision that you are a home improvement fanatic or that you are particularly handy — you don't need to be.

All you need is a song in your heart, a smile on your face, and an insatiable desire to see your home be the best that it can be. A few tools are of infinite value when it comes to home maintenance. However, the most complicated tool that you will need is a cordless driver drill for sinking a screw here and there. The tools that you will find yourself needing most often are a scrub brush, a paintbrush, and plenty of patience.

Most importantly, we assume that you will always seek help when needed, and that you will always put safety first when attempting a home-maintenance endeavor.

How This Book Is Organized

The chapters of this book are organized into the following parts so that you can easily find just the information that you're looking for.

Part I: Home Maintenance and You

This part introduces you to the benefits of home maintenance and to the major systems and components in your home. Even though you don't have to read this book from cover to cover, we strongly recommend that you check out the two chapters in this part so that you have a clear understanding of what parts of your home require maintenance and why you should pay attention to them.

Part II: Exterior Maintenance

In this part, we tell you about all the things you need to keep the outside of your home, and those parts of your home that are most affected by the outside, in good working order. Turn here for tips and guidance on maintaining everything from your roof to your home's foundation and doors.

Part III: Interior Maintenance

This part of the book shows you how to take care of, and extend the life of, the various elements and systems that make up the inside of your home. From ceilings to floors, this part of the book gives you an extensive roadmap to maintaining the innards of your house.

Part IV: Safety, Security, and Shutdown

Sometimes taking care of your home involves more than lubricating and tightening screws. When it comes to safety, security, and shutdown, planning is key. In this part of the book, we tell you how to plan for, and avoid, some of life's emergencies.

Part V: The Part of Tens

In this part, you find three chapters full of quick-lists that will help you focus your thinking about the most important maintenance tasks associated with your home. We also give you some home-maintenance tips to keep in the back of your mind as you go about caring for your house.

Part VI: The Home-Maintenance Schedule

Here you find a series of lists that you can use to keep your home-maintenance tasks organized. We tell you what you need to do and when. Follow this schedule, and your home will love you for it.

Icons Used in This Book

Some information in this book is so important that we want to emphasize it by placing these little pictures (called icons) next to certain points.

This icon flags text that's important and not to be forgotten.

When we go out on a limb to suggest something you should do, we use this icon. It represents your basic good idea.

We use this icon to steer you clear of things that we don't want you to do.

This icon points out dangers and health hazards that you should be wary of.

When we feel like telling you a little story, you'll see this icon.

We use this icon to highlight products that we've come to know and trust over the years.

Part I:
Home Maintenance and You

The 5th Wave   By Rich Tennant

"Honey, I thought you checked with the neighborhood committee before having the house painted magenta."

In this part . . .

Everyone knows that a bit of caulking or a coat of paint can make a home look better. What many folks don't know is that beauty isn't only skin deep. Both of these maintenance tasks, like most maintenance tasks, do much more than meets the eye. In this part, we help you see beyond the obvious and show you what to look for when it comes to keeping your home fit.

Chapter 1

Why Home Maintenance Is Important

In This Chapter

▶ Making your home a safer and more comfortable place to live

▶ Enhancing your home's value

▶ Saving money on repairs and energy

*H*ome maintenance is no one trick pony. There are actually five major benefits to maintaining your home, including improved safety, increased comfort, enhanced home value, money savings, and energy efficiency.

With these five huge benefits, an ounce of prevention is indeed worth a pound of cure. These, as you will soon discover, are words to live by when it comes to your home.

Here's to Your Health (And Safety)

A poorly cared for home can turn into a breeding ground for illness, injury, and even death:

- ✔ Drafty windows and doors can cause a cold which could cost you time and money at the doctor's office.

- ✔ A spongy subfloor can result in an unexpected visit to the floor below — complete with bumps, cuts, bruises, and maybe a trip to the hospital.

- ✔ A poorly maintained furnace can produce deadly carbon monoxide gas — known as the "silent killer" — the leading cause of poisoning deaths in America.

> ✔ An air conditioning system that fails in the heat of summer or a furnace that takes a hiatus in the worst of winter can produce an especially dangerous or even fatal environment for the elderly or very young.
>
> ✔ A smoke detector with a dead battery is, literally, like playing with fire.

Simple home maintenance can avert these disasters and make your house a safer place to live for you and your family. For example, the one nine-volt battery and three minutes that it takes to maintain your smoke detector could prevent you from loosing your home, a pet, or loved one.

So how do you spell safety when it comes to your home? M-a-i-n-t-e-n-a-n-c-e!

Comfort: You'll Miss It If It's Gone

You may not realize it, but your house contains a group of systems that makes it a comfortable place to live. (You can read more about each of these systems in Chapter 2.) Most of us take the systems in our house for granted. We don't even think about them until the day when one of them breaks down. The result: a distinct lack of comfort.

For example, your home probably has an electrical system that powers lights, a refrigerator, a water heater, and a clothes washer and dryer, among other things. You may not think about your electrical system as you turn on lights, take a cold can of pop from the refrigerator, take a hot relaxing shower, or fold your freshly laundered clothes. But if that electrical system breaks down, you'll quickly realize how much of your day-to-day comfort depends on it.

Because many of these systems have motors and moving parts, they are especially vulnerable to a high degree of wear and tear that, without preventive maintenance, could result in major inconvenience and lots of swearing.

Home maintenance starts on day one

We grew up in house that was built by our grandfather shortly after the turn of the twentieth century. Our family (which included our Mom and Dad, Morris and Alvera, plus our two sisters, Suzanne and Margaret) continually did maintenance on that old house, be it painting, plastering, plumbing, or repairing a broken window screen.

However, maintenance is not reserved for or specific to older homes. Home maintenance should begin the day you move in and continue for as long as the structure exists. But please don't think that you've signed up for years' worth of maintenance drudgery. We show you how home maintenance can be fast, efficient, and — could it be? — actually fun.

Maintaining and Enhancing the Value of Your Home

If you're like most people, your home is the single largest investment of your lifetime. Besides giving you a place to live, you may have also made this investment with the hopes of making some money on it when you sell the house. Thus, it makes good sense (and big bucks) to keep your home in tip-top shape.

We learned a valuable phrase from real estate professionals we encountered throughout the years in our building and remodeling business: *curb appeal.* This phrase refers to how the outward appearance of a home affects its value. A home with a roof, windows, doors, siding, fencing, and landscaping that are well cared for is more appealing to potential buyers and, hence, more valuable. Conversely, a poorly maintained home can be a real eyesore and worth significantly less than its well-maintained counterpart (see Figure 1-1).

Even if you don't intend to sell your home in the near future, you still need to maintain your home in order to maintain your initial investment. Simple repairs, like replacing a furnace filter, can make a big difference in maintaining this investment. How, you ask, can a home's value be affected by replacing a furnace filter? Seem like a stretch? Not in the slightest. With a clean filter, a furnace doesn't work nearly as hard, placing less stress on the motor, fan belt, and other components. Consequently, the furnace has a longer life, and, in turn, you avoid having to replace the furnace prematurely.

Figure 1-1: Your home's curb appeal translates directly into dollars.

Reaping more than you sow

Performing one maintenance task can trigger several benefits. A good example is replacing a dirty furnace filter, which can improve safety and comfort, enhance the value of your home, save you money in electrical bills, and help the environment.

More importantly, you just may find that by performing a bit of preventive maintenance, you actually save time by avoiding time-consuming repairs. Wouldn't you rather be playing with your friends or kids instead of making repairs to your home?

Avoiding Repairs: Like Money in the Bank

Here's where the "ounce of prevention" thing really applies. It's almost always less expensive to perform preventive maintenance tasks than it is to make repairs.

For example, the metal flashing that surrounds a chimney can be the source of a nasty roof leak if it's not maintained. The less than $20 in materials that it costs to caulk and paint the flashing is a fraction of the hundreds or thousand of dollars you would spend to repair leak damage to ceilings, walls, and flooring. Bet you can't find a blue-chip stock that pays those kinds of dividends! Ka-ching!

Gaps in siding and trim around windows and doors allow cold drafts and moisture to make their way into the wood skeleton of your home. Aside from driving up utility bills, the moisture produces rot that, in turn, weakens the structural elements in your home, and provides a veritable smorgasbord for structural pest, such as termites and other wood ravagers, as well as breeding dangerous mold. These small gaps can result in thousands of dollars worth of repairs, and if left unrepaired long enough, they can actually lead to the demise of your home.

You get what you pay for

Here's the first rule of home maintenance materials: Buy the best that you can afford. Doing so gives your home the maximum benefit and protection. If you buy inferior materials, you'll likely be doing the job over again soon. Worse yet, you

may end up spending a hefty sum to make repairs that otherwise would not be needed had you spent a little more up front. Not a bad proposition if you enjoy spending all of your free time and spare change fixing up your home.

ANECDOTE

Roots: A good place to begin

Before there were the Carey brothers (or Carey sisters — there are two), there were the Carey parents: Morris and Alvera. We can attribute our interest in building, remodeling, and repair to our parents — a couple of dyed-in-the-wool do-it-yourselfers. Both gone now, they made one heck of a home improvement and repair team. They were hard working, creative, and industrious. If ever a sow's ear could be turned into a silk purse, Mom and Dad could indeed do it.

Mom's favorite source for sprucing up the home was the local thrift shop, while the "dump" was Dad's hang out. Upon any given shopping spree, Mom would return home with unusual items, such as an old metal milk can, an assortment of picture frames, and a light fixture or two. Armed only with her innate creativity and a can of her infamous gold spray paint, she would convert trash into family treasures. The milk can became a lamp, the ailing frames were transformed into

sought-after antiques, and the light fixtures would rival those of Liberace. What they all had in common was their radiant gold finish, her trademark.

Meanwhile, Dad would be pulling an old piece of furniture off his truck that he "rescued" from the local landfill. His favorites were old console radios and television sets. Once, Dad took a vintage radio cabinet and transformed it into an elegant glass cabinet that Mom used to showcase all of her fine crystal and china. The hinged top that once served as the hatch to a turntable allowed convenient access to her treasures.

Be it painting, plastering, plumbing, there was always something that needed to be done around our house. With some ingenuity, our parents showed us that these tasks could be fun — that's something we want to show you, too.

The flip side: Spend five minutes and five bucks to caulk the trim around a window. Your home will love you for it, and you'll love yourself for saving so much of your hard-earned cash.

Making Your Home into a Lean Mean Comfort Machine

Most people know that the more efficiently a mechanical device works, the less it costs to operate. A well-tuned automobile engine renders far better fuel efficiency than a clunker.

The same holds true with many of the machines that you have around your home. Your furnace is a great example. A clean furnace filter, coupled with other preventive maintenance tasks, makes the furnace operate more efficiently, consuming less energy and making it less susceptible to breakdowns.

Energy savings equal money savings. Keeping the appliances in your home running efficiently also helps the environment — a major benefit for yourself and the planet.

Chapter 2

Getting to Know Your House and Its Systems

In This Chapter

▶ Getting an overview of your home and its important parts

▶ Looking at the common maintenance tasks for each part of the home

*H*ome maintenance reminds us a lot of the Monopoly board game. Both involve a bit of a gamble with real estate. In the game, dice decide your destiny. A favorable roll can turn you into a real-estate baron with holdings that rival those of Donald Trump. On the other hand, the wrong combination can land you straight in the pokey!

Each time you postpone a maintenance task, you are "rolling the dice" with your home's structural and aesthetic integrity and value. Moreover, while it isn't very likely that failing to keep up your home will have you doing the jailhouse rock, sadly, there are occasions when such negligence can result in tremendous damage for which you can conceivably be held liable — not to mention the personal loss that you can suffer.

In Chapter 1, we tell you about the importance of maintaining your home. If you simply couldn't wait to delve into this chapter, and you skipped Chapter 1, we encourage you to go back and give it a few minutes. While we haven't written this book with the expectation that you begin with Chapter 1 and continue page-by-page to the end, we believe that certain chapters are valuable to each and every reader. Chapter 1 qualifies as one of these. Accordingly, with our Monopoly metaphor in mind, we suggest that you neither pass "GO" nor collect $200 until you have given Chapter 1 its due.

In this chapter, we want to show you that your home is more than just four walls and a roof; your house is actually made up of a group of systems and fixtures, all of which need your loving care and attention from time to time (see Figure 2-1). We introduce you to each of these systems, which are then examined in great detail in the various chapters of this book.

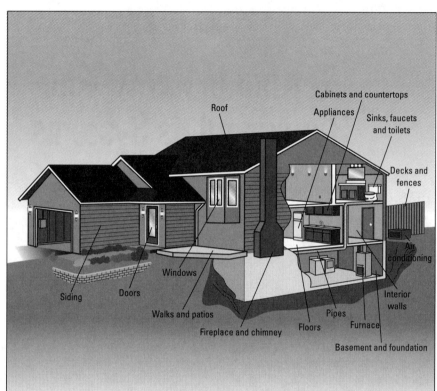

Sometimes It's Nice To Fool Mother Nature

Every area of a home needs ongoing maintenance, but some areas require more care than others. At the top of the "needy" list is a home's exterior. The exterior is subject to constant deterioration thanks to the forces of Mother Nature — the sun, wind, and rain. Consequently, it's no accident that you may find yourself spending a majority of your home-maintenance time on the exterior.

The following sections discuss the elements of a home's exterior that will, from time to time, require maintenance.

The foundation and the floor frame

The foundation, which we discuss in detail in Chapter 3, is a home's infrastructure. It is the element of construction that helps a home stay put. For homes with a basement, the foundation also holds back earth and limits the intrusion of unwanted water. Furthermore, a level foundation can usually contribute to a level floor, windows and doors that operate smoothly, and the absence of cracks in walls and ceilings.

Checking cracks before they spread and dealing with moisture control are among the most common maintenance tasks associated with a foundation.

The floor frame along with the foundation is a part of the home's infrastructure. The foundation and the floor frame work together to support the walls, roof, and other structural elements.

The floor frame consists of floor joists and/or girders (beams) and the subfloor. The joists and girders travel horizontally and rest on the foundation. The subfloor consists of lumber or plywood that is fastened to the floor framing. Finish flooring (carpet, vinyl, hardwood, and so on) is installed above the subfloor.

If for no other reason, the floor frame is notorious for the maddening creaks and squeaks that occur when traipsing across it. Aside from the fact that floor squeaks can drive you nuts, they are considered a sign of inferior construction, which can lower your home's perceived value. While this can surely be true, the reality is that even the best-built homes can suffer from a squeak now and again.

Thus, silencing squeaks is the most common maintenance task when it comes to the floor frame. Not far behind are preventing rot and leveling up an out of level floor before it damages the structure of the entire home. It's all in Chapter 3.

Roofing and siding

Most people think of siding as either vinyl or wood. We use the term to describe a wider class of materials — whatever can be used as a finished, protective coat on the exterior walls of your home, such as brick, wood, vinyl, stucco, aluminum, or a composite siding.

Siding is, by design, expected to endure forces that simply aren't an issue with interior walls. In the children's story, "The Three Little Pigs," the Big Bad Wolf didn't have a chance blowing down the house with the brick walls. What the story failed to mention was that the Little Pig that lived in the house with brick walls made sure to keep the mortar joints in good condition, the brick well sealed, and all the gaps caulked.

Take a lesson from this smart Little Pig and follow the maintenance routines suggested in Chapters 4 and 10 for your siding. You will discover that exterior wall maintenance is all about preserving the integrity of the siding.

We think of the roof as the fifth wall of the house. Because the roof is a horizontal surface, it is subject to all of the same forces that siding is, and then some. Like siding, rain and sun are a roof's biggest enemies.

Keeping a roof clean is one of the most important maintenance tasks. A debris-free roof improves watershed and prevents rot, mold, and fungus growth. Metal flashing at vents, chimneys, skylights, valleys, and other critical areas are most prone to leak, thus requiring special care.

Maintenance on your roof isn't much different from what you do to maintain your siding. We have, therefore, combined roofing and siding into Chapter 4.

Although not officially a part of the roof, gutters and downspouts are essential to proper watershed and, when well maintained, can prevent everything from a roof leak to sticking windows and doors. Cleaning, caulking, and painting count among the most common gutter- and spout-related maintenance tasks.

Keeping your eye on the doughnut

Although we were born 12 years apart, we shared many of the same teachers throughout school. One teacher who has a special place in both of our hearts is Mrs. Roxie Gibbs. Mrs. Gibbs was our high school English and Journalism teacher. She was your classic eyeglasses-sliding-down-the-nose, beehive coifed, mid-length skirted, prim-and-proper school marm straight out of *Little House on the Prairie.*

One of Mrs. Gibbs's favorite adages was "Keep your eye upon the doughnut and not upon the hole." Although these words were initially a total mystery to us, we eventually discovered their meaning. What Mrs. Gibbs was so eloquently saying was to focus on the issue (the doughnut) and not the minutiae (the hole). What does this have to do with home maintenance? Plenty!

When dealing with home maintenance, concentrate on the root of a problem (the doughnut) rather than focusing on the symptom (the hole). For example, people often ask us how to keep a door from sticking. A door sticks for one reason and one reason only! The uniform gap between the door and the frame no longer exists. The gap (which should have been there at installation) allows the door to be opened and closed without interference from the frame.

The sticking door is a symptom of a larger problem, like an out-of-level floor. Accordingly, we don't want you to be stuck on the stick — rather, we want you to chew on what causes the door to stick. Are we making ourselves clear, or are you stuck? (Chapter 5 tells you all about unsticking stuck doors.)

Windows and exterior doors

Without a doubt, windows and doors are two of the most important elements of a home. They give you access to the outdoors and, when armed with a key, access to the indoors! Windows and doors also provide natural light and ventilation — two of the most valuable commodities a home can have.

Unfortunately, windows and doors are frequently among the most maintenance-intense elements. This is true primarily because, unlike siding and roofing, windows and doors have moving parts that suffer from wear and tear. What's more, in most homes, windows and doors are also responsible for the majority of energy loss.

Water leaks, air leaks, and condensation are a few of the most common window-related maintenance issues. As for doors, a touch of lubrication to hinges and hardware, shimming a hinge, and adjusting a strike plate or door bottom can be the saving grace to any door.

Chapter 5 offers tips on these window and door maintenance tasks.

Decks, fences, and retaining walls

A deck can account for the majority of your outdoor entertaining area. For example, if you have an apartment in New York, a rooftop deck may be where you sunbathe, tend to your garden, and entertain guests. A rooftop deck isn't unique to a New York high rise, though. Many homes consisting of no more than two stories can have a roof deck or "veranda" located above a living space. Although these above-ground decks perform essentially the same function as their "on grade" counterparts, their maintenance needs can be completely different, as you can read about in Chapter 6.

Depending on what kind of deck you have — on grade or on the roof — the surface can consist of wood, vinyl, a composite, concrete, tile, roofing material, or a synthetic elastomeric product. In any case, the biggest maintenance challenges are keeping the surface clean, preventing leaks, and prolonging its life by patching, painting, staining, or sealing. Chapter 6 is chock full of information that you can use to make your deck the envy of your neighborhood.

Fences, like decks, come in all shapes, sizes, and materials. Wood, steel cyclone, ornamental iron, vinyl, concrete, block, and plaster are the materials most widely used. In spite of the vast array of material choices, most fences are constructed of wood, including wood posts, wood frame, and wood fence boards (or pickets).

Regardless of the material used to construct it, keeping a fence *plumb* (upright); preventing posts, framing, and fence boards from deteriorating or being ravaged by pests; keeping fence boards securely attached to the framing; and taking the sag out of a gate are the items that can be found on most homeowners' checklists. Chapter 6 tells you all about these tasks, and more. If your fence is constructed of ornamental iron or brick, check out the tips for caring for these materials in Chapters 9 and 10, respectively.

If your home is built on anything other than a flat lot, you already know that a retaining wall holds back earth that would otherwise come crashing through your home. It can also keep your home or yard from sliding down a hill. You can also use a retaining wall to expand the "usable" area of your property by terracing a slope.

Although more and more retaining walls are being constructed of interlocking decorative block, the vast majority of residential "garden variety" retaining walls are constructed of wood posts and wood boards. The information in Chapter 6 about maintaining retaining walls can add years to the life of your retaining wall.

The swimming pool and spa

Many people reject the idea of owning a swimming pool due to the perceived mound of maintenance that goes along with it. People have visions of spending all of their free time scrubbing tile, brushing plaster, and flushing filters. While each of these tasks does need to be performed from time to time, with a pool, a little preventive maintenance can save performing bigger or more frequent maintenance tasks down the road. For example, keeping an automatic pool cleaner well maintained permits it to run at peak efficiency and, thus, cut down on the need to manually brush it. The same is true for cleaning grungy tile. Regularly brushing the waterline tile with a nylon brush prevents a major cleaning due to scale buildup.

Regardless of its construction — aboveground, inground, fiberglass, vinyl, or plaster — a swimming pool or spa requires regular care and maintenance to ensure safe and healthy swimming conditions. This regular maintenance keeps the equipment in your pool operating at peak efficiency, which, in turn, extends its useful life — saving big bucks in repairs or replacement. Well-maintained equipment can even result in a friendlier utility bill since the equipment won't have to work quite as hard and can be run fewer hours each day.

Pumps, filters, and skimmers need cleaning, a heater needs cleaning and burner adjustment, and an automatic cleaner needs an occasional "tune-up" (lubrication and parts replacement). Decks, coping, tile, and lining need to be kept clean. And most importantly, the water needs to be balanced to prevent damage to the pool and equipment and to ensure a safe swimming environment. Chapter 7 helps you get into the swim of things when it comes to maintaining your pool or spa.

Landscape irrigation

An irrigation system is a convenient and efficient means of making sure that all of your precious plants receive the water they need to keep them perky and robust. Furthermore, a system equipped with a time clock can provide freedom to come and go as you please without worrying whether your garden is being watered.

However, as you can discover in Chapter 8, there is more to an irrigation system than a bunch of pipes, sprinkler heads, and a time clock. Simple maintenance tasks, such as cleaning a clogged sprinkler head and installing a battery backup in your time clock, can preserve what can take many years of tender loving care and nurturing to create.

We are sure that after you green thumb your way through Chapter 8, everything will be coming up roses.

Ornamental iron

Ornamental iron is a fancy term for steel fencing, handrails, or other decorative steel elements. It's no surprise then that the biggest maintenance challenge associated with ornamental iron is rust — the reddish brittle coating that results from attack by moist air. Therefore, the key to preventing rust (and the damage it does) is to prohibit moist air and water from making contact with the steel. Painting, as you can see in Chapter 9, is the most effective means of stopping rust dead in its tracks.

Unfortunately, rust may have already sunk its ruthless teeth into your helpless handrail. Before you pull out the old hacksaw to start cutting out bad spots, have a look at Chapter 9 for information on how to remove rust — chemically and mechanically — and what to do to patch the damage left in its tracks. You'll not only learn our secrets to getting rust off, but how to prevent it from returning.

Walkways, patios, and driveways

Walks and patios are to a home's exterior what halls and entertaining areas are to a home's interior. Can you imagine directing a houseguest down a hall with an uneven walking surface or attempting to entertain a group of people in a room with chunks of carpet, tile, or hardwood missing? Doing so would inevitably result in a twisted ankle or a nasty fall — talk about putting a damper on a party! Why, then, would you be any less attentive to the condition of the walking and entertaining surfaces outside your home?

In the grand scheme of things, chances are good that the walks, paths, and patios that surround your home are subject to as much or more traffic than many spaces within your home. In addition to the safety aspects, these and other paved areas, such as a driveway or carport, can have a tremendous influence on the overall appearance (the "curb appeal") of your home. Accordingly, they should be given the same degree of attention when it comes to home maintenance.

Paths, patios, and other paved areas typically consist of concrete, brick, stone, or asphalt. None of these materials is immune to the need for periodic maintenance. Uneven surfaces, cracks of varying proportion, potholes, and staining are conditions that cry out for attention. Ironically, the need for many of these repairs can be prevented down the road with ongoing mainte- nance. For example, a driveway remains more resilient and water-resistant and, hence, is less likely to crack when a sealer is periodically applied.

If your driveway looks like an Indy 500 pit stop or your front walk looks like the San Andreas Fault, you can clean 'em, patch 'em, seal 'em, or even stain or paint 'em using the information found in Chapter 10.

Your Home's Insides

As with the exterior of your home, basic elements of the interior require maintenance from time to time. The following sections help you identify these elements and the ongoing maintenance they require.

The plumbing system

Of all of a home's systems, the plumbing system is likely the most demanding when it comes to maintenance. Leaking pipes, clogged drains, and a banging water heater are just a few of the many plumbing-related maintenance chal- lenges that pop up.

Let us be the first to tell you that Chapter 11 is all wet. That's because its focus is on running water in the home. It discusses locating and shutting off your water main, dealing with your water heater, and caring for wells and water softeners.

Although the plumbing system is one of the most maintenance-intense, it really isn't particularly complex. Even beginners can easily perform the most common plumbing maintenance tasks: cleaning, lubricating, adjusting, and replacing worn parts. Make your plumber jealous by reading all about these simple maintenance tasks in Chapter 11.

Plumbing fixtures

The best thing you can do for your sinks, faucets, toilets, tubs, and showers is to keep them clean. Chapter 12 offers straightforward guidance on this very topic.

The drain, waste, and vent system

Chapters 11 and 12 discuss two essential elements of a plumbing system: running water and plumbing fixtures. Where does all of the running water produced by faucets and all of the waste produced by people and collected by fixtures go? Thankfully, it ends up in your on-site septic system or a municipal sewer system. The key is to get it from the fixture (tub, shower, sink, toilet, and so on) to one of these locations as quickly and as easily as possible.

The part of the plumbing system that performs this very important task is the drain, waste, and vent system. The drain and waste system uses gravity to carry wastewater and solid material to your home's main sewer line located in the basement, in the crawlspace, or under the concrete slab.

The vent system prohibits dangerous sewer gases from making their way into your home. A "trap" or water door at each fixture accomplishes this chore by being full of water at all times. You are probably familiar with the chrome or black plastic U-shaped pipe under your kitchen sink. What you may not know is that the same configuration exists below your bathtub and shower and is an integral part of the design of every toilet in your home.

If the foul odors don't make it into your home, where do they go? They are carried out vent pipes that are connected to drainpipes and go through the roof. The vents also serve another important function. They equalize pressure in the drain and waste system that facilitates drainage and prevents the siphoning of water from the traps.

What can go wrong? Plenty! Toilets, tubs, showers, and sinks can back up and cause chaos. What's more, slow running drains and the foul odor that accompany them can drive you nuts. Don't wait another moment. Set yourself and your drains free with the information in Chapter 13. Don't "waste" another moment, for all of your plumbing problems will soon be down the drain.

The heating, cooling, and ventilating systems

Heating, ventilation, and air conditioning (HVAC) — without these systems our homes would be little more than the caves that primitive civilization once occupied. How important are these systems? You tell us. Try turning your heating system off in the dead of winter or the air conditioning system off when a heat wave sends the mercury soaring above 100 degrees. It's no wonder that these systems are routinely referred to as "comfort systems" by heating and air conditioning professionals. After all, their mission is to provide comfort, regardless of the climate or weather conditions.

Home heating systems, also known as furnaces, come in various shapes, sizes, and configurations and are fueled by a host of different types of energy, including natural gas, oil, propane, wood, coal, and even the sun. The common system styles include forced air, hydronic (water), steam, gravity, and electric resistance, radiant, and solar. One thing that all of the systems have in common, regardless of the style or the energy that powers them, is their need for periodic maintenance.

Cleaning, lubrication, burner adjustment, and filter replacement, which we tell you about in Chapter 14, are among the most common maintenance tasks needed to keep a furnace running at peak efficiency. The more efficient a system, the less it costs to operate, the less energy it uses, and the longer it lasts.

In 1902, Dr. Willis Carrier invented refrigerant air conditioning. Concerned that his new invention would receive a "cool" reception, he staged a boxing match to showcase this never-before-used technology. While boxing remains a popular sport, it can't begin to compare to the phenomenon that air conditioning has become. Today, a whopping 30 million homeowners cool their homes with central air conditioning. In addition, another 18 million home owners cool one or more rooms in their homes with a room air conditioner. That's a lot of cooling!

All air conditioners, whether window- or wall-mounted units or whole-house central air conditioning systems, operate on the same principle. A fan sucks warm indoor air across a series of cool coils that contain a refrigerant. The cooled air is then blown back into the room. Amazingly, the refrigerant absorbs the heat and then exhausts it outdoors through another system of coils and fans.

The maintenance requirements for a home cooling system don't differ dramatically from those of its heating counterpart. In many cases the systems are connected sharing the same ductwork, blower, or other components. Cleaning, lubrication, and keeping the refrigerant level up are the most common maintenance tasks associated with a cooling system (many of these tasks should be performed by a professional, depending on what kind of system you have). Maintain your cool by checking out Chapter 14.

There's more to a home comfort system than heating and air conditioning. Since studies show that most Americans spend more than 90 percent of their time indoors, the quality of the indoor air has as much to do with health as it does comfort. That's where ventilation comes in. Without adequate ventilation, heat, humidity, air pollutants, and odors can build up inside a home causing serious health problems.

There are two types of ventilation: passive and active. The former uses physics and natural air currents, while the latter incorporates some type of energized mechanical device. Passive systems can include a mechanical device so long as it is not energized. A roof-mounted wind turbine is an example of passive attic ventilation.

Mechanically powered exhaust fans in the attic, bathroom, kitchen, laundry, and basement are active means of improving ventilation, reducing indoor humidity, removing pollutants, and improving indoor air quality.

Here, again, cleaning and lubrication top the list when it comes to maintaining a home's ventilation systems. After you read Chapter 14, you can breathe easy knowing that you can keep your home's ventilation system, and the people it serves, healthy.

Fireplaces

Today, a fireplace is rarely used as a primary source of home heating due to its poor efficiency. Nevertheless, fireplaces remain popular because they provide a cozy atmosphere and romantic appeal. More than any other element of a home, a fireplace represents warmth and comfort.

Not all fireplaces are created equally. Fireplaces built 50 to 100 years ago were constructed of solid stone or brick. After World War II, the fireplace became more of a decorative feature than a viable source of heat. Accordingly, solid stone and brick were replaced by less pricey variations, such as the free standing metal fireplace and "zero-clearance" prefabricated models. The latter have been used almost exclusively in new construction in the last 20 years as a means of trimming building costs.

Cozy and romantic as it may be, a poorly maintained fireplace can be one of your home's most deadly elements. It's imperative that you follow the information contained in Chapter 15. Regardless of the age or style of construction of a fireplace, there are maintenance routines to ensure that the fireplace is safe.

The firebox, glass doors, screen, damper, spark arrestor, flue, and chimney require ongoing maintenance. While all aspects of a fireplace are important, the integrity of the firebox and flue are of prime importance. Creosote, a byproduct of burning wood, can collect on the interior of a flue, and, when ignited, can explode with the force of several sticks of dynamite. Consequently, one of the most important fireplace-related maintenance tasks is cleaning to prevent creosote buildup.

In addition to regular chimney inspection and cleaning, cleaning and adjusting the glass doors and screen, cleaning and lubricating the damper, and making sure the spark arrestor is in tip-top shape are the most common preventive maintenance tasks.

Feel like a fire? Check out Chapter 15 first! It may save your life and your house.

Walls and ceilings

For the purposes of home maintenance, there isn't much that you can do to maintain interior wall structure, per se. It's the material that is *on* the interior walls that requires attention now and then — the same for the ceiling.

Drywall is the most common finish for walls and ceilings in homes built since the 1950s. Before that time, plaster was the material of choice for interior wall covering.

While drywall is both a time- and cost-efficient building material, it doesn't have the rigidity and resistance to damage that plaster does. By the same token, maintaining drywall is a heck of a lot easier than upkeep for plaster. A nick here, a gouge there, a hole here and a crack there — these are, without doubt, sites that are seen on the walls and ceiling of almost any home. They are often the result of a doorknob crashing through the wall, a shift in the earth, foundation settlement, and the ever-present roughhousing by little ones.

Patching holes and cracks in walls and ceilings, cleaning grit and grime, and painting are by far the most pervasive maintenance tasks that folks encounter with their walls and ceilings. Cleaning, patching, and painting — it's all in Chapter 16.

Appliances

A well-maintained appliance is both energy efficient and safe. In Chapter 17, we tell you how to maintain your cooktop, oven, range hood, microwave, refrigerator, freezer, automatic dishwasher, garbage disposal, trash compactor, washing machine, and clothes dryer, so that you get maximum efficiency and safety from them. As a bonus, we've included a host of our special "people friendly" cleaning solutions that require less elbow grease and are safer for you, your family, and our environment.

Cabinets and countertops

In the building trades, cabinets and countertops are referred to as _finishes_. We, on the other hand, like to refer to cabinets, countertops, appliances, and plumbing fixtures as your home's furniture. Like your home's furniture, aside from occasionally tightening a screw here or there, the biggest maintenance challenge that faces each is cleaning. Grit and grime from cooking and sticky fingers and mildew and scale buildup due to hard water are the most common cleaning tasks with these fixtures. The cleaning means and methods vary from finish to finish, as you can read about in Chapter 18.

Aside from keeping your cabinets looking good, cabinet doors, like interior doors, have hinges and hardware that, from time to time, need lubrication and adjusting, as do the cabinet drawer glides and hardware. After you read Chapter 18, your cabinets will indeed be like other fine furniture in your home.

In days gone by, countertops in most homes consisted simply of ceramic tile, plastic laminate, or linoleum with a metal edge. As with other home finishes, countertops have come a long way. Today, linoleum has all but disappeared, ceramic tile has remained strong, plastic laminate is enjoying renewed interest, and an array of solid surface materials are the rage.

Scratches in plastic laminate, stained, cracked or mildew-laden grout, and grungy caulk are among the most common complaints that folks have about their counters. Accordingly, Chapter 18 offers solutions to all of these problems and then some.

Flooring

You can't live with them, and you can't live without 'em! Maintenance-starved floors can be summed up in three words: squeaky, creaky, and dirty. Sounds more like the members of a punk rock group than a list of maintenance woes.

In Chapter 3, we tell you that out-of-level floors have virtually nothing to do with the floor itself and almost everything to do with the foundation and soil that support it. Nonetheless, an out-of-level floor can make doors and windows tough to operate and can be the cause of cracks in walls over windows and doors. If you're tired of patching cracks and wrestling with doors and windows, Chapter 3 was written with you in mind.

Are squeaks in your floor driving you to the edge? You're not alone. They are, without a doubt, one of the most common home-maintenance issues and, aside from leaks, a contractor's biggest nightmare. Good news! Quieting a squeaking floor isn't brain surgery. Better news: We tell you how to do it in Chapter 3.

Floors get the most wear and tear of anything in a home. Cleaning is the single most effective means of cutting down on the deterioration of a floor. Frequent vacuuming and spot cleaning can more than double a carpet's life span. And if you're looking for a way to keep the finish on your vinyl and hardwood flooring looking good, the answer is as close as a broom and dust pan. The grit and grime underfoot that we track into our homes acts like sandpaper that can turn a rich finish into a work in progress. The same holds true with ceramic tile and other types of flooring. Chapter 19 explains that when it comes to flooring, cleanliness is next to godliness.

Part II:
Exterior Maintenance

In this part . . .

*I*t's time to roll up your sleeves, put on your safety goggles, crawl on your belly, and sometimes stand on your head. It's you against one of the strongest forces imaginable — Mother Nature. Sun, wind, rain, and snow can give your home a real run for its money. In this part, we show you how to protect and care for the exterior elements (roofing, siding, windows, decking, and so on) of your home. It's not nice to fool Mother Nature. It's even worse to let her get the best of your house.

Chapter 3

The Foundation and the Floor Frame

In This Chapter

▶ Keeping your basement dry

▶ Stopping cracks in the foundation

▶ Caring for brick and block foundations

▶ Silencing creaky floors forever

▶ Leveling uneven floors

A home is only as good as its foundation. Now there's a familiar phrase. We couldn't agree more! A sound foundation keeps other parts of a home in good working order.

This chapter tells you how to care for one of the most important components of your home. We show you how to keep cracks in concrete from spreading, maintain mortar surrounding brick, control excess water, and keep your basement or crawlspace dry.

First, some clarification. We include the foundation and floor frame in this part of the book because, for all intents and purposes, their integrity is influenced primarily by the exterior — wind, rain, irrigation, grading, drainage, and earth movement.

A Little Foundation about the Foundation

The foundation is a home's infrastructure. It supports the floor, wall, and roof framing. Moreover, the foundation helps keep floors level, basements dry, and, believe it or not, windows and doors operating smoothly.

The foundation is also an anchor of sorts. This can be especially important if your home is built on anything other than flat ground or is in an area prone to earthquakes.

Interestingly, the origin of many leaks and squeaks can be traced to the foundation. A cracked or poorly waterproofed foundation, for example, can result in excess moisture in a crawlspace or basement. Without adequate ventilation, this moisture can condense and lead to, at best, musty odors, leaks and squeaks, and, at worst, rotted floor framing.

If your foundation is built of brick, be sure to read the sections of this chapter on dealing with efflorescence, moisture control, grading and drainage, and especially tuckpointing. If your brick foundation is not reinforced with steel or is crumbling, you should immediately consult a structural engineer to determine what means can be used to improve the integrity of the foundation. (Although this goes beyond the scope of home maintenance, you should be aware that an unreinforced brick foundation that is in good condition can be reinforced by capping the foundation with concrete reinforced with steel.)

If your home was built after the 1930s, chances are good that the foundation consists either of poured-in-place concrete (grade beam), concrete block, or a concrete slab (see Figure 3-1). The latter has become especially prevalent in the last couple of decades by builders seeking to cut costs and create more affordable housing.

Is There a Fungus Amongus?

One of the most common foundation ailments is a white powdery substance that appears on the ground under your home, on the floor framing, or on your foundation or basement walls. Although most people mistake the white powder for a fungus (fungus is typically green or black), it's really *efflorescence*, which is a growth of salt crystals caused by evaporation of salt-laden water.

Efflorescence appears when mineral salts in the concrete or mortar leak to the surface. While efflorescence is not particularly destructive, it is unsightly and can, in some cases, result in splintering or minor deterioration of the surface it grows on.

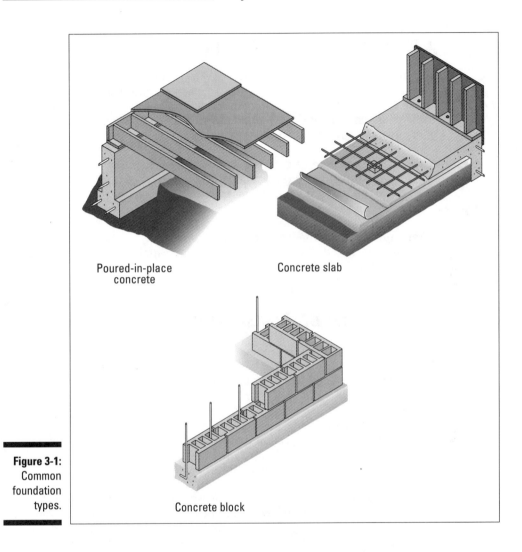

Poured-in-place
concrete

Concrete slab

Concrete block

Figure 3-1:
Common
foundation
types.

The area below the main floor and within the foundation walls can consist of
a concrete slab, a crawlspace, or a basement. With each of these configurations come a host of specific maintenance routines that can safeguard your
home's integrity.

Cleaning up efflorescence

A solution of 1 cup vinegar in 1 quart of warm water applied with a nylon brush removes efflorescence in a jiffy. To clean stubborn areas, use a wire brush and a 10-percent solution of muriatic acid in water. (Muriatic acid is swimming pool acid. It can be found in swimming pool supply stores as well as many hardware stores and home centers.)

Working with acid can be dangerous. Always wear safety goggles, rubber gloves, and protective clothing, and always have plenty of ventilation. Add the acid to the water in a plastic bucket. Adding the water to the acid can produce a dangerous reaction.

After applying either the vinegar or the acid solution, you should rinse the area thoroughly with fresh water. More than one application may be required to achieve the desired result.

Preventing efflorescence

Often, efflorescence can be prevented from recurring by sealing the concrete, block, or brick with a high-quality silicone concrete and masonry sealer. These sealers are generally clear and last for six months to a year depending upon the climate.

We don't recommend using inexpensive "water seals" because they don't offer the high level of protection that better quality, more pricey products do. Keep in mind that you need to apply the cheaper stuff more frequently, which generally ends up costing more money in the long run.

You can apply concrete sealers with a brush, roller, or a pump garden sprayer. It is imperative, however, that the concrete be clean before you seal it. A good power washing with a pressure washer or water blaster prior to application of the sealer offers the greatest penetration and lasting quality.

Avoiding Moisture under Your Home

If you see efflorescence on your basement walls and/or crawlspace and your crawlspace is perpetually damp and mildewy, you've got a moisture problem!

A natural spring, a high water table, a broken water or sewer line, poor grading and drainage, excessive irrigation, and poor ventilation are some of the most common reasons for a damp and mildewy crawlspace or basement.

What's a little water under the house going to hurt, you ask? Lots! Aside from turning a trip into the crawlspace into a mud-wrestling match or your basement into a sauna, excess moisture can lead to a glut of problems such as repulsive odors, rotted framing, structural pests, foundation movement, efflorescence (see the previous section), and allergy-irritating mold. We can't stress enough the importance of doing everything you can to keep excess moisture out from this area of your home.

Rooting out the cause of the moisture

A musty or pungent odor usually accompanies efflorescence and excessive moisture. Accordingly, a good sniffer proves invaluable in investigating the problem.

Start by checking for leaks in water and sewer lines under the home. A failing plumbing fitting or corroded pipe is often the culprit. Fitting a replacement or installing a repair "sleeve" around the damaged section of pipe almost always does the trick. See Chapter 11 for information on how to perform these maintenance tasks.

Believe it or not, a wet basement could be the result of a leaking toilet, tub, or valve located in the walls above. When it comes to finding the cause of a damp basement or crawlspace, leave no stone unturned.

Overwatering planters surrounding the house is also a common cause of water down under. Adjusting watering time, watering less often, installing an automatic timer, and adjusting sprinkler heads are the simplest means of solving this problem. Better yet, at planters next to the house, convert the traditional sprinkler system to a drip irrigation system. Doing so not only helps dry things out under the house, it also makes for a healthier garden.

Using gutters to reduce moisture

Contrary to what you may think, rain gutters are more than a decorative element to the roofline of a home. Their primary purpose is to capture the tremendous amount of rainfall that runs off of the average roof. Without gutters, rainwater collects at the foundation and, consequently, ends up in the crawlspace or basement. So, if you don't have gutters, install them. And if you do, keep them clean. (See Chapter 4 for more information on cleaning gutters.)

Make sure that your gutters and downspouts direct water a safe distance away from the house. Even worse than not having gutters and downspouts is having downspouts jettison water directly onto the foundation. We recommend piping the water 20 feet away from the foundation. You can use a length of rigid or flexible plastic drainpipe (without perforations) to carry water away from the downspout outlet to a safe location. Better yet, to avoid an eyesore and a potential trip hazard, bury the drainpipes below the ground.

Draining away from the house

Be sure that the soil around your home slopes away from the foundation. This helps to divert most irrigation and rainwater away from the structure.

The earth within 30 inches of the foundation should slope down and away at a rate of $\frac{1}{10}$ of an inch per foot. We think that a $\frac{1}{4}$ inch per foot is better. A good rule of thumb is "more slope equals less ponding." Keep in mind that grading should be built up with well-tamped dirt and not loose top soil, which will easily erode.

If you are having a difficult time determining the slope, you can use a measuring tape and a level to help you. Rest one end of the level on the soil against the foundation and point the opposite end away in the direction the ground should slope. With the bubble centered between the level lines, use the measuring tape to measure the distance between the bottom of the level and the top of the soil. For example, if you are using a 3-foot level and are establishing a grade of $\frac{1}{4}$ inch per foot, the distance between the level and the soil should be at least $\frac{3}{4}$ inch.

Generally speaking, grading requires a pick, a shovel, a steel rake, and a strong back. You also need a home-made tamp that consists of a block of wood attached to a wood post that serves as a handle. Use the pick to loosen the soil and to break large clumps into smaller, more manageable soil that you can grade with the steel rake. Rocks and large clumps should be removed and replaced with clean fill dirt that can be well tamped.

After you complete your grading work, use a garden hose to wet down the area to further compact the soil. Wetting down the area also gives you an opportunity to test how the soil drains.

The same holds true for paths and patios. A patio or path that slopes toward the home discharges water into the basement or crawlspace, a condition that breeds foundation problems and structural rot. Unfortunately, the only sure way to correct this problem is to remove and replace the source, and replacing a path or patio can get really pricey.

Giving the problem some air

Ventilation is another effective means of controlling moisture in a crawlspace or basement. There are two types of ventilation:

- ✔ **Passive ventilation:** This is natural ventilation that doesn't use mechanical equipment. Foundation vents (metal screens or louvers) and daylight windows for basements are the best sources of passive ventilation.
- ✔ **Active ventilation:** This type of ventilation involves mechanical equipment, such as an exhaust fan.

Passive ventilation should always be your first choice because it allows nature to be your workhorse and doesn't necessitate the use of energy to drive the mechanical device. You save on your utility bill and help the environment by not relying on fossil fuel. Having said that, never hesitate to use active ventilation when your crawlspace or basement needs it.

If you use passive ventilation, you must keep vents clean to allow maximum air flow. Thinning shrubbery, vines, and ground cover may be necessary from time to time. If vents are clear and moisture is still a problem, you may be able to add additional vents. Because adding vents can affect the aesthetic and structural elements of the home, consult a qualified engineer for this project.

All of the passive ventilation in the world may not be enough to dry out some problem basements. In these case, an active source of ventilation, such as an exhaust fan, should be installed. Installing an exhaust fan requires some minor carpentry and an electrical source. (See Chapter 14 for more information on ventilation.)

Installing a vapor barrier

Excessive dampness in a crawlspace or basement can condense, causing floor framing to become damp, covered with fungus, efflorescence, and rot. To avoid this damage to the floor framing, you can install a vapor barrier consisting of one or more layers of sheet plastic (six mil visqueen) on top of the soil in the crawlspace or basement (see Figure 3-2).

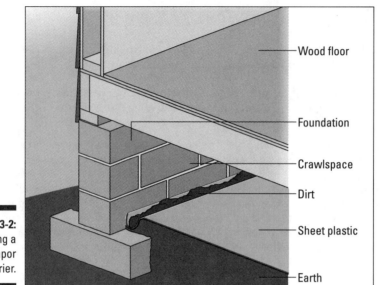

Figure 3-2:
Installing a vapor barrier.

Wood floor

Foundation

Crawlspace

Dirt

Sheet plastic

Earth

The plastic should be lapped a minimum of 6 inches and sealed with duct tape at the seams. Cut around piers and along the inside edge of the foundation. In severe cases, the plastic can run up the sides of piers and the foundation and be secured with duct tape or anchored with a line of soil at the perimeter.

Not so quick! Just because you installed a vapor barrier doesn't mean that your work under the house is done. With the plastic in place, you have a nice, dry surface on which to work to remove efflorescence or mold that has propagated on wood framing. Wearing safety goggles, use a wire brush and a putty knife or paint scraper to clean the affected areas (see Figure 3-3). Also, see "Cleaning up efflorescence" earlier in this chapter.

Figure 3-3:
Brushing off efflorescence and mold after installing your water barrier.

As you remove efflorescence or mold, have a blunt tool handy, such as a flat blade screwdriver, to test for evidence of rot (see Figure 3-4). If you can insert the blade of the screwdriver into the wood fibers using moderate pressure, it's time to call in a pest control specialist to make an inspection and suggest needed repairs.

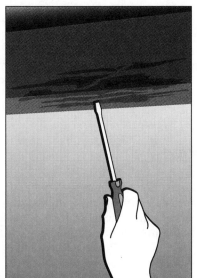

Figure 3-4:
Testing for
rotting
wood.

Wood framing that was previously damp, but not severely damaged, should be treated with a wood preservative that contains a pesticide such as copper or zinc naphthenate. The wood preservative is a liquid that can be brushed on with a throw-away paint brush.

Use extreme caution when working with wood preservatives that contain pesticides because they can be hazardous to your health — not to mention the fact that they have a fierce odor for the first week or so. Follow the manufacturer's directions on the label to the letter.

Using floor insulation

Poor or non-existent floor insulation can be another contributing factor to heightened condensation or dampness in a crawlspace or basement. See Chapter 5 for more information on insulation and the importance it plays.

Saying oui to a French Drain

If the advice we give in the previous sections doesn't help, and you are still faced with a crawlspace or basement that looks like the La Brea Tar Pits, it's time to call in a soils engineer to determine if the condition requires the installation of a French Drain, which is an elaborate drainage system.

If you already have a French Drain, even it needs maintenance. The inside of the pipe should be cleaned once a year using a pressure cleaner, which is a high-powered water blaster with a hose and nozzle for specific use within drainpipes. You can rent this equipment from a tool rental company, or you can have a plumbing contractor or sewer and drain cleaning service clean a French Drain for you.

Being Wise about Cracks

You just can't ignore cracks in a foundation or concrete slab. They are not only unsightly, but can often lead to more extensive damage where water is involved. Filling in these cracks and stopping them from spreading is essential to preventing serious structural issues in your foundation.

Foundations or structural slabs with an excessive number of smaller cracks or with cracks that are larger than ¼ inch in width should be examined by a structural or civil engineer to assess the extent of the damage and to determine the source. If the damage is severe, a geotechnical or soils engineer should be consulted to suggest solutions to correct the problem once and for all.

Even in the best of conditions, concrete moves a fraction of an inch here or there, not always resulting in a crack. And, believe it or not, concrete expands and contracts in conjunction with the temperature. That's right! Concrete expands on hot days and shrinks when the weather is cold.

Therefore, when patching cracks in concrete, we suggest that you use a product that gives a little here or there. The more elastic the product, the less likely a crack will reappear. One of our favorite patching products for cracks that are wider than ⅛ inch is a vinyl concrete patch, which usually comes packaged dry in a box.

We like to mix the dry patch powder with latex instead of water to give the product some added elasticity and adhesion. Latex additives, like patching compounds, can be found at most hardware stores or home centers.

Just as with painting, the key to successful crack repair lies in the preparation. To begin, the crack should be clean and free of any loose chips. For cracks wider than ⅛ inch, use a small sledgehammer and a cold chisel to chip away loose material (see Figure 3-5).

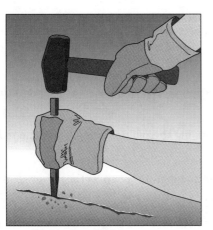

Figure 3-5:
Chipping away loose material in a crack.

Always mist a crack with water before installing a patching product. The water prevents the moisture in the patch material from being drawn out by dry concrete, which causes the patch material to crack and not form a solid bond.

Mix the concrete patch to the consistency of a thin paste and trowel it into the crack with a trowel. Scrape away any excess paste to create a smooth and uniform finish (see Figure 3-6).

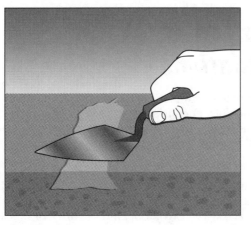

Figure 3-6:
Using a trowel to apply and smooth a patch.

Mix only a small amount of paste at a time because most products tend to dry pretty quickly. Tools and buckets should also be cleaned up immediately to avoid drying.

If you can't find vinyl concrete patch material, mix 1 part Portland cement to 3 parts sand, then add enough concrete bonding agent to make a stiff mixture about the consistency of mashed potatoes. Take a small part of the mixture and add more bonding agent so that it becomes a soupy consistency. Brush the soupy mixture into the crack using an old paintbrush and then pack the stiff mixture into the crack with a metal trowel. Use the trowel to create a smooth finish.

If the existing concrete surrounding the patch is rough, you can match the finish by sweeping it with a broom.

Large gaps of ¼ inch or greater in concrete (such as those between a concrete slab and foundation wall) require a slightly different patching method. Here, a latex caulk that contains silicone or a polyurethane caulk should be used. These products are pumped into the joint with a caulking gun and remain pliable to allow for ongoing expansion and contraction. Because most of these caulking products are self-leveling, no troweling is required.

Be sure to lightly spray the patch with water twice a day for a week to help it cure and prevent cracking.

The cost of a small box of concrete patch and a tube of concrete caulk along with a small investment of your time will do wonders to improve the overall appearance and longevity of your home's foundation.

A Few "Pointers" on Brick and Block Foundations

Bricks, at one time, were used extensively to construct foundations. Today, however, if a foundation doesn't consist of concrete, it is probably constructed of concrete block. In either case, brick and block have one thing in common. They are both joined together using mortar, a combination of sand and cement.

Unfortunately, over time, the mortar tends to deteriorate. Cracked and deteriorating mortar joints are not only unsightly, they also diminish the integrity of the surface and can allow water to get behind the brick or block causing major damage. This can be avoided by *tuckpointing* the brick or block foundation, which means the removal and replacement of cracked or missing mortar.

If the cracked or deteriorating mortar is extensive (an entire foundation, wall, or wainscot), tuckpointing is a project that is best left to professionals.

If the area is manageable, the task can easily be performed by a do-it-your-selfer by following these steps (see Figure 3-7):

1. **Chip away cracked and loose mortar using a slim cold chisel and a hammer. Remove the existing material to a depth of approximately ½ inch.**

   Be sure to wear safety goggles to avoid catching a piece of flying mortar in the eye. Use the cold chisel slowly and carefully to avoid damaging the surrounding brick. Clean up all of the loose material and dust using a brush after you finish chiseling.

2. **Prepare your mortar and allow the mix to set up for about 5 minutes.**

   Mortar can be purchased pre-mixed, or you can create your own batch using 1 part masonry cement and 3 parts fine sand. In either case, you want to add enough water to create a paste — about the consistency of oatmeal. It's best to keep the mix a touch on the dry side. If it is too runny, it will be weak and will run down the wall, making it difficult to apply.

3. **Brush the joints with fresh water.**

   Doing so removes any remaining dust and prevents the existing mortar from drawing all of the moisture out of the new mortar. Otherwise, the mortar can be difficult to apply and will most likely crack.

4. **Apply the mortar using a pie-shaped trowel called a "pointing trowel."**

   Force the mortar into the vertical joints first and remove the excess (to align with the existing adjacent mortar) using a brick jointer. The brick jointer helps create a smooth and uniform finish. After all of the vertical joints are filled in, tackle the horizontal ones.

   Avoid applying mortar in extreme weather conditions because the mortar won't properly set up.

5. **In a week or two after the mortar has had the opportunity to set up, apply a coat of high-quality acrylic or silicone masonry sealer.**

   The entire surface (brick, block, and mortar) should be sealed. The sealer prevents water damage, which is especially important if you live in an area that gets particularly cold. Unsealed brick, block, and mortar absorb water that freezes in cold weather. The water turns to ice and causes the material to expand and crack. Periodic sealing prevents this from occurring.

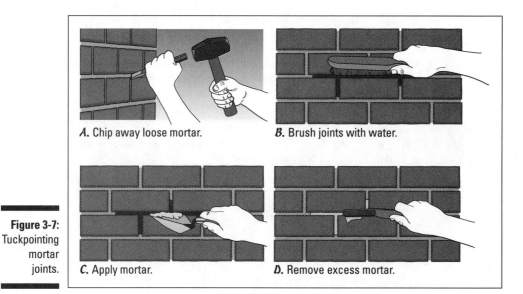

Figure 3-7:
Tuckpointing
mortar
joints.

A. Chip away loose mortar.

B. Brush joints with water.

C. Apply mortar.

D. Remove excess mortar.

Floors That Go Bump in the Night

The only good thing about squeaky floors is that no one can sneak up on you in the shower like that scene in *Psycho* where Anthony Perkins quietly tiptoes across the bathroom and surprises an unsuspecting Janet Leigh. If you don't live anywhere near the Bates Motel, you probably want to get rid of any squeaks in your floors.

Except for dragging a fingernail across a chalkboard, we can't think of a more irritating sound than a floor squeak. You know — you've paced that room hundreds of times. The one where the glasses in the cabinets chime and where the furniture wobbles. That special room where the builder left a built-in shrill that announces its presence (and yours) every time you walk by.

Boy, have we got good news for you. It doesn't have to be that way. Floor squeaks aren't difficult or expensive to repair, but without a little guidance, the task can be frustrating.

Why squeaks get started in the first place

No matter what's underfoot in the way of finish flooring — carpet, vinyl, tile or hardwood — unless your home is built on a concrete slab, underneath is wood. It's that wood that causes the squeaks — well, sort of. Conventional wisdom explains that wood sings when it flexes. Not so! Usually the squeak is a loose nail rubbing inside the hole it was originally driven into.

Lumber that is used to build a home contains a certain degree of natural moisture. This makes the wood easy to cut and minimizes splitting when it is being nailed together. Unfortunately, as the wood dries, it shrinks — a natural process that can take years. When the wood shrinks enough, once tightly seated nails can loosen and rub when the wood flexes below the pitter-patter of foot traffic, creating the familiar irritating sound: a floor squeak.

The first step in repairing a floor squeak is to find the nail that is rubbing up against the wood floor. This can be like trying to find a needle in a haystack. Here's a trick that we use to pinpoint a floor squeak so that we can make a repair. Use a short length of garden hose as a stethoscope. Hold one end of the hose to your ear and the other end on the floor while someone else walks across the floor to make it squeak (see Figure 3-8).

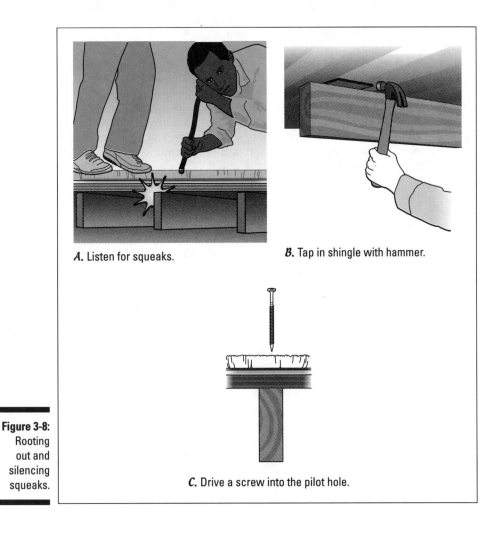

A. Listen for squeaks.

B. Tap in shingle with hammer.

C. Drive a screw into the pilot hole.

Figure 3-8:
Rooting
out and
silencing
squeaks.

If you can listen to the floor from a basement or subarea, the makeshift stethoscope yields more accurate results. If the problem is loose subfloor (the wood floor below the carpet, vinyl, hardwood, and so on), the repair can get sticky depending upon the type of finish flooring. However, if access below is available, installing a wood shim shingle between the subfloor and the floor joist is a quick and easy means of preventing the subfloor from flexing and quiets the squeak. Just squirt some carpenters glue on the thin end of the shingle and tap it in with a hammer (see Figure 3-8).

Another means of quieting a squeaking floor by preventing it from flexing is with a nifty gadget called a SqueakEnder. It consists of a metal plate and threaded-rod assembly that's screwed to the underside of the subfloor and a steel bracket. The bracket is slipped beneath the joist and over the threaded rod, then a nut is tightened onto the rod to pull down the floor and close the gap. For more information on the SqueakEnder, contact E&E Consumer Products, 7200 Miller Drive, Warren, MI, 48092; (800) 854-3577.

If access below is not available, after you locate the culprit nail, the next step is to create a better connection. Don't use nails to make the repair — use screws.

We recommend Grabber construction screws because they are easy to drive and grip like crazy. They have a finish head (like a finish nail) which makes them a particularly good choice when working on a hardwood floor. The head can be slightly countersunk and puttied. In addition, they can be driven directly through the carpet, pad, and subfloor and into a floor joist. For more information on Grabber Construction Screws, visit their Web site at www.grabberman.com.

Just follow these steps (refer to 3-8):

1. **Locate the squeak using the method discussed earlier in this section.**

2. **Drill a small pilot hole through the carpet, pad, and wood subfloor and into the floor joist.**

   The floor joist is the horizontal floor framing member that the wood sub-floor is attached to. Drilling a small pilot hole makes the job easier. The pilot hole and new screw should be installed near the existing nail that is making the noise. The old nail can remain or, if loose, should be removed using a nail puller or pry bar.

3. **Drive a construction screw into the pilot hole, through the carpet, pad, and so on.**

   When working on a hardwood floor, countersink (recess) the screw head so that it can be concealed with hardwood putty. Use a putty knife to install hardwood putty. Touch up the floor finish with 400 to 600 wet/dry sandpaper.

If you do decide to use nails, choose a ring shank nail which has a barbed shank for superior holding power. (Ask a clerk at the hardware store to help you find these nails if you don't know what they look like.) Like construction screws, ring shank nails can be driven through the carpet and pad; however, due to the size of the nail head, they are not a good choice for hardwood flooring.

We have found that talcum powder works particularly well in quieting a squeaky hardwood floor. Sprinkle a generous amount of the stuff wherever the floor makes noise. Work the powder into the joints and around any exposed nail heads. This method also works well on wood stairs. Unfortunately, this method generally provides only temporary relief for a few weeks or months. The talcum powder works great when you have company coming or are expecting houseguests for a week and don't have time to make the repair.

If the squeak persists, it may mean that settlement has occurred in the foundation, and pier post shimming may be required. This is similar to installing a shim shingle as discussed earlier. Instead, the shingle is inserted between the top of the pier post and the bottom of the girder (see Figure 3-9). Coat the end of the shingle with glue and tap it in snuggly using a hammer.

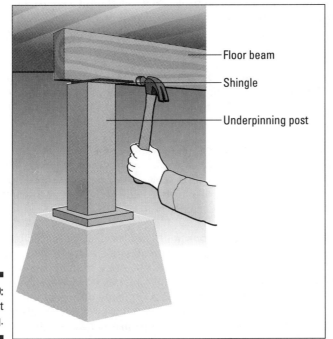

Floor beam

Shingle

Underpinning post

Figure 3-9:
Pier post
shimming.

Still struggling with a squeaking floor? Major foundation settlement or an out-of-level floor could be the problem; see the following section for more information. Because this is a more expensive repair, you may want to consider the positive aspects of owning your own floor squeak. Think about how different the movie *Psycho* would have been if Janet Leigh had heard Anthony Perkins coming.

Getting on the Level with Your Floors

Is a stroll across the floors in your home like negotiating the decks of a ship upon the high seas? If so, it's probably time to consider leveling the floor. Out-of-level floors are not only nuisances to go across, if severe enough, they can also become a real safety hazard.

Out-of-level floors can also cause cracks over windows and doors or make doors and windows stick and tough to operate. Thus, by repairing your out-of-level floor, you may find the windows and doors in your home are a whole lot easier to operate and last longer. Talk about preventative maintenance!

Not sure whether your floor is out of level and by how much? Don't head to the work shop to pull out a fancy level just yet. Simply swipe a marble (we like peeries) out of the little tyke's toy box and place it in various locations on the floor throughout the home. If the marble doesn't stay put, your floor isn't level.

The majority of homes with floors "not on the level" probably didn't start out that way. Poorly compacted soil, excessively damp soil, excessively dry soil, and shrinking support posts under the floor are a few of the most common causes of this condition.

Homes constructed on a hillside, on expansive soil (soil that expands when wet), or in earthquake country fall into a totally different group. While some of the fixes suggested in this section may indeed apply to these homes, chances are that the services of a licensed soils engineer and structural engineer will be required to do the maintenance.

If the marble test proves that your floor isn't level, be prepared to venture into your basement or crawlspace to investigate and make the necessary repairs. Unfortunately, floor leveling can't be done from above, unless you are willing to tear out the finish flooring to install a troweled-on floor leveling compound. This alternative is rare and is typically only performed when flooring is being replaced. Furthermore, you'll want to leave this one to the pros because the material that is used dries pretty fast. If you don't know what you are doing, you could end up with a bigger problem than you had before you began.

Trying some easy fixes first

Before embarking on the floor-leveling project we describe in the next section, we suggest that you take a simpler and more immediate approach that may set things straight with your floor. Start by stabilizing the moisture content of the soil near the foundation. Installing gutters and downspouts (and keeping them clean), installing downspout diverters (splashblocks), installing underground drainage systems, controlling landscape irrigation, and grading soil to shed away from the foundation are all effective means of controlling excessive moisture. (See "Avoiding Moisture under Your Home" earlier in this chapter for information on how to perform the maintenance tasks discussed in this section.)

Don't expect miracles. This isn't one of those conditions that will straighten itself out overnight. Depending upon the climate and temperature (based on the time of year that you take action), this "passive" stabilization process could take from a few weeks to the better part of a year. Try the marble test every month or so to see if your work is making difference.

If controlling the moisture near your foundation doesn't help or if there was a change for the good, but it simply wasn't enough, you need to move to plan B.

Giving the support posts some support

All right, now you can whip out that fancy level you've been dying to use. Start your floor-leveling project with a 6-foot level and a Sherlock Holmes approach. Walk the floors of your home to identify the areas that appear out of level. Place the level over the floor in various directions and read the level to determine how far out of level it is. Doing this enough times in various locations will reveal where the high and low spots exist.

Don't be intimidated by that big, fancy level. All bubble levels are read the same way, regardless of length. True level is established when the bubble in the glass tube is located equally between the centermost lines on the glass vial. Lifting one end of the level will send the bubble in one direction while lifting the opposite end will send the bubble the other way. Playing with the level, raising and lowering one side or the other, will familiarize you with how it works.

Now comes the fun part. Here's where you get to work on your belly, side, or back in a space similar to that of graves in ancient times. Seriously, working under the house can be no fun, so make sure you wear coveralls, carry a drop light, and have all the tools you'll need with you. It doesn't hurt to have a helper topside to assist because crawling in and out of the subarea can get old mighty fast. Better yet, let the helper go below while you do the "investigative" work above.

Most crawlspaces are accessed in one of two ways: through an access door in the foundation (an opening in the foundation with a door or removable panel) or through a trap door somewhere inside the home (typically in the floor of a closet). If your house is on a concrete slab or has a full basement, you don't have a crawlspace. Lucky you: no spiders to do battle with.

Sometimes you luck out when the support post that needs adjustment runs from your basement floor to the support framing of the floor above. Therefore, instead of having to work in a dark crawlspace on your belly, you can work upright in a well-lit basement.

However, if you are among the unfortunate, after you get into the crawlspace, you get to have a look around. If you've had the great misfortune of visiting the crawlspace below your home, you're familiar with the foundation at its perimeter and the various piers scattered about the interior. You may even have already bumped into a spider or two. Atop these piers, which vary in depth from home to home, are support posts called *underpinning posts*. The bottoms of underpinning posts are attached to wood blocks embedded into the tops of the concrete piers. The tops of the underpinning posts are also fastened to floor support beams called *girders*.

Sometimes the subfloor is attached directly to these girders; other times, for a more "beefy" floor, floor joists (horizontal floor framing) are installed above and perpendicular to the girders. The subfloor is then attached to the floor joist. In either case, the repair to the support posts is the same.

Over time, the piers may either sink or rise depending upon the type of soil that they are embedded in and how moist it is. If there is a lot of irrigation occurring on one side of the home along the foundation, and the water is making its way into the crawlspace, the piers in that location will likely be pushed up causing the floor to rise in that location. On the other hand, the soil at the other side of the home may be extremely dry which can cause piers to sink.

This may be contrary to what you consider logical. Mud sinks, right? Wrong! Most soil expands when wet. Hence the term "expansive soil."

In addition to your drop light, you'll need a few feet of replacement post material, a couple of lengths of 2 by 6, a handful of 16 penny nails, a circular saw, a hydraulic jack, and some patience. And don't forget your anti-anxiety medication if you're the least bit claustrophobic.

At those locations where the floor is high, place the floor jack over a block of wood directly under the support beam and a couple of feet from the pier. Using a short piece of post material, jack the floor up slightly (just enough to relieve any pressure on the existing support post) and knock out the existing post (see Figure 3-10).

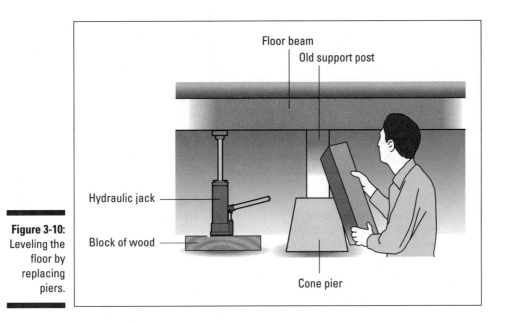

Figure 3-10:
Leveling the
floor by
replacing
piers.

Floor beam
Old support post
Hydraulic jack
Block of wood
Cone pier

Cut a new support post (shorter than the one removed by the amount calculated with your level from above) and place it between the pier and the support beam just like the one that you removed.

To determine the length of the new support post, from above, place one end of the level on the high spot and direct the opposite end to a predetermined level area on the floor. Hold the level so that the bubble is between the centermost lines in the glass vial. Then, measure the distance between the bottom of the level and the level area of flooring. The new post should equal the length of the old post less the measurement taken using the level.

Slowly lower the jack until the support rests firmly on the new support post and toenail the new support post to the pier and the support beam with two 16-penny nails at opposite sides. That's four nails at the top and four nails at the bottom. To toenail, drive nails obliquely through the end of one board into another, when the end of the first board abuts the face of the second.

You can also use approved metal connectors at both locations for a more positive connection. A metal connector is made from galvanized sheet metal that is fabricated to accommodate a specific size framing member. For example, the metal connector that would be used to anchor an underpinning post to the wood cap on a pier block is called a "post bottom." In the case of a four-by-four post, the post bottom is square (slightly larger than the size of the post and about two and one half inches high. There are holes in all sides of the connector through which nails are driven. Nails are driven through the holes in the bottom of the connector into the pier cap.

A girder-to-post connector is used at the top of the underpinning post. This connector consists of two straps that attach to opposite side of the post and two straps that attach to either side of the girder. As with the post bottom, this connector has holes in all of the faces for nailing. Both connectors must be in place before the new post is installed. Use a short level to make sure that the post is "plumb" — at a right angle to horizontal. Remember, the bubble in the glass vial needs to be centermost between the lines.

At the locations where the floor is low, the process is the same with one exception. The new support posts being installed will need to be cut longer by the amount calculated with your level from above.

In some severe cases where the condition has existed for a long period, a deep saw cut may be required at the underside of the support beam in one or more locations to make the timber more yielding and to facilitate movement of the floor up or down. The saw cut should penetrate approximately ⅔ the thickness of the timber. So, if the timber is 6 inches thick (measured vertically) the cut should be about 4 inches deep. For added strength, a splint consisting of short pieces of 2 by 6 should be glued and nailed with 16-penny nails onto either side of the support beam at the locations where cuts are made.

If your home is built on expansive soil and, thus, subject to regular movement, a screw jack is the ticket (see Figure 3-11).

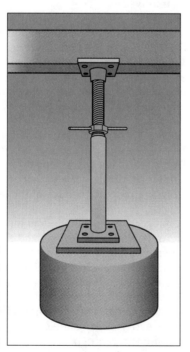

Figure 3-11:
Using a
screw jack
to shore up
your floor.

Screw jacks, also known as adjustable floor jacks, are used in lieu of solid wood posts between the concrete piers in the crawlspace and the girders (horizontal beams) that support the floor framing (joist). A screw jack is a metal support post that can be adjusted to level the floor. It consists of two heavy steel pipes, one inside the other. The inside pipe is threaded and is adjusted up and down by turning a large wing nut. The screw jack is attached with nails to the underside of the girder and to the wood block atop a concrete pier.

Screw jacks can generally be found at a local hardware store, home center or nail and tie specialty supplier. Here's how to install a screw jack:

1. **Use an hydraulic jack (like the one shown in Figure 3-9) and a short post to shore up the floor during this process.**

2. **Use a hammer, nail puller, and a sledge hammer to remove the existing underpinning wood post and nails.**

3. **Center the screw jack below the girder and on top of the wood block on the concrete pier.**

4. **Adjust the screw jack so that the top and bottom plates are flush to the wood surfaces above and below.**

5. **Drive 16-penny nails through the holes in the plates and into the wood framing.**

6. **Lower the house jack to transfer the floor load to the new screw jack.**

7. **Adjust the screw jack up or down to achieve a level surface.**

Besides not having to take motion sickness medicine anymore, don't be surprised if a few of those once-sticking doors and windows now operate just fine. It's amazing what a little trek under the house can do!

Chapter 4

Your Roofing and Siding

*Y*our entire home and its contents depend on the integrity of your roof and exterior walls in the same way that you depend on protective clothing to keep you dry in foul weather. Getting temporarily stuck in bad weather can make you slightly uncomfortable and maybe even ruin your hairdo, but left unchecked, a roof leak — even a tiny one — can end up costing a fortune in damage to a home's interior and its precious contents. Damage to flooring, plaster, wallboard, furniture, important papers, and more is no small matter.

Your Roof: The Fifth Wall of Your Home

Most folks are pretty conscientious about maintaining the exterior walls of their homes. On just about any day during good weather, you can drive through a neighborhood and find the sides of at least one home under siege by painters. But rarely do you see anyone on the roof of a home unless the roof is being replaced. For some reason, people just don't pay as much attention to their roofs, which we think is a mistake.

The whole idea of maintenance is to ensure longevity, reduce costs, and improve value. We think this concept should apply to the roof in the same way it does to the walls. In fact, we like to think of the roof as the fifth wall of the home that should be maintained with the same regularity as the walls that support it. With proper care and maintenance, a roof can outlast its warranty without leaking a drop or suffering any ugly damage.

Staying safe on the roof

A pitched roof is an alien plane. No — not a space ship from another planet. Rather, it is an unfamiliar surface to walk upon. And for the novice, an angled surface can be even more dangerous than the dastardly space ships that tried to destroy the earth in the movie *War of the Worlds*.

If you aren't agile or athletic, or if you have a fear of heights, think about hiring someone else to maintain your roof. If you do go up there, be sure to wear rubber-soled shoes. They grip better than leather. Finally, don't be afraid to wear a safety harness; it could prevent broken bones or even save your life. One carpenter who worked for us dislocated his shoulder when he grabbed onto the edge of the roof as he was sliding off during an accidental fall. Thank goodness the fall was from one story and onto soft dirt! Then again, how soft can dirt be when you fall onto it from 10 to 12 feet above?

Cleanliness is next to godliness

Streaking or discoloration can cause a perfectly good roof to look worn and tattered. And ugly is not a good thing — remember curb appeal? So, for appearance sake, use the following universal roof cleaning formula when your roof gets dirty. The concoction also gets rid of mildew or moss on your roof, which can cause extensive damage if left unattended.

You'll need these supplies:

- 1 cup liquid chlorine bleach
- 1 cup powdered laundry detergent
- 1 gallon hot water
- 1 bucket or large mixing bowl
- 1 stir stick (the kind for paint is okay)
- 1 pair of safety glasses or goggles
- 1 pump garden sprayer
- 1 stiff bristle broom
- 1 tall ladder (how tall will depend on the height of your roof)
- 1 pair rubber-soled shoes
- 1 garden hose

Do this project on a cool, humid, overcast day to make sure that the cleaner doesn't dry too fast on the roof. Wait until the weather's right and then follow these steps:

1. **Mix the hot water, bleach, and detergent until the soap granules dissolve and then pour the mixture into the garden sprayer.**

2. **Once on the roof, spray the cleaner on a strip about 3 feet high and 10 feet wide and let it sit for about 15 minutes.**

   Begin cleaning the lower portion of the roof, moving up as you clean each lower section. That way, you always stand on dry ground and reduce the chance of slipping (see Figure 4-1).

3. **If the cleaner begins to dry out, spray on a bit more.**

4. **Use the broom to scrub the area as needed to get it clean.**

5. **Rinse the cleaned area with fresh water.**

   Repeat the process until the roof is clean.

Figure 4-1:
Cleaning
your roof.

A wood shake or shingle roof covered with pine needles, leaves, moss, and other debris may retain water, causing the shingles to rot prematurely. An annual sweeping with a stiff bristle broom cuts down on fungus damage by enhancing proper watershed. Cleaning to promote proper watershed is important with other types of roofs, as well. Built-up debris can create a dam which can cause a leak.

A few uplifting words about ladders

There are as many different ladders as there are tasks that require one. They range from the small two- and three-rung "step-stool" type to the common six- and eight-foot "folding" models, to the big daddy of them all, the extension ladder. The extension ladder is the kind that "telescopes" in length. You know, like the ones used by firemen.

If your home-maintenance budget can afford only one ladder, get a six-foot stepladder. It gives you the length you need when tackling most home-maintenance and repair projects. You can change light bulbs at ceiling-mounted fixtures and paint ceilings and walls. However, if your ceilings are ten feet or greater, you need an eight-foot ladder instead. If your project involves a multi-story roof, you need an extension ladder.

Don't try to save money by purchasing a cheap ladder unless you intend to give it to someone you don't like. A cheap ladder falls apart in no time — usually with someone on it. When buying a ladder, look for secure connections, metal-supported wood steps, and superior hinges. Anything less eventually ends up failing you in the long run. As the ladder gets older, keep an eye out for loose connections, splits, and cracks and missing rivets.

Follow these tips to help you avoid any unplanned downward trips off your ladder:

- A sinking ladder can tilt and throw you to the ground. When working on dirt or turf, you may need to stabilize the ladder by placing the feet on boards or a sheet of plywood to prevent them from sinking into the earth. For added stability, place the bottom of the ladder away from the wall ¼ of the ladder's length.

- When working on the roof, the ladder should extend a minimum of two feet above the edge of the roof. The extension provides support so that you can steady yourself as you traverse from ladder to roof and vice versa.

- Never climb onto a roof from the gable end where the roof crosses the ladder rungs at an angle. Instead, mount the roof from a horizontal side. The plane of the roof should be parallel to the ladder rungs at the point where you leave the ladder to mount the roof.

- To maintain proper balance, keep your hips between the side rails when climbing the ladder or when reaching out. Keep one hand on the ladder and the other free for work.

The naked truth about flashing

Roof flashing creates a watertight connection where the roof is adjoined by a wall, as when a first-story roof connects to a second-story wall. Roof flashing also creates watertight connections between the roofing and items that penetrate it, including plumbing pipes, furnace flues, skylights, and chimneys.

The metal trim around the chimney — where the chimney intersects the roof — is a type of roof flashing. The metal trim surrounding a skylight where the base of the skylight connects to the roof is another type of roof flashing.

The metal plate laced between the shingles at a pipe penetration is yet another example of roof flashing. All roofs have roof flashing. Although some flashings are made of lead, most are made of galvanized sheet metal or aluminum. And that means rust or corrosion. And rust or corrosion means leaks.

To prevent flashings from leaking, you need to keep them from rusting. The application of a good coat of paint every few years generally does the trick.

After you apply the first coat of paint to your flashing, maintaining it is easy. You want to focus on removing any rust that appears and keeping the paint in good condition. You need the following items:

- 1 box of Tri Sodium Phosphate (TSP), mixed to manufacturer's specifications
- Sandpaper or 1 wire brush
- 1 paint brush
- 1 can of rust converter
- 1 can of latex paint

Follow these steps to maintain rust on your flashing:

1. **Wash the surface with the TSP.**

   The TSP etches (chemically roughens) the painted surface.

2. **Use the sandpaper or the wire brush to remove all rust.**

3. **Clean away the dust and use the paintbrush to apply the rust converter.**

   The rust converter acts as a primer while converting leftover rust to an inert material.

4. **Apply the latex paint as a finish coat.**

   We like to paint our roof flashings, vent pipes, and flue caps the same color as the roofing material, making them less obtrusive and more esthetically appealing.

 One type of flashing, called vent flashing, incorporates a rubber grommet that seals the connection between the centermost portion of the flashing and the plumbing vent pipe. Keep this rubber grommet in good condition with a shot of rubber preservative every year or two.

Wood shake and shingle roof preservation

No matter how clean you keep it, and no matter what condition the flashings are in, a wood shake or shingled roof usually starts looking a little worn out after only a few years. The intense ultra-violet rays of Good Old Mr. Sun cause the majority of the damage, drying shingles out and causing them to split and literally burning holes into others. The shingles can lose virtually all of their moisture (water and natural resins) in as little as five years. This can result in cupping, curling, splitting, and an almost certain early demise. However, with proper care and maintenance, you could double or even triple the life of a wood shake or shingle roof.

Want to inspect a roof and don't want to climb up there to do it? Get a good pair of binoculars. Then you can — stand back and take a close look! Split shingles, shingles with holes, cupped and curling shingles, and other damaged shingles will be as easy to spot as if you were standing right there next to them.

Super-cleaning to open the pores

The roof preservation process begins with a much more thorough cleaning than the general roof cleaning technique that we describe earlier in this chapter — roof preservation requires a super-cleaning that completely exposes all the pores of the wood. Then, later in the process, the preservative can easily penetrate deeply and completely into each and every pore. This super-cleaning also cuts through the grime and makes your wood shake or shingled roof look almost as good as new.

We recommend a pressure washer for super-cleaning a roof. This small device converts water supplied from a garden hose to a high-pressure mix of forced air and water. This mixture comes through the hose with enough force to cut through soft wood. Talk about eliminating elbow grease. Wow! You can get a power washer from a tool rental place — and some paint stores — for about $50 to $75 a day.

When using the pressure washer, hold the spray tip approximately 8 to 12 inches from the roof's surface while working backwards from the lowest part of the roof up to the highest part.

Never stand downhill of your work. You can very easily slip on the wet surface.

Special attention when mold exists

When mold is present, the pressure washing should be followed by an application of mold-killing bleach (1 quart of bleach to 1 gallon of hot water) to eliminate remaining spores that may reside deep within the pores of the wood.

Place the mixture in a garden sprayer and thoroughly wet the entire roof. Keep it wet for at least 15 minutes and then rinse with fresh water. It is important to perform this process after pressure washing — after thorough cleaning has opened the pores of the wood.

Replacing damaged shingles

After super-cleaning the wood roof, wait until it dries, and then follow these steps to replace any damaged shingles (see Figure 4-2):

1. **With the blade of a hack saw, cut the nails anchoring a damaged shingle and carefully slip it out.**

   Attempting to pry nails loose or pull a shingle out may damage surrounding shingles and make it more difficult to install the new one.

   Use the shingle you just removed as a pattern to custom cut a replacement.

2. **Slip the new shingle up and under the building paper until the butt end (the fat end) is within 1-inch of the adjacent ends.**

3. **Toenail (nail at an angle) two barbed roofing nails as high up as possible without damaging the butt end of the overlapping shingle.**

4. **Finish the repair by placing a wood block against the butt end of the new shingle and striking the block firmly with a hammer. Drive the shingle until it aligns with the surrounding shingles.**

   This process conceals the new nails, providing a more watertight installation.

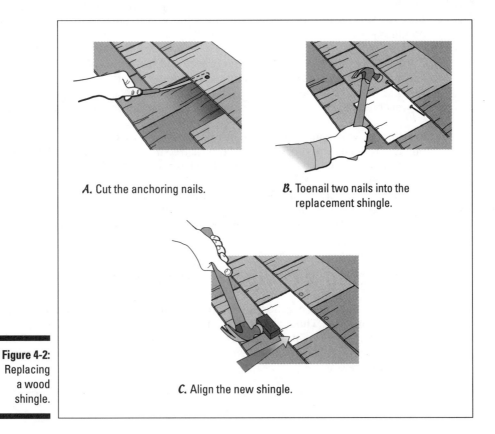

A. Cut the anchoring nails.

B. Toenail two nails into the replacement shingle.

C. Align the new shingle.

Figure 4-2:
Replacing a wood shingle.

Applying the preservative

The preservative restores the natural oils to the wood fibers, safeguards the roof from fungus and rot, and protects the roof from the harmful ultraviolet rays of the sun.

You see both oil-base and water-base preservatives at the stores. We prefer the oil-base type because it penetrates deeper, combats weather stress better, and lasts longer.

Non-pigmented preservatives can have pigments added to improve ultra-violet protection. The pigment actually masks the sun's ultraviolet rays preventing them from damaging the wood. The pigment also blends together, into one color, the older shingles and the new ones that were used to make patches.

Although you can apply preservative with a garden-type pump sprayer, the process can be done more professionally and in less time by using an airless paint sprayer. You can rent one in the same fashion as the pressure washer and for about the same cost. The process really is simple. Just spray the oil onto the roof. When the surface becomes shiny, stop spraying in that area and move on.

Apply preservative when there is no breeze and the air is still, ensuring that the majority of the product ends up on the roof and not on the neighbors' new car. Work backwards from the low end to the high side being careful not to walk on an already treated area which could be slippery (see Figure 4-3).

Most preservative applications last three to five years, depending upon the climate. Keeping the roof clean and debris-free helps extend the lasting quality of the preservative and therefore the life of the roof.

For more information on wood roof maintenance, you can contact the Cedar Guild on the Internet at www.cedar-guild.com. They offer a terrific pamphlet entitled "How to More Than Double the Life of Your Wood Roof."

Replacing a composition shingle

Replacing a damaged composition shingle is a little different than changing one made of wood. The composition shingle is more flexible and therefore somewhat more forgiving. Because composition shingles become more flexible when warm, this task is best saved for a sunny day. Here's all you have to do (see Figure 4-4):

Figure 4-3:
Applying oil
to the roof.

1. **Fold back the shingle(s) above the one to be removed.**

2. **Use a flat pry bar to remove the nails that hold the damaged shingle in place.**

3. **Slip a new shingle in position to replace the one that was removed.**

4. **Nail the new shingle in place using a flat pry bar as a hammer extension.**

Using a flat pry bar (flat bar) as a hammer extension is a really neat trick. This technique allows a nail to be driven in from beneath an overlapping shingle. First, the nail is pressed into the shingle by hand. This requires reasonably strong fingers and a bit of force. Once the nail is in place, the bottom of the flat bar is positioned so that the straight end rests atop the nail head. As the hammer strikes the flat bar, the offset below drives the nail home.

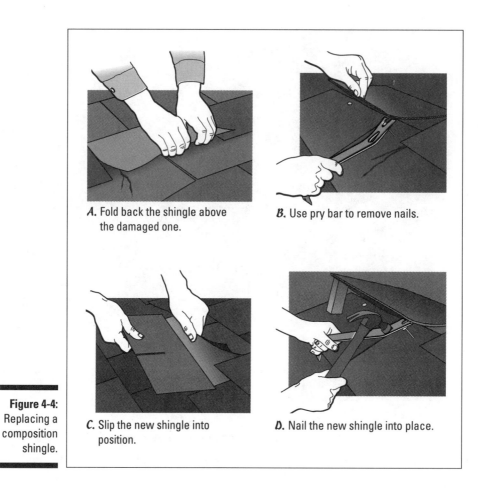

A. Fold back the shingle above the damaged one.

B. Use pry bar to remove nails.

C. Slip the new shingle into position.

D. Nail the new shingle into place.

Figure 4-4: Replacing a composition shingle.

All That Dam Ice

Did you ever wonder where icicles come from? Did you know that if you have icicles you might have an ice dam as well? And if you have an ice dam, you may soon be fighting a roof leak.

When snow falls on a roof, it seals the roof, which becomes almost airtight. As the house is warmed to a nice toasty temperature, heated air escapes into the attic. As the attic gets warmer, it melts the snow atop the roof, and water rushes downward toward the overhangs. The moment the liquefied snow hits a cold overhang it begins to freeze. The water that freezes after it rolls over the edge becomes icicles (see Figure 4-5).

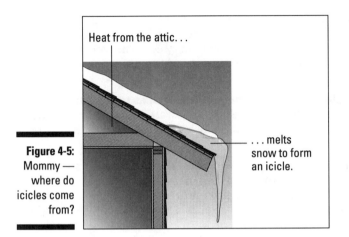

Heat from the attic. . .

. . . melts snow to form an icicle.

Figure 4-5: Mommy — where do icicles come from?

Water that freezes before it rolls over the edge builds up to create a barrier known as an *ice dam,* which becomes larger and larger as runoff continues to freeze. Finally, the ice on the overhang widens to the point where it reaches the edge of the attic. At this point, the water remains liquid and the ice dam causes it to back up over the attic where it can leak into the home.

All too often, this is precisely what happens — water held back by the ice dam backs up and leaks into the home. There are other negatives about ice on your roof. Ice buildup can damage rain gutters, causing costly repairs. By preventing ice buildup, you might be able to save your house from being flooded during a freeze and add a little life to your gutters, as well.

To prevent an ice dam, you need to keep the attic cold. Not the house — the attic. If the attic is cold, the snow on the roof won't melt, and ice dams won't form. Here's how to make it happen:

- ✔ **Don't close off eave and roof vents during the winter.** This traps the warm air that melts snow on the roof.

- ✔ **Fill all penetrations between the living space and the attic area with foam sealant.** You can buy it in a spray can. Look for penetrations in the ceiling in the following places (many may be hidden beneath attic insulation): plumbing vents, ventilation ducts, heat registers, electric wiring, and ceiling light fixtures.

- ✔ **Don't caulk around furnace flues.** A flue that contains hot gasses should not come into contact with combustibles such as wood or foam sealant. Contact your local heating or sheetmetal contractor and have a metal draft stop installed. It can be sealed to the pipe and the house frame without creating a fire hazard.

✔ **Check your attic insulation.** Be sure that your attic insulation is loose (as opposed to compacted) and that there is a more than sufficient amount up there. Check with your local utility company. Most offer free energy audits. Your local building department is another inexpensive inspection alternative.

✔ **Consider installing an eave-heating device such as heating tape or heating wire (see Figure 4-6).** They prevent water from freezing on your eave. Eave heaters operate on extremely low voltage, making them inexpensive to operate.

✔ **Install special metal flashings at problem eaves.** Ice doesn't stick to the metal as readily as it does to most types of roofing. The nice thing about metal flashings is that they can be made to order by your local heating or sheetmetal contractor. You may be able to save money by looking for a product at your local home center known as "Ice and Water Shield."

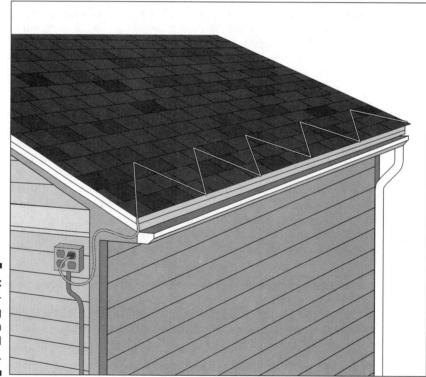

Figure 4-6:
An eave-heating device can help avoid dam ice.

ANECDOTE

A true story

When we were kids, our Aunt and Uncle had a cabin in the mountains that we visited for a week in the summer and again each winter — our ritual summer and winter vacations. Every summer we watched our Uncle and, in later years, his sons mix graphite and oil together and then apply it to the "A-frame" roof of their cabin. The concoction preserved their wood shingles and caused the snow to run off more quickly each spring. In 35 years we never saw the roof replaced once.

Find That Leak!

The first step in repairing a leak is finding its point of origin. This can be extremely difficult on a flat roof, so we recommend that you hire an industry professional to find and repair a leak in a flat roof. However, on a pitched roof, do-it-yourselfers can find the leak themselves. You'll still need to hire a contractor to repair the leak, but being able to tell the contractor where the leak is saves time and shows the contractor that he or she is dealing with an informed home owner.

While water testing a pitched roof is not a difficult process, it can be time-consuming and tedious. Be prepared to exercise a bit of patience. The process requires two people, one on the roof and one in the attic (or living space below if no attic exists). You also need the following tools:

- 1 ladder
- 1 garden hose
- 1 flashlight

Then follow these steps (see Figure 4-7):

1. **Use the garden hose to run a modest amount of water over the roof at a point below the area where a leak is suspected.**

   Don't run the hose full blast. Don't use a spray nozzle, and don't force the water between the shingles. Doing so may force water into the home, creating the illusion that you've found a leak when, in fact, you did nothing more than temporarily create one.

   Work from the lowest point of the roof (near the eaves or gutters) in an area of about 4 to 6 feet wide. Work your way up the roof a couple of feet at a time. Standing on dry roofing above the water helps prevent a sudden and unexpected slip.

2. **Station your partner in the attic and tell him or her to holler at the first sign of water.**

The moment your helper sees water, he or she should let you know. A whaling screech will usually do the trick. An inexpensive pair of kids' walkie-talkies allows you to communicate clearly without yelling.

Figure 4-7:
Water
testing a
pitched roof.

It's Okay If Your Mind Is in the Gutter

Gene Kelly would probably not be remembered as well for his part in *Singin' in the Rain* if the movie set had been equipped with rain gutters. As a matter of fact, the producers would probably have changed the title of the film to something like *He Stayed Dry While Singing Near The Rain*.

When it comes to the place you live, singing in the rain isn't what you'll be doing if you haven't properly maintained your gutters and downspouts.

Cleaning gutters and downspouts

Gutters and downspouts filled with debris can back up, causing roof leaks, rot at the overhang, and structural damage.

Once a year, you need to get up on the ladder and give those gutters and downspouts a good cleaning. Gutters that have not been cleaned for a while may be filled with a mud-like substance, which you can scoop out with a small garden trowel or a putty knife. You may even want to invest in a gutter scoop (a plastic trowel-like scoop made especially for cleaning gutters).

After you remove the majority of the debris, flush the rest away using a garden hose with a spray nozzle. If the water pressure at your place is insufficient, you can rent a small pressure washer to help flush out debris. We both own pressure washers just for this purpose.

Patching up leaks

When galvanized sheet metal gutters aren't properly maintained (regularly cleaned and painted) they tend to rust. As we mention earlier in this chapter, unpainted metal rusts, and rust results in leaks. The same technique used to maintain roof flashings can be enlisted on gutters.

When a rusty area turns into a leak, try this quick repair. You need the following tools:

- ✔ 1 wire brush (or a wire wheel mounted on an electric drill)
- ✔ 1 throw-away paint brush
- ✔ Strips of tin foil or plastic (for pinhole leak repairs) or small strips of galvanized sheet metal (for larger hole repairs). Whether the strips are made of foil, plastic, or metal, they only need to be slightly larger than the hole being repaired.
- ✔ Rust converter
- ✔ Paint
- ✔ Roofing cement
- ✔ Putty knife

If the gutter is sagging, replace the mounting brackets before fixing leaks. You don't want the gutter shape to change once the leak has been fixed. This could cause a patch to open.

With your tools assembled, follow these steps to patch the leak:

1. **Use the wire brush or a wire wheel on a drill to remove as much rust from the area as possible.**

2. **Apply a coat of rust converter over the repair area.**

   The converter renders any minute remnants of rust inert. With rust you can't be too careful. Allow the converter to dry completely.

3. **Apply an ⅙-inch-thick coat of roof cement around the leak. Before the cement dries, add a strip of tin foil to the repair area (kind of like taping a Band-Aid to your arm). Use a putty knife to gently flatten the foil and squeeze out the excess cement.**

   The total thickness of the repair should not exceed ⅙ inch. A dam can be created if too much roof cement is used.

   For larger repairs (bigger than a pinhole), the tin foil should be replaced with a piece of sheet metal. Heating contractors typically have a trash can full of scraps that are perfect for this type of repair. Chances are you can get the scrap you need for a handshake and a thank you. For badly damaged areas, sheet metal plates can be pop-riveted into place and sealed with liquid aluminum. However, this is a maintenance task that you may want to leave to the sheet metal contractor.

4. **With the foil in place use a putty knife to add another thin layer of roof cement sufficient to completely cover the patch.**

If the repair area is too large, then you should consider replacing the damaged sections. The style you have is probably still available. You would be amazed at how little gutter shapes have changed over the years.

Occasionally, a gutter seam or joint will open producing a leak. Catching this problem early on will reduce the chance of rust and, possibly, a major repair. Seams in aluminum and galvanized sheet metal gutters can be caulked with liquid aluminum. Plastic gutters can be repaired with polyurethane caulk. Be sure to thoroughly clean the area before applying the caulk.

Siding: A Raincoat to Keep You Dry

Water can attack and damage wood siding. Stucco walls crack when the house shifts as winter rains expand soil. Metal siding dents easily. Vinyl siding pits as it oxidizes. Even bricks chip and crack with winter freezes and summer ground settlement.

No surface is perfect; no material perfectly withstands the rigors of nature and the force of the elements. But you can do a thing or two to add life and beauty to your home's siding.

Wood siding

When wood's moisture content reaches 20 to 30 percent, fungi deep within its fibers begin to grow and flourish causing dreaded *wood rot.*

Wood siding should be treated with an application of oil, stain, or paint to prevent rot. These materials act as a barrier, preventing water from coming into direct contact with the wood. Which finish you choose is mostly an esthetic choice:

- Oil, a clear finish, is absorbed into the wood, filling all pores and voids, thereby displacing water that would otherwise be absorbed.

- Oil stain is the same as oil except that a pigment gets mixed into the oil.

- Paint penetrates and protects in the same way that oil does. Additionally, paint coats the surface of the wood with a thin, durable waterproof hide.

Oil is easier to apply than paint, and if the oil is clear (or almost clear), mistakes are nearly impossible to detect. Therefore, oil is pretty forgiving. When the oil contains stain, the added pigment makes application slightly more difficult (mistakes show more readily). But, the added pigment helps to filter out more of the sun's damaging ultraviolet rays. Unfortunately, oil has a tendency to evaporate and won't last as long as paint. However, unlike paint, oil and oil stains do not split, chip, or blister.

Everything's a trade-off. With oil you won't ever have to sand, scrape, or chisel the surface to prepare it for another application. But, be ready to re-apply a new coat every several years. With an oil stain, figure about three to five years of lasting quality. A good grade of paint, applied to a properly cleaned surface, lasts seven to ten years or more. Paint certainly lasts longer, but it is by far the most difficult to apply.

Follow this general rule of thumb to determine the lasting quality of oil and oil stains: The more wood that you can see when the job is complete, the more often you can expect to redo the finish.

Paint experts agree that 80 percent of a good oil, stain, or paint job is in the preparation. But the exterior of your home is no small area. And when it comes to preparation (removing old layers of loose paint, a tattered layer of stain, a discolored layer of wood, or just plain dirt), you can expect to do some major work.

Fortunately, tools are available at home centers, paint stores, and rental outlets that help make cleanup and removal an almost fun job, including sand blasters, soda washers, and pressure washers. All these tools involve some degree of work on your part, but they are a breeze to use compared to a hand-scrapper, a hand-chipper, or a blowtorch. Our personal choice is a pressure washer.

Painted surfaces

Prepare for repainting by insuring that all old loose paint has been completely removed. A new coat of paint won't stick any better than the old paint below it.

Whether you hand scrape or pressure wash, be sure to sand spots where a painted surface meets a bare spot. Tapering or feathering these transition points makes them less visible and guarantees a nicer looking finished product.

Prime all bare spots with a high-grade oil-base primer. Then caulk all joints with a high-grade 50-year, paintable silicone or polyurethane product. Joints are caulked to prevent water from getting behind the siding. Any joint that will allow this to happen should be caulked.

Tinting a standard white primer a shade or two lighter than the finish coat can improve coverage. For example, a light brown finish coat covers a beige primer more effectively than it covers a white primer. This is not an exact science. In fact, the primer can be almost as dark as the finish coat or several shades lighter. Anything is better than painting a dark finish coat over a light primer.

Oiled surfaces

Oiled surfaces are prepared for refinishing differently than painted ones. Clean the wood with a pressure washer, apply a coat of wood bleach, let it stand (per manufacturer's instructions), and pressure wash again. At this point a fresh coat of oil or oil-stain can be applied. Your oiled siding will look so good you won't believe you did it yourself.

Stucco maintenance

Stucco is really cool stuff. It doesn't rot, and compared to other types of siding, it's relatively easy to maintain. Stucco is very porous and holds on to paint better than most other kinds of siding. Also, stucco is one of the easiest surfaces to prepare and paint. So, if you have stucco — count your blessings.

Unfortunately, its brittle, damage-resistant surface can sometimes be a drawback. When the house shifts, rigid things crack.

Caring for cracks

For cracks up to a ¼-inch wide, caulking solves the problem. Just follow these simple steps:

1. **Clean all loose debris from the crack.**

   A can opener and a vacuum cleaner work wonders here.

2. **Use a paintable silicone caulk — and your finger — to make an invisible repair.**

   Don't use a putty knife. Doing so prevents you from matching the existing texture. With your finger you can force the caulking in the crack to align with the irregular surface of the stucco.

 Don't use just any caulk; use the 50-year kind, which really does hold better and longer.

Taking a chunk out of gouges

You can repair wider cracks and gouges with a latex patching compound. Follow mixing instructions carefully. The amount of water you use can change the properties of the patching compound. If this happens, it may not hold as well. Then follow these steps:

1. **Clean all loose debris from the crack or gouge.**

2. **Use a latex patching product and a putty knife or trowel to fill the area.**

3. **Apply a second coat to match the surface texture.**

   Thin the patching compound to a pancake-batter consistency. Dip the end of a paintbrush into the mixture. Holding your hand between the wall and the paintbrush, slap the handle of the brush against your hand. The patching compound splatters onto the surface, matching the texture of the stucco. If the texture is flat, wait for the splattering to become slightly firm and then wipe it to the desired flatness with a putty knife or a trowel.

Painting stucco

Really porous stucco absorbs gallons of paint causing a great deal more paint to be used than is really need. If you're painting stucco for the first time, save paint by using a water hose to completely wet the surface of the stucco before applying paint. The water fills the pores in the stucco thereby preventing excess amounts of paint from absorbing deep into the stucco. Wait for surface water to evaporate first and then begin painting.

Vinyl siding

Vinyl siding is a great looking product. It doesn't warp, split, or buckle and, according to what several manufacturers espouse, it doesn't ever have to be painted. The fact is — it can't be painted. Paint simply will not stick to vinyl in the same way that it sticks to wood.

This wouldn't be important except that, like all types of exterior siding, vinyl does have its shortcomings. The surface of vinyl siding etches in time. As the surface deteriorates, the pitted result causes the material to become dull and prone to stain.

The only way to combat this problem is to regularly clean the siding. Twice a year is good — once in the spring and then again in the fall. Use a pressure washer with laundry detergent to get the surface sparkling clean. Most pressure washers have a plastic dip tube that can be used to blend in things like chemicals and detergents.

Keeping the surface of the vinyl clean won't prevent it from oxidizing, but it will prevent corrosive chemicals in the air from attacking the surface. Ever seen what bird poop can do to a car's paint job? Regular washing at least slows the process of deterioration.

Aluminum siding

Aluminum is another beautiful siding that man has created in an attempt to outdo nature. They said it wouldn't rust like steel, that it would never have to be painted, and that it would simply last forever. Well, the truth is it probably will last forever. But, by then, it won't look new at all.

Think of aluminum siding in the same way that you think about a car body. It's a smooth metal surface covered with paint that needs to be regularly cleaned, polished, and waxed. Really, think about it. Aluminum siding is metal that is formed and polished and given a factory paint job just like a car body. So what automobile paint job do you know of that will last forever?

The fact is that aluminum siding, like all the others, does need to be maintained and occasionally painted. If you want to see a good case of chalked (oxidized) paint, then get up close and personal to a 20-year-old home sided with aluminum that has never been cleaned or painted. So, how do you prevent chalking? You don't prevent chalking, but you can make light work of getting it to disappear. All you have to do is attend to it on a regular basis.

Pressure wash regularly, once or twice a year, and don't forget the laundry detergent. Your aluminum siding will remain bright and shiny for years. And the task won't ever seem overwhelming.

When the time comes to paint your aluminum siding, follow these tips:

- Aluminum siding should not be scraped. Aluminum has a smooth surface and should be sanded with a finer 400- to 600-grit sandpaper.
- A zinc oxide primer (metal primer) is best for bare aluminum.
- An aluminum surface is smooth and should be spray painted for best results.
- An aluminum surface should be patched with a filler made especially for metal — like car Bondo.

Chapter 5

The Energy Envelope

M ost home maintenance projects save you money over time. But only a few of them produce an immediate and measurable return. Maintaining your home's energy envelope is one such project. The floors, walls, ceilings, doors, and windows of your home combine to make up its energy envelope. When the energy envelope is properly maintained, your personal comfort level reaps the benefits by better protecting you from the elements. And your wallet also notices a difference when you aren't paying such high heating and cooling bills.

Saving Energy with Insulation

The furnace is running "full bore" and yet you feel a chill all the way down to your bones. There isn't a window open in the house, and the walls and ceilings are fully insulated. You simply can't figure out where the cold is coming from.

Well, if your home is 20 years old, or older, you may need to perform a little maintenance on your insulation. And the attic is the first place you should look. Believe it or not, most heat is lost through the ceiling — 60 percent or more. Heat rises! Walls account for about 20 to 30 percent of the heat loss, with the rest escaping through the floor. Properly maintained insulation can significantly reduce this heat loss.

Types of insulation

There are two basic kinds of insulation:

✔ **Loose-fill insulation:** This kind of insulation is made out of small individual chunks of fibers. It is also known as "blown" insulation because it is installed with a blower, a giant vacuum cleaner that works in reverse.

✔ **Batt insulation:** Insulative fibers are woven together to create a continuous blanket of material. Batt insulation is available in 16 and 24 inch wide rolls (or 8 foot strips) to fit standard spacing between ceiling and wall framing members. A paper or foil moisture barrier is glued to one side of this type of insulation. (We prefer not to use the foil-backed type because it tends to promote condensation that can result in mildew growth.)

When installing batt insulation, always place the side with the backing toward the inside of the home. For example, with ceilings, the backing goes down, and for floors, the backing faces up.

Filling holes in insulation

Loose fill insulation can cause many problems — especially in the attic. Powerful air currents are created in your attic as air enters through eave vents and exits through higher gable or ridge vents. Natural air currents can actually move loose fill insulation as if being swept by a broom, resulting in piles of insulation in some areas and none in others (see Figure 5-1).

Figure 5-1:
Loose fill
insulation
that has
shifted.

If you have loose fill insulation, look to see if the insulation in your attic has shifted. If some areas of your ceiling are bare, the problem can be solved with a plastic lawn rake. Use the rake to gently move the insulation from high spots onto the bald areas. Note that we said plastic. With electrical wires present in the attic, it would not be wise to use a metal rake.

A piece of batt insulation also could be used to cover a hole. Hey, it would save raking. And it couldn't be easily blown out of place. Just follow these steps:

1. **Measure the approximate area to be filled — the bald spot.**

2. **Use a razor knife or a pair of scissors to cut pieces of batt insulation to the approximate length required. Cut as many pieces as necessary to fill the space.**

   This is not an exact science. The batts of insulation can overlap the loose fill material. Or, the loose fill material can be pushed out of the way to make room for the new insulation.

3. **Lay the material in place.**

If your insulation appears to be in good shape, but you still feel a chill, you may need to add more. Check with your local public utility or your local building inspector for advice on what to do.

Keep attic insulation clear of light fixtures. If the light boxes are covered with insulation, they can overheat and a fire can result. And above all, don't make the mistake of plugging attic vents. An attic must be able to breathe, otherwise, trapped hot air can convert even the best insulated home into a sweatbox on a hot summer day. Not to mention that a build-up of humidity can occur, which over a long period of time can result in wood rot, mildew, mold, and fungus growth.

A skylight chase is the walled area that immediately surrounds the skylight between the roof and the ceiling. Skylight chases that run from the roof to the ceiling should also be insulated.

Over the years insulation requirements in homes have changed. R-19 was once sufficient for use in attics. Today, in moderate climates, R-38 is required. In extreme climates, R-60 makes is necessary. You may not have enough to meet new requirements. Check with the building department in your area to determine the correct R-value for your home. With insulation, thicker is better. Loosely packed, but thicker. You really can't use too much. However, there is a point of diminishing return.

Choosing an insulation material

If you discover that you do need to repair, maintain, or upgrade the insulation in your home, you will find that there are several types of material that are available. You can choose from fiberglass, rock wool, or cellulose. They all work. Here is what we think about each type.

Fiberglass

Fiberglass insulation is the most popular and widely available type of insulation. You can buy it as either batts or loose fill. Also, it is relatively inexpensive, and the batts are very easy to install. Finally, it is non-flammable and resists damage from water.

Unfortunately, the fibers can irritate your skin and lungs, so take precautions while handling it. Use gloves, breathing apparatus, protective clothing, goggles, and a hat to reduce an itchy aftermath. In fact, these safety precautions should be followed regardless of the type of insulation.

Taking a cold shower after working with insulation helps remove tiny fibers that make their way to your skin. Don't take a hot shower. Doing so opens the pores of your skin and allows the pesky fibers more opportunity to make you uncomfortable.

Rock wool

Mineral wool or "rock wool" is very similar to fiberglass insulation. It is a little more expensive and somewhat more difficult to find, but doesn't usually provoke the itchy reaction caused by fiberglass. It looks a great deal like lint from a dryer and can be equally dusty when handled. Rock wool can be blown in like fiberglass. It is also available in bags that allow it to be poured in place. Rock wool can cake when wet and naturally settles over time. Either of these conditions will diminish its insulating value.

Cellulose

Cellulose insulation is an organic, loose-fill material made from recycled paper. This requires it to be chemically treated to resist attack from moisture and pests. Moisture absorption can make cellulose heavier causing it to pack down and lose its insulative value.

If you have cellulose insulation in your walls or ceilings, the insulative value has probably diminished substantially since it was first installed. When loose-fill insulation compacts, you should vacuum out the old and start fresh.

Mixing and matching

The various kinds of insulation can be mixed and matched. If cellulose insulation exists, and more material is needed, you can add any type of fiber you wish. It is also acceptable to use batts over loose-fill material and loose-fill material over batts.

The nice thing about attic insulation is that it doesn't have to be glued, nailed, stapled, or otherwise held in place. All it does is lay there. Adding more simply means going up there and spreading it evenly around. With batts this can mean unrolling it and placing pieces side by side, and with loose fill it can be as simple as shaking it out of a bag. The toughest part of this maintenance project is protecting your lungs, skin, and eyes.

Wall insulation

If mildew grows on the inside surface of your exterior walls, or if your exterior walls are sweating (you see excessive condensation), it may mean that there is no wall insulation or that the insulation has settled and compacted. In either case insulation should be added. When wall insulation is up to snuff, condensation doesn't occur as readily, diminishing the possibility of fungus growth. No condensed water means no fungus food, and therefore, no fungus growth.

Adding insulation to a wall is a bit more difficult than adding it to an attic. In an attic the insulation is usually exposed. In a wall the insulation resides between the interior and exterior wall coverings. To insulate a wall, you have to either remove the wall covering or create small penetrations and blow the insulation into the wall cavity. It is simply not cost effective to remove a wall covering to insulate the wall cavity. Therefore, blown insulation is usually used to insulate the walls of a completed home.

Because wall framing members (studs) are spaced every 16 inches or so, penetrations to add insulation must be made at the same intervals, thus filling one cavity at a time. In some homes a horizontal block exists midway between the top and bottom of a wall cavity. In such cases two penetrations must be made into each wall cavity: one above the horizontal block and one below it.

Floor insulation

An insulated floor substantially reduces the loss of heat (thank you energy gods), helps to eliminate mildew- and rot-causing condensation, and generally helps to keep your tootsies warm when you go barefoot through the kitchen (and other areas where carpet doesn't exist).

If you have hardwood floors, you should be especially interested in maintaining your floor insulation. We have seen instances where lack of floor insulation caused planks of hardwood flooring to twist, buckle, and curl.

Periodically you should crawl beneath your home with a flashlight to check the condition of the floor insulation in your basement or subarea. You want to insure that it is properly positioned. Here, sagging is the biggest problem. Floor insulation is normally held in place (between the floor joist) with netting or bailing wire attached from one joist-bottom to another (see Figure 5-2). If the insulation netting sags, it should be reattached or replaced. Nails hold better than staples but are hard to drive in tight spots. Staples are easier to install, but it may mean buying a tool. Construction-grade staple guns can be purchased at your local hardware store or home center.

Lightning rods (named for their speedy installation) are a handy alternative to netting or bailing wire when maintaining sagging floor insulation. These lightweight, flexible steel rods hold the insulation in place by spring tension. You place one end of the rod against the side of a floor joist and bend it slightly so that the other end is forced into place against the face of the opposite joist (see Figure 5-2). Use one hand to hold the insulation up and the other hand to whip the lightning rod into place. Lightning rods are available at hardware stores, home centers, and from insulation contractors.

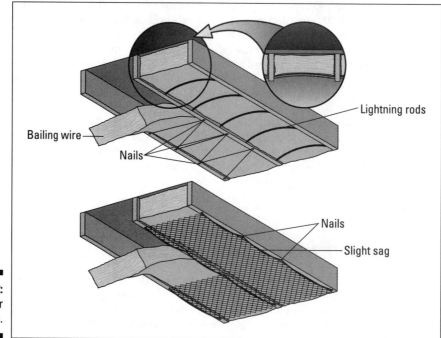

Figure 5-2:
Floor
insulation.

Insulating pipes

Putting insulation around all accessible water pipes saves energy, prevents freezing during most moderate to medium chills, and reduces condensation when pipes flow through attics and crawlspaces (see Figure 5-3).

Properly maintained pipe insulation can be cheap insurance. A pipe that bursts in the crawlspace is no joy to experience or repair, but it's bearable. A pipe that bursts in the attic is an altogether different story. An attic burst can literally destroy a substantial portion of your home before the leak is stopped. We know. Years ago, long before we were old enough to spell contractor (let alone be one) a pipe in our attic burst. What a mess.

Be sure that the tape, which holds the insulation in place, is in good shape, and make sure the insulation is still in good condition, as well. If either the insulation or the tape crumbles to the touch, the material should be replaced. If the insulation is crumbling, removal requires nothing more than a gentle tug. With the insulation removed, all you have to do is slip a new piece in place.

Pre-formed, tubular, foam pipe insulation is slit lengthwise to insure easy installation. All you have to do is open the slit and lay the insulation onto the pipe. Pipe insulation comes in 6-foot lengths and is easy to cut with scissors or a razor knife.

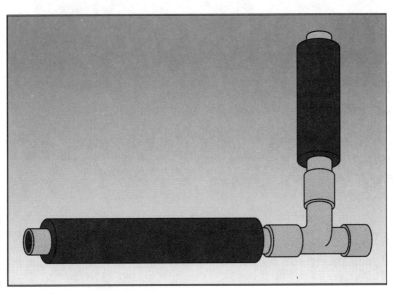

Figure 5-3:
Insulated
pipes.

If you live in an area where temperatures frequently reach below freezing, and you have installed pipe heaters (wire or tape), don't insulate these pipes without first getting the approval of the company that manufactures the pipe heaters. By the way, pipe heaters also deteriorate. If you see signs of deterioration or fraying, it may be time for replacement.

Heat duct insulation

As with other kinds of insulation, the material that surrounds your heat ducts reduces energy costs while improving the effectiveness of your central heating and cooling system. It also helps prevent unwanted condensation in attics and crawlspaces, thereby reducing the chance for mold, mildew, and the foul odors associated with them.

Insulation is wrapped around and around the duct in a corkscrew fashion (see Figure 5-4). Air currents, rodents, house movement, and vibration in the heating system can cause the insulation to loosen and fall away from the ducting. Reattaching or adjusting the insulation to cover the ducting is a good thing. While you're there, add an extra layer. It couldn't hurt.

A nail can be "stitched" into insulation to hold it together. This is done in the same way that a seamstress uses a sewing pin to hold two pieces of fabric together.

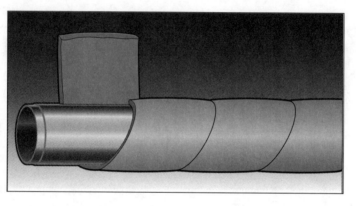

Figure 5-4:
Heat duct
insulation.

A thin layer of plastic, which acts as a vapor barrier, surrounds modern insulated heat ducts. The plastic prevents moisture from attacking the insulation and the ducting. Isn't plastic wonderful! Again, rodents, house movement, and sloppy workers can damage the thin plastic vapor barrier. Plastic sheeting (any kind) and metal tape can be used to fix the barrier.

Metal tape looks like duct tape only shiny. Metal tape won't rot in moist areas where duct tape can. Actually, for small tears, just tape over the damaged area in the same way you would cover a cut with an adhesive bandage. For areas of larger damage, use a piece of plastic as a patch held in place with metal tape. The tape should seal all four sides of the patch.

Infiltration control

If your home is like most, your attic and exterior walls are insulated. If you're a real smart consumer, you also have insulated floors. Congratulations if all three areas are insulated!

The good news is that insulation is pretty easy to maintain. The bad news is that there is more to the energy envelope than maintaining insulation. Insulation alone will not do the trick. Another maintenance step, known as *infiltration control,* also must be performed periodically.

Infiltration control refers to the control of air leaks through penetrations in ceilings, walls, and floors. Believe it or not, infiltration control is critically important to a proper insulation job. No matter how much insulation exists in your home, if major air leaks exist, your insulation won't work effectively.

Locating leaks

Unwanted air can leak into your home from all sorts of places: at weather stripping, door and window frames, attic and subarea plumbing and electrical penetrations, at heat registers, yes, and even at electrical switches and receptacles.

Infiltration also occurs where pipes and wires in walls penetrate into the attic or subarea. When this condition exists, air can travel freely between the attic or subarea and the inside of the house. Air travels through the inside of a wall and out into the living area via wall penetrations, such as a heat register, a wall switch, or a plug.

Finding a penetration in an attic or crawlspace isn't terribly difficult when it comes to plumbing pipes, flues and ventilation, and heating ducts. Just check the point where a pipe or duct penetrates the ceiling or floor and look for gaps.

Unfortunately, wiring poses a different problem — especially in an insulated area. Short of removing the insulation, there is no way of seeing where penetrations exist. That's because the wiring normally doesn't stick up beyond the insulation like a pipe or a flue. This means searching through insulation until you find a point where a wire travels down through the top of a wall. Normally, a large gapping hole will need to be sealed.

The amount of infiltration from walls, ceilings, and floors is simply amazing. Fortunately, you can easily locate these leaks in the myriad places they occur: around light switches, electric plugs, drain and water pipes, heat registers, thermostats, wall and ceiling light fixtures, smoke and carbon monoxide detectors, floor plugs, door bell chimes, doors, and windows.

Just light a candle and hold it next to suspect leak point. If a leak exists, the flame flickers. Using a smoky incense stick also works and may be safer.

Be careful when using the flame around drapes. They can easily catch fire when you're busy looking for leaks.

Stopping infiltration

In the days when we were the maintenance men aboard the ark, we filled small cracks (no wider than ¼ inch) with caulking. For larger openings we stuffed insulation or steel wool into the gaps. For the largest and most gaping of holes, we used tin plates or wood covers.

Today, things have changed. Expanding polyurethane spray foam in a can is now available. No more time consuming tin plate installations or replacing insulation or steel wool that has fallen out. Simply spray a little expanding foam into the gap, and it immediately expands to permanently seal the hole (see Figure 5-5). Home maintenance in a can. What a country!

Where polyurethane spray is now best for large gaps, then and now, caulking is still best for narrow cracks. The kind of caulking to use will depend on the area being caulked. Glass, metal, wood, plastic, and other surfaces each respond differently to caulk. Read the manufacturer's label carefully before making your purchase.

Another new and very recent development in infiltration control is precut gasketing for electrical switches and outlets. The gasketing is thin foam material that fits neatly between the plug or switch cover and the wall. Each gasket is precut to match either a plug cover or a switch. Holes are also precut for the mounting screws that hold the cover plate to the wall.

If your electrical boxes aren't gasketed, we suggest that you add them. An entire home can be gasketed for under $50. Outlets on interior walls also should be covered. Don't forget that air can get into interior walls via wire and pipe holes that penetrate through to the attic and crawlspace.

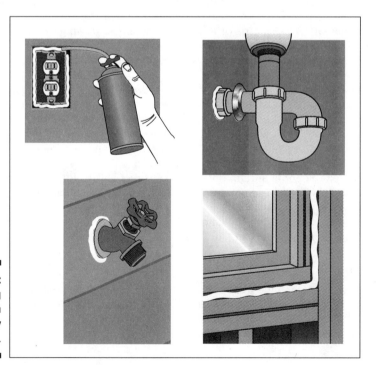

Figure 5-5:
Stopping infiltration with spray foam.

Windows: See the Light and Feel the Cold

As beautiful as they are, windows aren't as energy efficient as insulated walls. Unfortunately, you can't see through a wall. Imagine your home with no windows — it's probably not a place where you would want to live. Fortunately, you have a choice.

Here are a few maintenance suggestions for your windows that will make Here are a few maintenance suggestions for your windows that will make them more energy efficient, add longevity to their existence, and make them easier to operate.

Caulking to prevent water leaks

Often water leaks at a window result from a breakdown in the connection between the frame of the window and the frame of the house. To prevent leaks, the window should be caulked where its frame meets the exterior siding (see Figure 5-6). If the window is surrounded by wood trim, all gaps between the trim and the siding (and the trim and the window frame) should be sealed with a high-grade polyurethane caulk. Take special care to seal the top side of the top piece of trim. Puddling water at this location causes many window leaks.

Figure 5-6:
Caulking an
outside
window.

Preventing leaks with weather stripping

Leaks also occur when weather stripping wears out. You may have to remove the operable portion of the window to find the weather stripping:

✔ **Sliding windows:** Open them half way and lift the window out of the bottom track. Then pull the window out of the opening bottom first.

✔ **Single hung windows:** Usually, you just release a lever on the side track(s) of the window frame. Contact the manufacturer for specific instructions.

After you remove the operable portion of the window, it becomes pretty obvious where the weather stripping is and how it will have to be replaced. Most home centers offer replacement weather stripping in peel-and-stick rolls. If you aren't sure about what to do, take the section that you removed to the store with you or photograph the area that needs attention. A picture is definitely worth a thousand words!

You may need an adhesive solvent to "unstick" the weather stripping. Adhesive solvent is available in spray cans for easy application. Adhesive remover can be pretty caustic stuff. Read the can to be sure that it won't damage your window frame.

If you have metal or vinyl frame windows, check the drain holes at the outside edge of the bottom portion of the window frame. These holes exist whether a window slides sideways or up and down. During rains water can fill the track, leak to the inside of the home, and literally flood the area surrounding the window. Drain or "weep holes" allow water to escape from the frame thus preventing flooding. You can use a piece of wire, a pipe cleaner, a small screwdriver blade, or an ice pick to insure that the holes are clear and will drain freely.

Stopping air leaks

A window that leaks air can also mean excessive energy loss — and cost. Summer or winter, you don't want your house to leak air, especially if you spend your hard earned dollars warming or cooling it.

Test a window for leaks by holding a lighted candle near all its joints and connections. If the candle flickers, you have an air leak. Check

✔ Where one section of the window meets another

✔ Where the windows meet the frame

✔ Where the frame meets the wall

You seal air leaks in the same way that you seal water leaks — by caulking exterior leaks and replacing weather stripping. Also, foam sealant can be injected between the frame of the window and the frame of the house. This is a major deterrent to air infiltration and also prevents water from leaking into the house.

Preventing condensation on glass, frames, and sills

Condensation around windows can result when a window leaks air. Cold outside air mixes with warm inside air and creates a wet layer of condensation over the entire window. Help, you can't see! Condensation can actually form enough moisture to cause wood to rot. And don't forget mildew. Condensation is basically a feed bag for mildew. Condensation can be reduced by:

- ✔ Sealing air leaks
- ✔ Replacing single-pane glass with double-pane "insulated" glass
- ✔ Using wood frame windows
- ✔ Using storm windows

 If you have insulated windows and you see rainbows or condensation between the two sheets of glass, then your window has failed and should be replaced. The frame can remain, but the glass must be replaced. Here it is important to shop for the best guarantee. Where there are many who are ready to "sell to you" to get their piece of the almighty buck, there are a few who do offer a lifetime warranty. Study this aspect of your purchase carefully. A failed insulated window is expensive to replace at $150 and up.

Maintaining storm windows

A storm window is simply a second window that adds insulative value to the window that it covers. Make sure that storm windows are properly sealed at their edges when they are installed. Air leaking through the edges of a storm window can allow condensation to occur between it and the window it protects. Storm window condensation can become so heavy that the frost produced can prevent you from seeing through.

Don't leave storm windows up in the summer. Leaving them up year-round can cause rot to occur in the area between the storm window and the house. Also, ventilation is a must to reduce fungus growth in a home. Storm windows need to be taken down so that the house windows can be opened.

Replacing window film

Sounds like something from a Kodak moment doesn't it? Nope, no pictures here. But there is added comfort. Window film is a layer of plastic that is applied to a window to reduce heat transfer and to prevent furniture and drapes from being bleached. Window film comes in a variety of thicknesses, colors, and shades which influence the amount of visible light they let through.

Old window film can break down after time. Bubbles, cracks, splits, peeling, and chipping can occur, thus requiring a maintenance face-lift. Window film can be patched, but it is just as easy to replace. Some folks are threatened by its removal, but it really is easy. Here's how:

1. **Spray the film with sudsy ammonia.**

   Don't try this in direct sunlight. Anything that can cause the ammonia to evaporate and dry out prevents it from doing its job.

2. **While still wet, cover the entire area with a layer of plastic food wrap.**

   Overlap edges of the plastic wrap for complete coverage. The food wrap keeps the ammonia moist and active.

3. **Wait 15 to 45 minutes and remove the plastic wrap.**

4. **Use a window scraper to easily peel away the softened film.**

With the old sheet removed, application of a new layer of film is easy. Make sure the window is perfectly clean, and then follow these steps (see Figure 5-7):

1. **Cut a piece of window film about 2 inches longer and 2 inches wider than the size of the window.**

2. **Mix 1 teaspoon of liquid dishwashing detergent with 1 quart of water in a spray bottle. Soak the surface of the window with the soapy solution.**

3. **Peel back the liner-paper from the window film to expose its adhesive layer.**

   A helper makes this step easier.

4. **Drench the adhesive side of the film by spraying it with the soapy solution.**

   Have a drop cloth and towel handy to keep the mess to a minimum.

5. **Place the adhesive side of the drenched window film against the wet window, and using your hands, smooth the film against the surface of the glass, eliminating any wrinkles.**

6. **Spray the exposed surface of the film with the soapy solution. Using a rubber squeegee, continue to smooth it against the glass, working first horizontally from the center to the side and then vertically, moving the solution to the bottom of the window.**

   The trick is to use slow, gentle movements.

7. **Use a straightedge and razor knife to trim the film where it meets the window frame.**

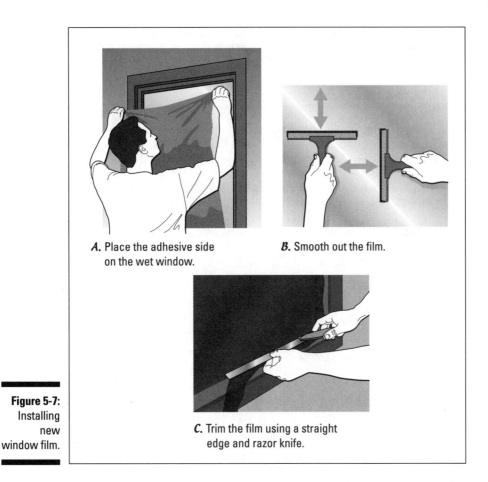

A. Place the adhesive side on the wet window.

B. Smooth out the film.

C. Trim the film using a straight edge and razor knife.

Figure 5-7:
Installing new window film.

Maintaining screens

Newer, more energy-efficient homes don't allow for the passive exchange of air through cracks, gaps, and penetrations as older homes did. Unfortunately, this condition creates stale trapped air within the home. In addition, some of the components used in the fabrication of construction materials emit gases that cause health problems, which can range from a minor case of the sniffles to a full-blown allergic reaction. Air in the home must be continually exchanged with a fresh supply from the outside. This fact makes screens really important.

Cleaning screens

You must keep screens clean in order to get a good exchange of air. Grit and grime can also hasten deterioration, thereby diminishing the life of a window screen. Dirty screens also prevent light from making its way into your home. Moreover, a gust of wind can blow dust from a screen straight into your home, aggravating allergies and increasing housekeeping chores.

To clean your screens, lay them flat on a smooth, cloth-covered surface, such as an old sheet on a picnic table. Scrub them gently with a soft nylon brush, rinse with a hose, and shake off excess water.

Patching a screen

Screen patch kits are available at hardware stores and home centers everywhere. They are inexpensive and easy to install (the process takes less than a minute). You can also use any of the following methods to repair window screens, depending upon the type of screen material.

Apply a small amount of clear nail polish to a small hole or tear in a vinyl or fiberglass screen. The polish acts as an adhesive, sealing the damaged area.

Small tears in metal or fiberglass screens can be mended with a dab of clear silicone adhesive. If necessary, dab it on in successive layers until the tear is completely filled.

You can "darn" small holes in metal screening. Simply unravel a strand or two from a piece of scrap screening and sew the hole shut, weaving the strands through the sound fabric with a needle (see Figure 5-8).

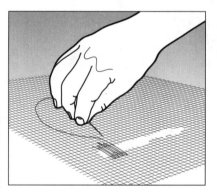

Figure 5-8:
"Darning" a
screen.

Large holes in metal screen material take a little more effort. Start by neatly trimming the damaged area to a ravel-free square or rectangle using tin snips. Next, cut a piece of patch screen material that measures about 1 inch larger (in both directions) than the damaged area. Unravel a couple of strands of material around the entire perimeter of the patch. Then bend the unraveled ends at each side of the patch at 90-degrees. Place the patch over the damaged area and carefully thread the bent wires through the sound fabric (see Figure 5-9). Then bend the wires flat again to hold the patch in place.

For fiberglass screening, simply cut a patch of similar material and affix it to the good material using transparent silicone glue.

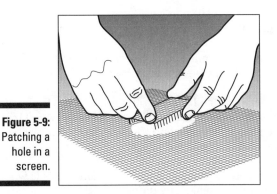

Figure 5-9:
Patching a
hole in a
screen.

Doors and Hardware

An exterior door may be more energy efficient than a window, but a door can leak just as much water and air. As the moisture content changes in soil, your home shifts. Your doors also shift, creating gaps large enough for a dump truck to pass through.

With doors, you need to regularly caulk the exterior trim even if the exterior door in question is protected by a covered porch. Remember that caulking is designed to keep out air as well as water. Caulk the doorframe to the door trim and the door trim to the siding.

If you find moisture on the entry floor, it could be a leak between the threshold and the door bottom. The threshold is the wood or metal platform at the base of the doorway. It usually tilts outward to shed water. The bottoms of most exterior doors are fitted with a metal door bottom or "shoe" that houses a rubber gasket. The door shoe is attached to the bottom of the door with screws driven through oblong slots in the shoe. The oblong slots allow the door bottom to be adjusted up and down as the house — and consequently the door — shift up and down. When the door is closed, the rubber gasket is supposed to rest tightly against the full length of the threshold preventing the influx of air and water.

No matter how successfully the door shoe and threshold work to prevent air and water leaks, there could be yet another problem. The threshold itself might leak. Exterior door thresholds are normally laid in a thick bed of caulk when originally installed. Occasionally, the caulk shrinks and the threshold leaks. The only way to prevent future leaks is to remove the threshold, recaulk the area, and replace the threshold. Be sure to readjust the door shoe once the threshold has been replaced.

Stopping air leaks

An air leak in a doorframe is pretty common. Use the candle test described earlier in this chapter to see just how severe the problem is.

Foam sealant can be added between the frame of the door and the frame of the house by removing the interior door casing. The casing is the wood trim that covers the joint between the doorframe and the wall. Use a flat pry bar to slowly remove the trim so that it won't be damaged.

Other air leaks can occur between the door and the doorframe. This is where weather stripping is handy. It doesn't make any difference whether the exterior door is painted or stained, large or small, solid wood or French style, the same type of weather stripping can be used. We like the kind of whether stripping that consists of a rubber bead attached lengthwise to a strip of metal. Standing outside the door, with the door in the closed position, gently press the rubber portion of the weather stripping against the door and frame at the same time. Attach the metal section of the weather stripping to the frame of the door with the nails or screws provided. Here, oblong holes allow the weather stripping to be adjusted later as house movement causes the door to shift.

Adjusting a sticking swinging door

When a door sticks, always check for a loose hinge first. Try tightening the screws that connect the hinges to the door and frame. Often that's all it will take to repair a sticking door.

If the hinges are loose and the screws won't tighten, chances are the screw holes are stripped. Replace them with longer ones. The screw that normally holds a hinge in place connects to the frame of the door only. A longer screw will penetrate through the door frame and into the house frame (where support is really solid). This technique works even if the existing holes are stripped.

If you aren't into buying and installing longer hinge screws, then you may want to repair the stripped holes. Use a golf tee or a few toothpicks and reuse the original screw. Dip a golf tee (or several toothpicks) into any good wood glue and drive the glue-laden material into the stripped hole. Wait several hours for the glue to dry and cut off the excess material. This repairs the stripped holes. Now you can then reuse the original screws to hold the hinge tightly in place. Fore!

Slightly shifty doors

When a house shifts, you never know which way it will cause a door to move. Sometimes the gap between the door and the frame increases. Other times, the normal distance between the door and frame diminishes to the point where rubbing or sticking results. The problem always seems to manifest itself either at the side of the door opposite the hinges or at the top of the door.

Before we tell you how to adjust the hinge to fix the rubbing, we must first give you a quick rundown on hinge anatomy. A hinge comes in three parts: the two hinge sides and the hinge pin. The hinge sides are held together when the hinge pin is driven through alternating rings known as the *knuckles*. Bending the knuckles can widen or narrow the gap between the hinge sides. At the same time adjusting the knuckles can change the position of a door and get rid of the rub.

To begin this repair, first decide which knuckle you need to operate on (All directions are as you view the door from the side where you can see the hinges and where the hinges are located on the left side of the door. Reverse the following repair procedures when the hinges are located on the right side.):

- ✔ **If the door sticks at the upper-right side:** Bend the hinge knuckles on the upper hinge only away from the hinge center. After you have bent the knuckles, the hinge sides will be closer together moving the upper-right side of the door away from the upper-right side of the frame.

- ✔ **If the door sticks at the lower-right side:** Bend the hinge knuckles on the lower hinge only away from hinge center. After you have bent the knuckles, the hinge sides will be closer together, moving the lower-right side of the door away from the lower-right side of the frame.

- ✔ **If the door edge sticks at both the top and bottom:** Bend the hinge knuckles on both the upper and the lower hinges away from hinge center. After you have bent the knuckles, the hinge sides will be closer together moving the upper and lower side of the door away from the upper and lower side of the frame.

- ✔ **If the door sticks at the top edge on the right side:** Bend the hinge knuckles on the upper hinge slightly toward center and bend the lower hinges knuckles slightly away from hinge center. After you have bent the knuckles, the upper hinge sides will be slightly farther apart and the lower hinge sides will be slightly closer together. This tilts the door in the opening. The trick here is to tilt the door enough to miss the top but not so much as to cause it to rub on the upper-right side.

To perform the hinge bending operation, just follow these steps:

1. **Remove the hinge pin with a hammer and a nail punch.**

2. **Use an adjustable wrench to bend each of the knuckles in the desired direction — one at a time.**

   The door doesn't have to be removed from the opening.

3. **Replace the hinge pin.**

When the hinge is repinned the door will have moved. Ain't home maintenance a kick? Who would have thought?

Sliding glass doors need love, too

Did you ever reach out to open a sliding glass door, give it a tug, and feel like the door was pulling back? Hey, patio doors need love and attention, too.

Unlike conventional exterior doors that swing on hinges, a sliding glass door moves on rollers. Little wheels made of neoprene or metal. Little wheels that wear out with use.

Since the wheels on the bottom of a sliding glass door run in a threshold often filled with dirt and sand, it's a wonder that they last more than a year or two. If you have sliding patio doors, here's how to convert loving care into lasting quality and a door that opens and closes as easy as pie.

First and foremost always keep the bottom track of the door clean and free of dirt and sand. In addition, regularly spray the track and the wheels with a waterless silicone spray. The absence of water in the spray reduces the chance for rusty wheels, and the silicone is a colorless lubricant that won't stain or attract dust.

Just like other doors in the home, a sliding patio door can be knocked out of whack when the house shifts. Adjusting the wheels at the bottom of the door can compensate for this problem. Raising or lowering opposing wheels (located at the underside of each end of the door) can straighten a crooked door, thus allowing it to close parallel to the doorframe. Raising both wheels evenly can prevent the bottom of the door from rubbing on the track as the wheels wear out and become smaller.

For wheels that are adjustable, simply turn the adjacent screw to make it happen. Normally you will find a hole at each end of the bottom track of the sliding door through which a screwdriver can be inserted. Use a pry bar to slightly lift the door to take pressure off the wheel while you turn the adjustment screw.

If the door is lowered when you in fact wanted to raise it, simply raise the door and turn the screw in the other direction. How's that for getting the best bang for your sliding door buck.

Rollers that are completely worn out (or those that can't be adjusted) can be replaced. Open the door about half way, raise it 1 inch by forcing it into the top track, and at the same time, pull out on the bottom. With the door out of the opening, snap the old rollers out and pop in a pair of new ones.

Double-action swinging doors

Double-action swinging doors give their hinges a real test. After your kids go through them 29 million times, treating them as if they were a new Disneyland adventure, the mounting screws loosen and the springs within the hinge weaken in spite of the fact that you may from time to time shoot them with a bit of silicone lubricant.

Many of these doors use double spring-action hinges that are self-closing and allow the doors to swing in both directions. Some have stops that allow the doors to remain open when they're swung past 90 degrees. Some of these hinges are mounted to a wood strip that you mount to the doorjamb. You may have two or three hinges on each door.

To adjust the hinge so the doors meet flush when closed, use the spring steel adjustment rod provided with the hinge. If you've lost the adjustment rod, use the long end of a snug-fitting Allen wrench. Push or pull the adjustment rod to increase the spring tension. This allows you to remove the pin that holds the spring in place. Move the pin so that the spring is one hole tighter; then check the door alignment. You may have to make adjustments to the springs on both doors.

Because there is a lot of pull on the screws that hold these hinges in place, replace the screws with 1½ or 2-inch-long screws that reach into the studs behind the doorjamb.

Another type of hinge on swinging doors uses a double-acting pivot consisting of a heavy spring and a cam. Some cams have stops that hold the door open when it's opened beyond 90 degrees. These hinges are mounted either in the bottom of the door or in the floor.

Dust and dirt is the biggest problem for these bottom-mounted spring devices. Keep them as clean as you possibly can by vacuuming frequently. If the spring is jammed, unscrew the cover plates from the hinge and vacuum. If you find any rust, scrape it off and vacuum again. Then spray the spring and the pivot with a silicone lubricant. Clean and install the cover plates.

Pocket doors

This style of door is appropriately called a "pocket" door because, when in the open position, the door neatly slides into a void space in the wall. A pocket door glides on rollers that hang from a track mounted on the frame above the door. Old-fashioned pocket doors always seemed to fall off the track. That doesn't happen with the newer doors. But it may be necessary to adjust the height of the doors because of changes in the floor covering. The procedures for doing this vary depending on the manufacturer and model of the door, but in general, here is how to do it:

1. **Remove one of the split headers that hide and trim the roller track.**

   Beneath the rollers, you find a hanger with an adjustment bolt and nut or screw.

2. **Use a thin-end wrench or a screwdriver to turn the nut or screw to raise or lower the door.**

To clean the tracks, use a vacuum to remove dust. Lubricate the rollers with spray silicone lubricant.

Silicone lubricant keeps the hardware locks functioning unless they become very dirty. In that case, remove the lock or lever and clean them in mineral spirits. Spray a coating of silicone on the interior parts; then reassemble.

Bifold doors

Bifold doors can misbehave due to worn or broken parts, a damaged track, loose hinges, lack of lubricant, and dirt. To fix any of these problems, you must remove the door by lifting up on the panel nearest the jamb until the bottom pivot clears the jamb bracket. (You may have to unscrew the bottom pivot until it clears the bracket.)

If any of the parts are worn, remove them and take them to your home center or hardware store and purchase identical replacement parts, if possible. You may find that the pivot holes aren't the correct size and the hole has to be enlarged to fit the replacement pivot. Follow the manufacturers instructions to do this.

If the pivot hole is worn and too large for the new pivot, drill out the hole and fill it with a dowel glued in place. After the glue dries, bore a new hole of the proper size in the dowel.

If the problem is with the bottom pivot or jamb bracket, replace the worn parts. Adjust the bottom pivot so that the top of the door is about ⅜ inch from the track for best operation.

Rusty, bent, loose, or paint-encrusted hinges hamper smooth operation of bifold doors. Rather than trying to clean a painted or rusty hinge, buy new hinges. They improve operation and make your door look like new. Well, almost.

Shower doors

When a snoopy guest uses your bathroom, the first thing he or she looks at are the shower doors. Are they clean? Here are ways to clean those doors and keep them that way:

- ✔ Using lemon oil polish and a scouring pad, scrub the glass panels with gusto. If the door has acrylic panels, go easy on the scrubbing or you may scratch the acrylic.

- ✔ Scrub with sodium carbonate. You can find a pure form of sodium carbonate, called *ph increaser,* at swimming pool retailers.

- ✔ Use a sponge and dishwashing detergent to clean the shower door (and the rest of the shower stall) after every shower.

- ✔ Place a couple of small suction cups that have small hooks on the inside of a shower door. Use the pair of hangers to suspend a vinegar-soaked rag on the inside of the shower door. Reposition the hangers and rag periodically to conquer small sections at a time. This may sound funny and look terrible, but it's inside the shower and your guests won't see it unless they are really snoopy. The vinegar will soften the mineral deposits. Really dirty shower doors may require some scrubbing with a nylon scouring pad.

If the doors get out of alignment, or the rollers come off the track, you can usually reset the doors by lifting them in the frame and resetting the rollers in the channel.

When the doors drag, or they don't stay in the bottom channel, the rollers need adjusting. Lift the outer door until the rollers clear the top track; then, pull the bottom of the door out and away from the bottom channel and set it aside. Do the same with the inner door.

Clean debris from the bottom track and clean the doorframes using the mildew solution we give you in Chapter 17. Loosen the screws that hold the rollers to the doorframe and adjust them to raise or lower the door as needed. If the screws are rusted, replace them with zinc-coated or stainless steel screws. A light spray of a dry silicone lubricant will keep the rollers operating smoothly.

Knobs, locks, and latches (oh my!)

How could anyone possibly write a biography about Martin without including Lewis? And what about Abbot and Costello? In the same vein, how could anyone expect us to write a chapter about doors without including door hardware? You know — knobs, locks, and latches.

Dirty knobs (not legal in every state)

Barring a damaged finish, just about the only problems you'll have with door-knobs and sliding door latches are screws that loosen and collected dirt that jambs up the mechanism. In our 21+ years as contractors, we haven't ever seen a doorknob fail — at least not yet! We've found that cleaning and lubrication can solve most problems.

When a doorknob, key lock, or sliding door latch begins to stick intermittently, or when it isn't operating as smoothly as usual, it's probably gunked up with dirt. When this happens, most of us have the tendency to use a lubricant to solve the problem. Not! Lubricant is used to reduce friction, not clean. If you have a sticky doorknob, we suggest spraying cutting oil into the works. Cutting oil cleans and lubricates. Better yet, take a few moments to remove the hardware and dip it into a bath of cutting oil. Follow the bath with a spray of light machine oil — sewing machine oil is great — and reinstall the knob. Ninety-nine-percent of the time it will operate like it's brand new. This procedure has worked successfully for us on doorknobs and levers, deadbolts, throw bolts, and patio door latches — just about any door hardware that we've ever had to maintain.

Someone told us your screws were loose

You reach for the doorknob, and as you grip it, you notice that it has shifted from its original position. You can see where the trim ring and the paint don't line up. You try wiggling the knob in hopes that it won't move, thinking to yourself that if it doesn't, further attention on your part won't be required. Hey, sooner or later you will have do deal with it. The nice thing is that the maintenance is unbelievably easy.

To solve the problem, tighten the screws that hold the knob in place. Often their location is pretty obvious. Usually they can be found at the interior trim ring. With some hardware the interior knob and trim ring must be removed to access hidden screws. This requires the knob to be removed first, then the trim ring. A small pushbutton release can be found in the shaft of the knob. Depress it with the blade of a small screwdriver and pull the knob away from the door. The pushbutton is usually located on the underside of the knob shaft. Once the knob is removed the trim ring can be popped off by applying pressure to a small spring lever located at the inside edge of the trim ring or by prying it off with a screwdriver. The screws will be found immediately beneath the trim ring — two of them. Tighten them snugly in place and replace the trim ring and the knob. First time around the process may confuse you slightly. After one time you'll wonder how anything so simple ever avoided your attention.

You can keep key locks lubricated with graphite powder, but it can be a bit messy and there is the chance that using too much could temporarily jamb the lock. However, there is an easy and inexpensive alternative. Rub a pencil onto your key. Then push the key into the lock. The lead, which is actually a graphite compound, will transfer to the lock and lubricate it. It really does a great job.

The other side of the coin

When is a plate big enough to hold a door closed, but not large enough to hold lunch? When it's a strike plate — that's when. If you just laughed, then you know that the strike plate is the small metal thing attached to the doorframe that interlocks with the bolt on the doorknob when the door is closed. The strike plate is so named because it is what the bolt "strikes" as the door is being closed. The strike plate actually serves three purposes:

- Its curved outer edge helps to gradually depress the bolt as the door closes.
- It acts as a shield preventing wear and tear to the doorframe.
- When interlocked with the bolt it holds the door snugly to the frame. With some strike plates, this function is adjustable.

One of the major causes of door (and window) misalignment is house movement. Actually, if a house didn't move there would probably never be a need to realign its doors. However, until homes stop shifting, doors will have to be tweaked one way or another, and the process will often have to include adjusting the strike plate to realign it with the door bolt.

Closing the door just enough for the bolt to lay on the outside edge of the strike plate can give you a good idea of why the bolt isn't interlocking with the strike plate. The bolt must rest centered between the top and bottom of the plate. If the bolt is lower than center, the plate must be lowered. If the bolt is higher than center, the plate should be raised.

Most often the adjustment needed is extremely minor. Place a chisel into the hole in the strike plate. To lower the strike plate, hold the edge of the chisel against the bottom of the hole and tap downward on the chisel with a hammer. One light blow is all that it usually takes to move the strike plate enough to clear the bolt. Hold the chisel against the top of the opening and lightly tap upward with the hammer to move the plate up. Keep in mind that if the strike plate has to be moved more than ⅛ inch, the door may have to be adjusted instead — maybe both.

A strike plate is held in place with two screws. Slam a door often enough and the screws will definitely come loose, resulting in a door that wobbles when closed. First, try tightening the screws. If they're stripped, which is often the case, use our golf tee trick to make the repair. Remove the screws and the strike plate. Dip two golf tees in glue. Drive one golf tee into each of the holes. When the glue has dried, cut off the excess golf tees with a razor knife. Then all you have to do is reinstall the strike plate. No more wobble after this repair.

Loving your locks

In addition to making sure that your locks are securely fastened to the door, you also need to clean and lubricate locks to keep them in good working order.

To remove the lock, first remove the knobs. Unscrew the screws holding the faceplate on the inside knob. Remove the knobs. Remove the screws in the latch plate and remove the latch bolt assembly. The latch is that part of the door hardware that fits into the strike on the door frame when the door is closed. Clean the latch bolt assembly with mineral spirits. Lubricate the assembly with silicone spray, and then reinstall the lockset.

Bolts that hang up on the latch plate may catch on paint. Remove the paint and lubricate the bolt.

Chapter 6

Decks, Fencing, and Retaining Walls

. . . .

In This Chapter

▶ Doing right by your deck (and other wood structures)

▶ Taking care of fencing

▶ Maintaining your retaining wall's health

. . . .

*T*his chapter features maintenance tips on some areas of your house that you may not think of too often — your deck, fencing, and retaining wall. Like other areas of your home, these items need regular upkeep and an occasional pick-me-up to relieve damage caused by lack of maintenance.

Preserving Your Wood Deck and Structures

Natural wood that is not protected begins to deteriorate the moment it is exposed to nature's elements. The ultraviolet rays of the sun, moisture from rain and snow, and various fungi soon take their toll. Although not a part of nature, irrigation water (any kind of water, in fact) also can damage unprotected wood.

Fortunately, your wood structures can be protected by the use of a high-quality oil-base wood preservative — the same kind we suggest for exterior siding in Chapter 4. In fact, the same cleaning techniques that we mention there can also be used to prepare the structures mentioned in this chapter. However, in this chapter, the wood structures we discuss are more difficult to protect than siding because each structure contains many pieces of wood, each piece having more than one side exposed to the elements.

Woody's wood deck

A few years ago, we appeared regularly on a cable network TV show entitled *Home and Family*. We were the home-improvement guys. During the early days of the show, we also cooked and sang. We were pretty good at home improvements, fair cooks, and lousy singers.

Executive producer "Woody" Fraser reveled in finagling the on-air talent (us included) into doing the unexpected and the outrageous. But even more fun than all the craziness that made the show so unique was our opportunity to teach. Woody insisted that our viewers learn something from each and every segment. "Laugh and learn," he always said.

During our tenure, we were involved in projects that ranged from concocting simple cleaning formulas to building a complete room addition for the Shier family — a Los Angeles couple that had been unexpectedly blessed with quintuplets.

One day, Woody decided that he wanted a stage built — outside — in the backyard on the backlot at Universal Studios in Hollywood. Woody

was dying to have a place outside where guest entertainers could sing, dance, and be interviewed. We suggested a covered wood deck.

There was a method to our madness. Our strategy was to build the deck as a "show-n-tell" project and then use the finished product as a stage. We also planned to use the deck later for segments on maintenance and upkeep. Woody loved the idea, and for three weeks, viewers shared in the planning, construction, and finally, the completion and use of our new deck and stage. The view from the deck was magnificent. It overlooked a beautiful mountain range as well as the *Jurassic Park* set — dinosaurs and all.

As we had hoped, the deck turned out to be an ongoing resource for segments on exterior home maintenance. The number of e-mails that we received asking about deck maintenance was incredible. During the next two years, many deck segments followed — on everything from wood preservation to deck brightening — and it all took place on Woody's special stage.

Painting

Unlike wood siding (which we discuss in Chapter 4), wood in decks, handrails, fences, retaining walls, and other complex structures expose several surfaces of each piece of wood to the weather. With these structures, achieving a positive waterproof membrane with caulking, sealing, and painting is difficult.

For example, painting a gazebo could require caulking hundreds — maybe thousands — of connections before painting. To top it all off, the structure may prevent you from painting all the various sides of each piece of wood. Imagine, for example, how you would maintain the underside of a deck that lies 12 inches off the ground? You'd have to be pretty skinny to get under there to apply a coat of paint.

Partially painted pieces of wood create a real problem. Even if the unpainted side doesn't get wet directly, exposed wood can absorb moisture in the form of vapors rising from beneath. A painted surface on that same piece of wood can become riddled with bubbles, splits, chips, and peeling paint. After the painted surface has been compromised, it can no longer fully protect the wood, and in fact, the damaged surface becomes a contributor to further moisture attack.

Our advice: Don't paint unless you can cover all six sides of every piece of wood. In situations where pieces of wood are sandwiched together, and the joined surfaces can't be painted, then the pieces should be joined as one by thoroughly caulking all connecting joints. If all sides can't be reached, an oil or oil stain finish is best.

Because of the chipping, bubbling, and splitting normally associated with painted decks and handrails, we are reluctant to suggest painting. However, a painted deck can be beautiful. If you do decide to paint, keep the following in mind:

- Make sure that the surface is thoroughly clean and that the wood is dry. Go to extremes to get the wood clean: pressure washing, sanding, and detergent scrubbing.
- Remove all loose nails and replace them with the next larger size.
- Use a hammer and nail punch to countersink all nails (see Figure 6-1). Fill the resultant nail hole with a high-quality, exterior-grade putty.
- Fill all other holes with a high-quality, exterior-grade putty. During application be sure to remove all excess putty. This will help to keep sanding to a minimum.
- Apply a high-quality polyurethane caulking at all joints.
- Prime all bare areas and puttied spots with a high-quality, oil-base primer.
- Finish decks with a high-grade, oil-base finish. Handrails can be finished with a good-quality, acrylic-base paint.
- Be prepared to recaulk and touch up paint every year.

Giving your paint the finger

Want to know how good a paint is? Give it the finger — the finger test, that is. Open a thoroughly mixed can and dip you thumb and finger into the paint far enough to rub the paint between your thumb and finger tips. If the paint feels smooth, you've got good stuff. If it feels gritty, the quality probably isn't so good. Poor-quality paint often uses clay as filler, giving it that gritty feeling.

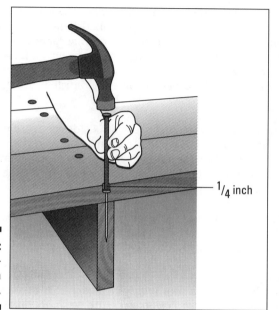

1/4 inch

Figure 6-1:
Counter-
sinking a
nail.

Never paint a wood surface that has previously been oiled. The paint won't stick, and you'll have a mess on your hands forever. The best rule of thumb is to repaint painted surfaces and re-oil oiled surfaces. However, oiled surfaces can be painted and vice versa if you take the time to use a paint remover followed by a thorough sanding. Once the wood is oiled or oil-stained, even the most minute spots of leftover paint show up like a headlight on lover's lane.

Oil

Oil doesn't last as long as paint, but it is easier to apply. Instead of laying on the surface like paint, oil penetrates deeply into the pores of the wood, preventing the attack of moisture from within. Oil also penetrates between joints and connections. For ultraviolet protection, fine wood preservatives also reflect or absorb ultraviolet rays.

With oil, there is no rigid surface layer (like paint) that can bubble or split. However, oil eventually evaporates out of the wood, leaving it unprotected. Oil takes 12 to 18 months to evaporate to the point where some areas of the wood may be unprotected. Wood that is protected with oil should be recoated every — you got it — 12 to 18 months.

Essentially, the oil for wood siding that we discussed in Chapter 4 also can be used for the applications noted in this chapter. However, remember that horizontal surfaces (especially decks) are less forgiving than vertical surfaces (such as walls, posts, and rails). When used on a deck for example, excessive amounts of oil can puddle, and puddled oil doesn't dry. Puddling scuffs easily and can stick to furniture, feet, and shoes. This can mean the destruction of interior floors.

Stain

If you want to stain a deck, look for a product designed specifically for decks. Well-meaning do-it-yourselfers often end up applying stains designed for vertical surfaces, such as siding. Stains designed for use on vertical surfaces are not as abrasion resistant as those made for decks. Deck stains are made to resist scuffing where lots of traffic is expected.

A semitransparent, oil-base stain is a good bet. The combination of oil and a pigment protects the wood from both sun and water and hides surface irregularities.

Plan to spend in the neighborhood of $20 to $35 per gallon on semitransparent, oil-base stain. A gallon covers approximately 300 to 500 square feet.

For vertical surfaces, a semitransparent or solid color stain shows off the beauty of the wood. The solid color stain won't show as much of the wood as a coat of semitransparent, but the solid color protects the wood for a longer period of time. Some folks wrongly assume that solid color stain is like paint. A solid color stain definitely does a good job of showing off the grain.

Our wood preservative: Clearly, it isn't clear

You can make your own wood preservative at home. However, keep in mind that even the most clear of finishes slightly darken wood. To see how dark the wood gets, simply wet your thumb with a drop or two of water and press the wet appendage against the wood. The wet wood will look the same when oiled.

You need:

✓ Boiled linseed oil

✓ Mineral spirits

✓ Pigment (the kind used to color paint)

✓ Mildicide (a pesticide that kills mildew that is available at paint stores)

Mix equal parts of oil and mineral spirits. Then add pigment to the intensity you like, and stir in a package of mildicide. (Follow the instructions for the mildicide as if you were adding it to an equal volume of paint.)

When applying the preservative, don't put it on too thick. A little bit goes a long way. Don't forget to backbrush and wipe up any puddling. As we mentioned earlier, oil and oil-stain puddles never dry. They turn into sticky messes that are nearly impossible to remove.

Always apply an oil or oil-stain finish either early or late in the day when the wood is not in full sun. The thinner that helps the oil penetrate evaporates too quickly on hot days. The oil can end up laying on the surface.

Help to force the oil or oil-stain into the surface by going back over the entire area with a paintbrush or roller (called *backbrushing*). A China bristle or natural bristle paintbrush is by far the best applicator for use with oil. A nylon paintbrush should not be used with oils, oil stains, or oil-base paints. One to three applications of a high-quality product may be required.

Clear finishes

If you like the natural color of the wood you want to protect and don't want to alter its appearance, try a clear finish. Just be sure that the clear finish that you purchase contains UV inhibitors to fight off an ultraviolet sunburn. One we know of is Penofin.

Beware of the popular "cure all" water seals. Many of these products contain petroleum jelly or paraffin, which offer minimal water protection and absolutely no UV protection. Furthermore, these products have little penetration and rapidly evaporate.

Protecting your deck against critters

Dirt is a world filled with tiny little insects (and some big ones too) and lots of moisture. Wood and water don't mix, and wood surrounded by dirt for any length of time simply deteriorates.

Wherever possible, move dirt away from the wood. For example, a flower bed tends to grow higher each time it is mulched. After years of mulching, the dirt may come into contact with your wood deck. When this happens it's smart to remove enough soil to eliminate contact. Eliminating earth-to-wood contact also makes it more difficult for termites to make it into wood structures.

Wood that has been exposed to moisture in dirt can be treated with a pesticide (such as copper napthinate). One we know of is Copper Green, which can be applied with a brush or sprayed on. Pesticides also help deter termites.

Cleaning your deck

Always keep a wood surface free of any debris. Leaves, pine needles, and dirt hold water and accelerate rot. An occasional sweeping is all that's required here.

Giving your deck a facelift with sanding

If your wood deck is too far gone to bring back to life with just a coat of paint or wood brightener and a coat of oil, then you may want to consider sanding. If you should decide to sand it yourself, you can rent a floor sander to make the job easier. Don't even consider hand-sanding unless you have a small deck and three or four months with nothing else to do.

Be prepared to spend a good while sanding. Start with 30-grit paper and work your way up to 100-grit. Sand first cross-grain, then in both diagonal directions, and then finally in the direction of the grain. Don't forget to use our hinge-pin trick to set all nails at least ¼-inch deep before sanding.

You can also give your wood surfaces (oiled, oil-stained, or painted) a good scrubbing using the following formula:

- ✔ 1 cup of powdered laundry detergent
- ✔ ½ cup liquid chlorine bleach (if moss is present)
- ✔ 1 gallon of hot water

Add the bleach to the water. Although this solution is mild, be sure to wear gloves and eye protection. Work the solution into the surface with a stiff bristle broom or a nylon brush. Once scrubbed, completely rinse the surface with water.

Severely neglected oiled or oil-stained wood may require washing with a wood-brightening product. Look for one that contains oxalic acid. Apply the product with a nylon brush in accordance with the manufacturer's instructions. (Remember to wear protective clothing, rubber boots, gloves, and safety goggles to avoid injury.)

Sea story

We were pressure washing a home one day, when momentarily, we became engrossed in conversation which distracted us. To make a long story short, the tip of the pressure washer got a little to close to the wall. By the time we turned around to pay attention to what we were doing, the high pressure jet of water had cut a hole completely through a ⅜-inch layer of plywood siding.

A thorough cleaning with a pressure washer saves on a lot of elbow grease and makes those hard-to-get-to areas, like handrails and trellises, easy to clean. Pressure washing natural wood that has turned gray can help remove discoloration and can bring the wood back to its natural color.

A pressure washer can be rented from a paint store or tool rental company. Use extreme caution when operating the device to avoid personal injury and damage to the surface of the wood.

If you plan to refinish the wood after cleaning, allow the wood to completely dry before applying the finish. Once dry, nail heads, which rise above the deck's surface, should be countersunk. One of the simplest ways to do this is by using a hinge pin removed from a door hinge. The hinge pin serves as an oversized nail set — much easier for a novice to use.

Roof Decks — A Breed Apart

A roof-deck, simply stated, is a deck that doubles as a roof, or vice versa (see Figure 6-2). A roof deck has all the properties of a roof without the ugly appearance associated with most types of flat roofing. The two most common types of roof decks are:

- ✔ **Decks where the top surface is not the waterproof membrane.** The top surface is usually ceramic tile, stone, or plain, patterned, or textured concrete. A waterproof membrane lies underneath the finish surface. This is the prettiest kind, but a leak repair often requires complete replacement of the finish surface.
- ✔ **Decks where the top surface is the waterproof membrane.** These are the least expensive to install and maintain.

Finding a leak in a roof deck can take time, but it isn't difficult. Sometimes leaks don't occur at the waterproof membrane, but at adjacent connections. The ticket is to find out where the leak is coming from to determine whether a repair can be made.

Continuous L-shaped metal flashing creates a waterproof seal where the deck membrane meets a wall. Part of the L shape travels vertically, 6 to 8 inches up the wall (beneath the siding) while the horizontal part of the L-flashing protrudes 6 to 8 inches away from the wall (beneath the waterproof membrane). The membrane sticks to the flashing, which extends up the wall beneath the siding to ensure waterproof integrity between the horizontal and vertical surfaces.

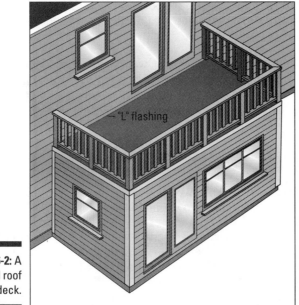

Figure 6-2: A typical roof deck.

"L" flashing

Unfortunately, flashings do corrode and rust. However, you can get a flashing to last almost forever by regularly cleaning and painting it.

Scuffs, scrapes, and lime deposit build-up can cause a roof deck to appear worn and tattered. So can cracked and chipped grout. Also, leaves and other debris are not only unsightly, but can prevent proper watershed or clog a drain, causing water to back up into the house. Here are a few tips:

✔ For tile decks, repair cracks and gouges in grout and seal the entire surface with a high-quality silicone sealant. This won't prevent a leak, but the deck surface looks better longer.

✔ For stone decks, repair cracks and gouges in mortar and seal the entire surface with a high-quality silicone sealant. This won't prevent a leak, but, again, the deck surface looks better longer.

✔ Keep drains free and clear of debris to prevent flooding.

Fencing

Fencing: The sport of kings, where two people, thought to be intelligent, wave long slender pointed objects at each other in an attempt to make the other person bleed profusely. Is that what they mean when they say "foiled again"? Whoops, wrong fencing.

We have just been advised that we are supposed to be talking about the kind of fencing that normally surrounds your yard, garden, or pet enclosure, or maybe even your entire property.

There are so many different types of fencing: wood, stucco, masonry, metal, chain link, plastic, wow! In this chapter, we discuss wood fences. Please refer to the appropriate chapters in this book for maintenance tips for fences made of other materials.

Wood fences

Review the section "Preserving Your Wood Deck and Structures" in this chapter and follow the same instructions to maintain a fence.

Wood is wood and whether the wood is used for a deck, a fence, a gazebo, or a retaining wall there is one common fact — wood and water don't mix. Using an oil-base wood preservative with ultraviolet inhibitors keeps your fence looking newer, longer.

Loose rails and fence boards also can be a problem with wood fences. The fence can suddenly begin flopping in the wind, looking tattered and sloppy. Reattach loose rails and fence boards with nails or screws to prevent the fence from flapping around. Be sure to use galvanized nails, ceramic-coated construction screws, or stainless screws. Regular non-coated nails can completely rot out in as little as a year or two.

Wood fence posts always seem to rot in the exact same place: at ground level. Why not — that's where the dirt and the water are. Make sure the earth around a fence post slopes down and away, which helps shed water and keeps the post dryer.

When a fence post begins to rot at the base, the fence it supports is usually not long for this world. In the old days when we were maintenance men on the Ark, a rotten fence post meant digging out the concrete pier surrounding the base of the post and replacing the whole kit and caboodle.

Today, a pair of metal connectors, known as *fence post repair brackets,* can be used to make such a repair. Hey, waste not, want not! Not every post can be reused. If the rot at the post base extends more than 8 or 10 inches above the concrete pier that holds the post in the ground, then the post should be replaced. Also, there must be at least 3 inches of concrete between the edge of the fence post and the outside edge of the concrete pier.

Fence post repair brackets are available in two sizes, 3½ and 4 inch. One size is for rough-cut posts (4 inches) and another for finished posts (3½). We tell you this because we brought back the wrong size our first time round.

Only a few items are required for this project:

- ✔ 1 small block of wood
- ✔ 1 piece of scrap 2 by 4, about 6 inches long
- ✔ 1 hammer
- ✔ 1 flat pry bar
- ✔ 1 shovel
- ✔ 1 sledge hammer
- ✔ A few screws or a handful of 10d galvanized nails

Just follow these steps:

1. **Brace the fence with the 2 by 4 to hold it in a plumb position until the repair can be completed (see Figure 6-3).**

   Holding the fence in an upright position, wedge one end of the 2 by 4 into the landscape and nail the other end of the brace to the fence near the post that you intend to repair. Don't drive the nail all the way in. The brace is temporary and the nail has to be removed once the repair has been made.

Figure 6-3:
Bracing your fence for repair.

2. **Using the hammer, remove fence boards that cover the area to be repaired.**

   Use a block of wood to buffer the blow of the hammer, which reduces the chance of damaging a fence board. Lay the block against the fence board and strike the block with the hammer. The flat pry bar can be helpful here.

3. **Shovel the dirt away and expose the base of the post and the top of the concrete pier.**

The area should be swept clean so that the outline of the post in the concrete can be clearly seen. This is important because attempting to drive a fence repair bracket in the wrong location can easily bend the bracket, causing the project to become more than an unhappy experience for everyone involved.

4. **Use the sledgehammer to drive in the brackets.**

As you drive the bracket into place with the sledgehammer, it crushes the post and wedges itself into the concrete. The first bracket usually goes in pretty easily. However, the second one is more difficult to install because the first bracket usually uses up all of the available space between the rotted portion of the post and the pier. Be prepared to apply more force to each blow of the sledgehammer to properly seat the second bracket.

5. **Bolt, nail, or screw the brackets into the post.**

Because the brackets are tightly wedged between the pier and the post, the method of attachment usually is not terribly important. However, where substantial post damage exists, bolting can prove to be wise.

6. **Replace the fence board(s), remove the temporary brace, and refill the post hole.**

You have just saved over $100. Go have a beer — you deserve it!

Setting a sagging gate straight

A sagging wooden gate is a nuisance at best, and can, at some point, become impossible to open. The problem must be pretty common because someone has already packaged and marketed a repair kit for exactly that purpose. It's called a gate repair kit and consists of a cable with corner mounting brackets and a turnbuckle. The nice thing about a turnbuckle assembly is that it can be tightened or loosened to raise or lower the gate. The turnbuckle kit contains:

✔ Two metal corner brackets with mounting nails

✔ Two lengths of wire cable with galvanized metal U-bolts, which are used to attach one end of each cable to one of the corner brackets and then the other end of each cable to the turnbuckle.

✔ A galvanized metal turnbuckle

Here's how it works. A metal bracket is attached to the upper corner of the gate (on the hinge side). Another bracket is mounted diagonally at the lower corner of the gate on the latch side. Cables are attached to each corner bracket and then to the two ends of a turnbuckle. As the turnbuckle is tightened, the latch side of the gate rises. As the turnbuckle is loosened, the latch side of the gate drops (see Figure 6-4).

Figure 6-4:
Giving your
gate a
facelift.

This system won't work if the upper bracket is not placed on the hinge side of the gate.

Termite treachery

Termites are a universal problem. And when wood buried in the ground is connected to your home — whether the buried wood is pest-resistant or not — that wood can act as a secret corridor from the ground to the interior of your home. For example, a fence attached to the house that has posts buried in the ground can act as a termite path.

However, you can protect your home from a secret attack by termites. All you need to do is add a layer of sheet metal at the point where the fence and house intersect. A layer of sheet metal between the fence and the house is all that it takes to termite guard your home.

Wood Retaining Walls

A wood retaining wall often doesn't get noticed until it begins to topple. The first thing we hear when someone calls us about maintenance, "Gee, the Great Wall of China has stood straight and tall for centuries." Our response is, "Yeah, but the Leaning Tower of Pisa is just about ready to fall over. It all depends on the construction, doesn't it!"

Wood retaining walls are considered temporary, but their life expectancy can be improved by keeping the wood as dry as possible. To keep your retaining wall dry:

1. **Dig a 6- to 12-inch-wide trench between the retaining wall and the hill it supports.**

   The trench should go to the bottom of the retaining wall.

2. **Line the bottom and both sides of the trench with burlap cloth.**

3. **Place 6 inches of drain rock over the burlap in the bottom of the trench.**

4. **Install a 4-inch perforated drainpipe (perforations down) over the first layer of rock.**

   The drainpipe should daylight at some point beyond the end of the retaining wall. If possible, extend the pipe so that it drains directly into the public storm drain system.

5. **Fill the rest of the trench with drain rock to within 6 inches of the top of the dirt being retained.**

6. **Cover the rock with a layer or two of burlap and cover that with 6 inches of soil.**

   Make sure that the support posts are not in unnecessary contact with any soil and that the surrounding earth is graded to shed water away from the posts and retaining boards.

Clean the wall and post annually with soap and water, and every year or so apply a fresh coat of oil-base wood preservative.

Chapter 7

The Swimming Pool and Spa

*T*he Beverly Hillbillies had enough money to hire a pool maintenance company to maintain their "cement pond." If you don't or would prefer to take care of the day-to-day maintenance of your pool or spa, this chapter was written with you in mind.

Regardless of its construction — above ground, in ground, fiberglass, vinyl, or plaster — a swimming pool or spa (or cement pond) requires regular care and maintenance to ensure safe and healthy swimming conditions. This regular maintenance keeps the equipment in your pool operating at peak efficiency, which, in turn, extends its useful life — saving big bucks in repairs or replacement. Well-maintained equipment can even result in a friendlier utility bill because the equipment won't have to work quite as hard and can be run fewer hours each day.

The support system for a pool or spa consists of the following:

✔ A pump

✔ A filter

✔ One or more surface skimmers

✔ An automatic cleaner (optional)

✔ A heater (optional with a pool, a must with a spa)

✔ Manual cleaning tools

✔ Automatic timers and/or electronic controllers

Each of these devices works in harmony to produce clean and safe swimming conditions. You are also an important part of your pool or spa's support system since automatic support can go only so far.

The Pump

The pump is often referred to as the heart of the swimming pool system for good reason. Like the human heart, the pump is a pool's circulatory system. It draws water from the main drain (located at the bottom of the pool or spa) and the surface skimmer(s); then it pushes the water through the filter and heater and back into the pool through the return lines. The pump also helps distribute chemicals that are added to keep the water pure and in balance.

The pump consists of an electric motor, an impeller that draws water, and a "pot" that holds a strainer basket. The strainer basket gathers objects large enough to be sucked through the main drain or skimmer, such as small pebbles, leaves,or hairpins, but are too large to be sent to the filter. Many pools, and most spas, have more than one drain designed to prevent a youngster from being drowned by being held underwater by the powerful suction of a single drain.

The pot typically has a clear plastic cover that monitors the amount of debris collected by the basket strainer. An accumulation of debris in the basket strainer restricts the flow of water, causing the pump to work harder and permanently damaging the pump. Therefore, the basket strainer should be checked and cleaned regularly — at least once per week or after a heavy swim load.

Instead of cleaning the pot on the spot, have an extra basket strainer on hand and rotate them. This allows the contents of the dirty basket (hair, string, leaves, and small pebbles) to dry out which makes cleaning a heck of a lot easier. What's more, you can clean the dirty basket at your convenience and the system won't need to be shut down for long.

Cleaning the basket strainer is easy. First, turn off the pump, unscrew the plastic cover, and remove the basket strainer. A rubber O-ring is generally located between the pot housing and its plastic cover to assist in making an airtight seal. The O-ring should be rinsed off with fresh water and periodically lubricated with Teflon or silicone lubricant. The lubricant keeps the O-ring supple and helps it withstand cracking and deterioration from chemicals and prolonged exposure to sun.

Since most modern pumps used for residential pools have self-lubricating bearings and seals, they typically don't require lubrication. Your best bet is to check the owner's manual for your pump to determine the suggested maintenance.

The Skimmer

The basket strainer in the pump is really the second line of defense when it comes to gathering debris too large for the filter to handle. The first is the surface skimmer.

The skimmer draws in surface water and whatever resides on that water (oil, leaves, and windblown dirt or other debris) and collects large material in a basket, much like the basket strainer in the pump. The skimmer keeps the surface of the water clean and minimizes the amount of debris that makes its way into the main body of the pool water. Most pools have at least one surface skimmer, and some have more. The skimmer is located in the waterline tile on the downwind side of the pool.

If you are considering constructing a pool or spa, keep in mind that a skimmer is most effective when located on the downwind side of the pool because the wind directs the water (and debris) toward the skimmer.

There isn't much to maintaining a surface skimmer other than making sure to empty the basket at least once each week — more often in the fall when leaves are a problem.

Often the interior surface of the skimmer develops an oil ring at the water line. This ring should be periodically cleaned using a non-abrasive tile cleaner or surface scum remover.

The other element of the skimmer that should be periodically checked for proper operation is the trap door at the mouth of the skimmer — called a *weir*. The weir contains a buoyant material at the top that allows it to close — prohibiting debris from reentering the pool when the equipment is off or when there is lots of wave-making activity in the pool.

The weir is attached to either side of the skimmer housing with spring-loaded pins that fit into holes in the housing. Over time (and with a little horseplay) the pins may become disengaged, which prevents the weir from operating freely. Or, the ground shifts and the weir no longer has a uniform gap at the perimeter, which can cause it to stick.

If the weir is sticking, it can be removed and trimmed at one or both sides using a hacksaw to prevent it from rubbing against the housing. If the weir is not rubbing against the sides, but is on the sluggish side, remove the weir from the housing using a flat blade screwdriver to pry back the spring-loaded pins. Lubricate the pins and springs with Teflon lubricant and reinstall the weir.

If all else fails, replace the weir with a new one. Universal replacement weirs can be found at most stores that sell pool and spa supplies and can be installed in a matter of minutes using the removal technique discussed earlier. Also, skimmer baskets may, over time, develop holes or their handles often break, thus requiring replacement. You might be able to reattach the handle using a couple of zinc-coated screws. However, if the basket contains holes, it's a sign that the basket may soon disintegrate. Time to invest in a new basket.

If you hear your skimmer gulping water, the water level in the pool or spa is too low. Air is entering the system which can cause the pump to lose its prime. Always keep the water level at about midlevel of the waterline tile. In warm or windy months this may mean adding water almost daily. A pool cover can significantly cut down on water lost through evaporation.

The Filter

If the pump is the heart of a swimming pool or spa, then the filter is its lungs. The filter removes impurities and particulate matter (oils, grease, and dirt) and returns clear water to the pool via the return lines.

If the skimmer and pump do their respective jobs efficiently, the filter does a better job. It is the filter — in combination with chemicals — that makes the water sparkle and safe to swim in.

Three types of filters are used primarily for home swimming pools (see Figure 7-1):

- The high-rate sand filter
- The diatomaceous earth (D.E.) filter
- The cartridge filter

What these three types of filters have in common is that they all need to be regularly cleaned. A dirty filter simply can't do its job effectively. Consequently, the pool water becomes cloudy, the pool walls become laden with algae, and chemicals can't be evenly dispersed into the water. Moreover, a dirty filter causes a build up of pressure in the system. This heightened "back pressure" diminishes flow and puts undue stress on the pump motor.

The best time to clean a filter is before the water becomes cloudy. To determine when a filter should be cleaned, monitor the pressure gauge that sits atop the filter tank. While filter pressure varies with different filter styles and systems, pressure usually ranges from 6 to 20 pounds per square inch (psi). It's time to clean the filter when the pressure has increased by 8 to 10 psi above normal.

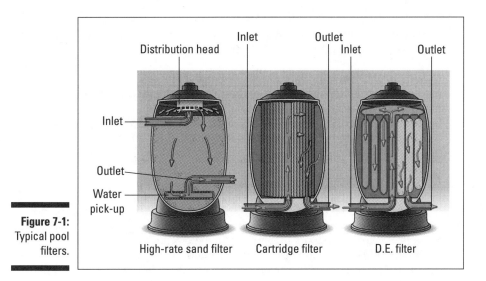

Figure 7-1:
Typical pool
filters.

High-rate sand filters

The high-rate sand filter is the most popular type, primarily due to its simplicity of operation and maintenance. You clean it by "backwashing" — a process that reverses the flow of water through the filter and out a waste line. Backwashing lifts the particles previously collected by the filter, raises the sand bed, and cleans it.

Most high-rate sand filter systems contain a clear section of pipe, called a *sight glass,* that shows you the clarity of the backwash water. The process is complete when the water is clear.

A sand filter can last indefinitely when regularly backwashed. And although a sand filter doesn't need to be recharged, it's a good idea to pour a degreaser into the top at least once each season. The amount of degreaser used is based on the size and capacity of your filter. Follow the label directions on the degreaser. The degreaser works its way through the filter system.

D.E. filters

Of the three types of filter media, the D.E. filter delivers the cleanest water. It is also one of the most maintenance-intense systems.

D.E. is a light-colored porous rock composed of the shells of diatoms — a type of one-celled algae. It is a white powdery substance similar to flour. D.E. is generally introduced into the filter through the skimmer and coats fabric-covered filter grids called *septa*. As with the high-rate sand filter, the D.E.

filter must be periodically backwashed to dispose of the waste that has been collected. However, unlike the sand in the sand filter, the diatomaceous earth must be removed and restored with fresh D.E.

Owners of D.E. filters often make the mistake of relying only on the backwashing process as a means of cleaning their filter. Unfortunately, this process usually doesn't remove the majority of D.E., which can become caked between the filter grids. Accordingly, a D.E. filter should first be backwashed and then taken apart in order for all of the filter grids to be washed with a degreasing product, fresh water, and a nylon brush.

A power washer can make the job of grid cleaning a snap.

After the grids have been cleaned, they should be reassembled and placed back into the filter tank and the tank put back together. As with the pot at the pump, a rubber gasket sits in a groove between the top and bottom of the filter tank. This hula-hoop-sized O-ring should be cleaned and lubricated with Teflon or silicone-based lubricant. Septa with worn fabric should be replaced.

Cartridge filters

In the case of a cartridge filter, the pool or spa water is circulated through a fibrous material. To clean this type of filter, simply remove the cartridge and rinse it off with a garden hose. To remove oils, soak the cartridge for about an hour in a solution of trisodium phosphate (TSP) — 1 pound for every 10 gallons of water. A clean plastic garbage can works great for holding the cleaning solution and the filter. When complete, rinse the cartridge with fresh water and reinstall it.

If the cartridge is covered with algae, clay, or other vegetation, soak it for a longer period (2 to 3 hours) in a stronger solution of TSP — 3 pounds for every 10 gallons of water.

After thorough cleaning, calcium deposits may be found on the cartridge. If this is the case, the cartridge should be soaked in a solution of muriatic acid and water — 1 part acid to 20 parts water. Mix the solution in a plastic container, adding the acid to the water, and soak the cartridge until the solution stops fizzing. Remove the cartridge, rinse it with a hose, and reinstall it.

Muriatic acid is dangerous stuff. Make sure to wear protective clothing, safety goggles, and rubber gloves, have plenty of ventilation, and follow the directions on the label to the letter.

If all of your cleaning efforts turn out to be futile and the cartridge fails to maintain clean water, or if a cartridge is showing signs of wear, it's time to replace the cartridge.

Keep in mind that, depending upon the specific configuration of your system, there may be a series of valves that may need to be opened, closed, or placed in different positions to facilitate the filter cleaning or backwashing process. Your best bet is to consult your equipment owner's manual, your pool or spa builder, or a qualified pool and spa maintenance technician.

The pressure gauge

The pressure gauge located at the top of most filters is one of the system's most important components. It displays the pressure inside a filter, which can build up to a dangerously high level. The gauge must be in top operating condition at all times.

Small bits of sand or other debris can get lodged in the opening at the base of the gauge causing it to display a false reading. Also, condensation and water can cause the gauge to rust and fail. Thus, part of a good pool and spa maintenance routine includes replacing the pressure gauge every few years. Fortunately, in the grand scheme of things, a pressure gauge is one of the least expensive parts of the filter system weighing in at about $10 to $15.

The Heater

What good is a pool if it is too cold to swim in? And there's no sense in having a spa if the water can't be raised to a therapeutic level that reduces the day's stress and eases muscle tension.

A heater is essential if you have a spa and can be necessary if you live in a cool climate where pool water may need an occasional boost. A heater, in combination with other devices such as a pool cover, can extend the swim season by several weeks or even months.

Pool heater maintenance varies depending upon the type of system that you have. A gas heater contains burners that should be vacuumed at least once each year to remove spider webs and other debris that can clog the burner ports. After you vacuum the burners, you should check for gas leaks at all connections.

To check for gas leaks, make a solution of liquid dish soap and water in a spray bottle (one tablespoon in a cup of warm water). Spray the soapy solution onto the pipe joints and look for little bubbles to become big ones. If you see big bubbles, turn off the gas and call your local utility company or a qualified plumbing contractor. Do not use the heater until the gas leak has been repaired.

Electric heaters contain heating elements (such as those on your stovetop) that can become covered with scale (mineral deposits). Often, scale can be stripped from an element by removing it and cleaning it using a wire brush. Some elements are so far gone that replacement is the only alternative. Bring the old element to your pool and spa supply store for an identical match.

To change an electric element, first turn off the power to the heater to avoid injury. Next, open a drain plug to remove excess water, remove the old element, and install the replacement. Make sure that the system is full of water and the pump is operating before powering up the heater to avoid damaging the new element.

When purchasing a replacement element, buy an extra to have on hand should one go out when you least expect it — such as during a backyard party. The water won't have a chance to cool off, and you'll be a real hero.

Putting a Lid On It

Aside from raising the pool temperature, a pool cover prevents leaves and other debris from entering the pool. It also reduces evaporation. This combination equals great savings — less energy to heat the pool, less energy to run the filter and automatic cleaner, and less water due to evaporation. What's more, a covered pool uses fewer chemicals.

Good quality pool covers, such as self-draining nylon covers that stretch taut across the pool, are also an important element in pool safety. Many of these covers are so strong that they can easily support the weight of a small child or even an adult who may have fallen into the pool.

To extend the useful life of your pool cover, scrub it with a nylon floor and wall brush and fresh water. Some cover companies recommend using a mild solution (one tablespoon to a gallon of hot water) of hand soap to clean a really dirty cover. The cover should be washed two to three times a year to prevent stains that can't be removed later. The floor and wall brush is something that comes with most pools, but can be purchased at stores that sell pool and spa supplies and accessories.

Open or remove (depending upon the type you have) the pool cover when adding chemicals. Chemicals and chemical vapors can break down the cover material. After adding chemicals, don't replace the cover until the filter has run for a couple of hours and the chemicals have been diluted throughout the system. ***Warning:*** Be sure to supervise the uncovered pool to prevent a potential accident.

Depending upon the type of cover material (vinyl or nylon mesh), small holes or tears should be mended before they become bigger problems. However, a deteriorating cover should not be repaired — replacement is in order. Vinyl and nylon repair kits consisting of a small piece of patch material and some adhesive are often provided at the time the cover is installed. A repair kit can be obtained by contacting a pool cover professional or through a pool and spa supply company. The damaged area must be clean and dry in order for the patch material to stick.

A brittle cover or one that is cracking is a sure sign that the cover needs replacement. Most covers have a life of about five years.

If you have an automatic cover, periodically check the motor to make certain that it is not in contact with water. This can cause the motor to short out and allow rust and corrosion to damage the motor, its housing, or mechanical parts attached to it.

An automatic cover that is sluggish or that isn't evenly aligned with the edge of the pool when fully closed or when in the full open position are signs of needed maintenance by a service professional. He will have the tools and expertise needed to adjust or replace wheels, cord, pulleys, glides, and other parts.

A Clean Pool Is a Happy Pool!

Even with all of the automatic-cleaning equipment available today, there is still no substitute for manual-cleaning equipment and some elbow grease. It permits you to get into nooks and crannies that are off limits to automatic cleaning equipment. Bagging leaves and brushing the surface will prevent staining, keep the surface smooth, and give your pool or spa that extra bit of sparkle.

Basic manual-cleaning equipment consists of a wall and floor brush with short nylon bristles and a net for scooping leaves or other debris from the water (see Figure 7-2).

If your pool or spa is made of fiberglass or has a vinyl liner, and it isn't surrounded by lots of trees, these are the only tools that you will likely need. If, on the other hand, your pool or spa has a plaster finish, you may find it useful to have a stainless steel brush for removing algae, rust stains, and scale. A large leaf net is especially useful for gathering leaves on the surface of the water or at the bottom of the pool or spa. Brushes and nets easily attach to lightweight aluminum telescopic handles that can make getting to the most remote locations a breeze. Manual-cleaning equipment can be purchased from a pool and spa supply store.

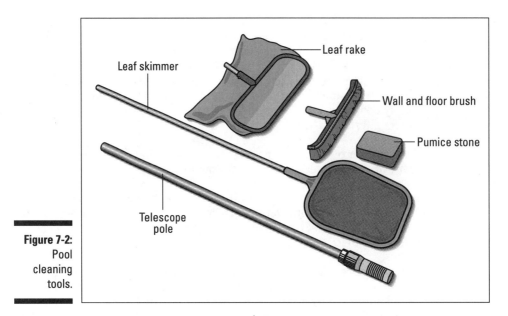

Leaf rake

Leaf skimmer

Wall and floor brush

Pumice stone

Telescope pole

Figure 7-2:
Pool
cleaning
tools.

The other bit of manual-cleaning equipment is really semi-automatic — a vacuum cleaner. Like a household vacuum cleaner, the pool vacuum consists of a suction head, hose, wheels, and sometimes a brush. One end of the hose connects to the suction head while the other typically connects to the suction port at the surface skimmer. Like the cleaning brushes and nets, the suction head attaches to an aluminum handle for easy maneuverability. The vacuum is slowly and methodically guided along a pool's walls and bottom. The material that is gathered by the vacuum cleaner is sent directly to the filter. Some models have their own on-board filter bag. A vacuum isn't really needed if you keep your pool covered, regularly bag leaves, sweep the surface and have an automatic pool cleaner. Brushing debris to the floor drain will perform essentially the same function as a vacuum.

Your pool cleaning plan

Pool maintenance programs vary from pool to pool; however the following maintenance program is adequate for most pools:

- ✔ Use a leaf net to remove leaves during each pool session. Leaves or other debris allowed to rest on the bottom of the pool or spa can cause staining.

- ✔ Clean the strainer baskets in the skimmer and pump at least once a week — more frequently in autumn if the pool is not covered.

- ✔ Clean tile with a soft brush and a pool tile cleaner. The cleaning of pool walls depends on your surface: plaster, vinyl, or fiberglass. Follow the manufacturer's suggested procedures.

- ✔ A good once over twice a week along the waterline with the nylon wall and floor brush prevents scale buildup and keeps the tile bright and shiny.

- ✔ Vacuum the pool at least once a week (if you don't have automatic pool cleaning equipment).

- ✔ Test the water frequently (at least twice a week during swim season and weekly during the off season) and add chemicals if necessary. Follow the manufacturer's directions.

- ✔ If the water appears cloudy, test it for chemical balance; if necessary, backwash and service the filter.

- ✔ Keep the deck clean and clear of debris by regularly rinsing it off with a garden hose.

Automatic pool cleaners

For pool owners, the automatic pool cleaner is the best invention since the lounge chair. Some automatic pool cleaners vacuum, others agitate; but the principle is the same — keep the pool as clean as possible with minimal manual effort (see Figure 7-3). A good automatic pool cleaner is worth its weight in gold.

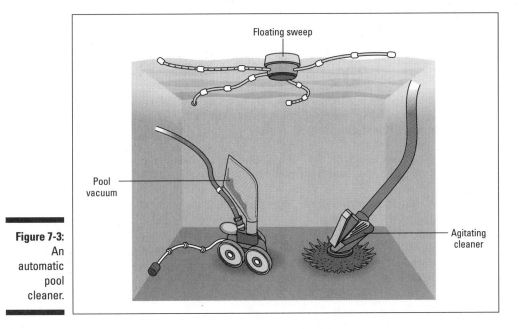

Figure 7-3: An automatic pool cleaner.

Floating sweep

Pool vacuum

Agitating cleaner

In order for an automatic pool cleaner to do a good job of maintaining your pool, it too must be maintained. Although most manufacturers make maintenance-free models, we have found that an annual "tune-up" during the off season makes an automatic pool cleaner work more efficiently, improves its dependability, and enhances its lasting quality. Depending upon the type of cleaner, a tune-up can include rotating or changing tires, replacing the filter bag, replacement of cleaning rings on agitator hoses, and gear and spring replacement, to name a few. Though this might sound complicated, all you need to do is pull the cleaner out of the pool and bring it down to your local pool and spa supply store. Most stores will replace the parts for you at no charge — provided you buy the repair/replacement parts from them. Or you can do the tune-up yourself with nothing more than a screwdriver and an adjustable wrench.

Caring for tile

Waterline tile can easily become marred with scum and scale. Short of whipping out a hammer and chisel (which may be necessary in some cases), there are a couple of effective means of staying on top of tile care.

The cleaning method that requires the least amount of energy involves using a commercial swimming pool tile cleaner and scale remover. This, in combination with a stiff nylon brush and a thorough rinsing with water, removes almost all scum and most scale. These cleaning products are pretty powerful, so be sure to wear safety goggles and long sleeves. Work from the decks with water in the pool. For the most effective cleaning, it is best for the water to be at the low side of the tile line, but never with the plaster or fiberglass exposed as the chemicals could damage the finish.

Always use cleaning products in strict accordance with the directions. Also, never use steel wool to clean tile. The metal particles can stain the plaster.

You can remove light scale deposits with a solution of muriatic acid and water — 1 part acid to 6 parts water. Add the acid to the water and use a stiff nylon brush to apply the solution.

When working with acid of any kind, wear safety goggles, rubber gloves, and skin protection and have plenty of ventilation to avoid injury.

Although it requires more elbow grease, a more effective means of removing scale involves using a block of pumice — similar to what our mom used to use on her feet. Oops! Not that mom's feet were covered with scale like pool tile — better stop here. In any event, the pumice block works well at removing scale buildup without damaging most tiles. Test a small area first because some brands of tile can be scratched (see Figure 7-4).

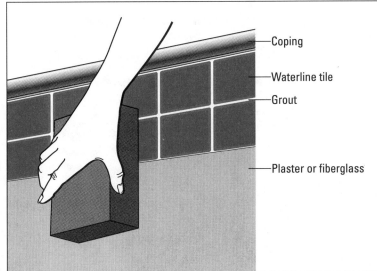

Coping

Waterline tile

Grout

Plaster or fiberglass

Figure 7-4:
Cleaning
pool tile
with a
pumice
stone.

In addition, wear a pair of rubber gloves or you won't have any skin left on your hands after going around the perimeter of the pool. Simply rub the pumice block back and forth until the scale disappears. Frequently dipping the block into the pool water will provide needed lubrication and flush out debris from the stone.

Both the commercial tile cleaner and the pumice block do an excellent job of renewing the grout surrounding the tile. Badly stained or discolored grout can be remedied with an acid washing or regrouting. Due to the potential for injury and damage to surrounding finishes, we suggest that only a professional perform this work.

If you have a prefabricated fiberglass or acrylic spa, use only the cleaning materials and methods suggested by the manufacturer.

Coping with coping

Coping is the trim at the edge of the pool (see Figure 7-5). It is above the waterline tile and beside the concrete decking.

When we were kids, almost every pool had a sand-colored coping with an upturned bullnose edge. As beginning swimmers, we clung to that coping as our security blanket until we became confident enough to venture out into the pool. It was our Rock of Gibraltar!

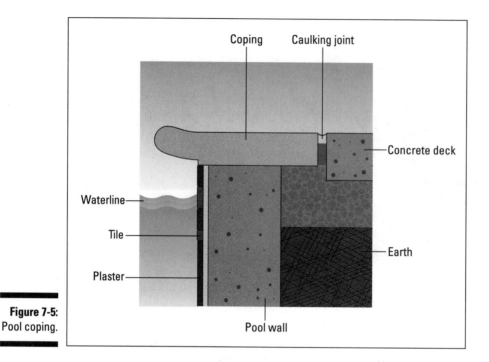

Coping   Caulking joint

Concrete deck

Waterline

Tile

Earth

Plaster

Figure 7-5:
Pool coping.

Pool wall

While some pools still have this traditional type of coping, bullnose brick and stone have become popular replacements for design-conscious pool owners. Many pools have done away with coping all together by cantilevering the decking over the pool edge.

As a rule, coping doesn't require much maintenance. Periodic cleaning with a garden hose and fresh water generally does the trick. However, the flexible joint between the coping and the decking may, from time to time, need to be repaired or replaced. The material in this joint is a special elastomeric self-leveling compound designed specifically for use around pools. Most pool supply stores stock the material in a host of colors. The old material can usually be removed by prying it out using an old chisel or putty knife.

With the old material out, pack sand into the joint to within ¾ inch from the top of the adjacent coping and decking. Install the material in accordance with the manufacturer's directions.

The freshly caulked joint should be lightly covered with small grit sand to enhance the appearance of the finished product and to blend in with surrounding finishes.

When Old Man Winter Arrives

Winterizing your pool protects it from damage by chemical imbalance and algae growth. A properly winterized pool is securely covered and, thus, protects little ones from drowning.

Many people believe that pool equipment can be can be shut down during winter months. This may be true in certain areas of the country where temperatures dip below freezing for a good part of the time, but the lack of circulation can allow algae to grow in a pool in a more moderate climate. Thus, if you live in warmer weather, you should run your equipment every day. However, you don't need to run it for as long a period each day. Reduce your timer to about half the time that you operate your equipment during swim season.

What's more, draining a pool is a no-no that can cause significant damage to the pool. The weight of the water actually keeps the pool from rising out of the ground. Emptying the pool can allow pressure to push the pool and surrounding decking out of the ground in a matter of days, causing thousands of dollars in damage. Yikes!

If you do live in a cold climate and don't plan to operate the equipment during the winter, the first step in preparing your pool for the off-season is to test your pool water to protect the pool from staining, scaling, and equipment damage. You can do this using a test kit, or it can be done on site by a pool maintenance professional. A third alternative is to bring a water sample into your local pool and spa supply company to be tested by a pool water professional. If the test reveals metal or calcium problems, follow the chemical treatment directions of your pool water professional.

Here's the quick once over when it comes to winter and pool water. If necessary, raise the total alkalinity to 80 to 125 parts per million (ppm) for plaster pools or 125 to 150 ppm for vinyl, painted, or fiberglass pools. With respect to pH, tests should show a pH of 7.4 to 7.6. Use acid to lower the pH or a pH increaser, such as soda ash (sodium carbonate), to raise the pH.

If necessary, raise the calcium hardness to 200 to 250 ppm for plaster pools and 175 to 225 for all others or as recommended by your pool water professional.

Prior to closing or covering the pool for the season, the pool walls and bottom should be brushed and vacuumed to remove any debris that could cause staining. Calcium and hard water stains at the water line tile should be removed using one of the techniques discussed earlier in this chapter. Remove all debris from skimmer baskets, the pump strainer basket, and the automatic pool cleaner, if one exists. Thoroughly clean the filter by backwashing the system or cleaning the cartridge in the case of a cartridge filter as discussed earlier in this chapter.

Never store a dirty filter. Deposits and scale may harden and cake over the winter leaving a tough repair or clean up job in the spring.

The pool should be super chlorinated for the winter to protect against unwanted bacteria. In addition, the filter pump should be run for several hours to thoroughly distribute the chlorine. If you own a pool with a plaster finish, you might want to consider using a chlorinating floater that contains chlorine tablets.

When the pump and filter are not operating, any algae present in your pool water has a chance to run wild. To prevent this, add an algaecide directly to the water around the edges of the pool. Run the pump and filter to circulate the water and to distribute the algaecide.

Extra precautions should be taken if your pool is located in an area that frequently reaches sub-zero temperatures. Damage due to frozen pipes can be avoided by partially draining the pool to about 4 inches below the skimmer. When in doubt, follow the advice of your pool builder or local pool water professional.

Other "cold climate" precautions include draining the heater manifold, strainer basket and pump, and the solar heating system (if one exists). The heater manifold is a distributor of sorts. It directs the unheated pool water into the heat exchanger (where the water is heated), back into the manifold and out to the pool or spa. The manifold can be drained by opening a small drain valve located on the heater housing or on the manifold itself. Refer to owner's manual for drain valve location.

Also, the skimmer expansion plug should be used to plug one or more pipes at the bottom of a skimmer. The skimmer expansion plug is a rubber plug with a wing nut at the top. Tightening the wing nut will cause the plug to expand for a secure fit in the pipe opening at the bottom of the skimmer. The plug is designed to prevent water from getting into the pipe at the bottom of the skimmer and freezing which could prevent damage.

Finally, cover the pool to keep leaves and other debris out. Consult the Consumer Products Safety Commission (CPSC) for an approved cover that can prevent children and animals from drowning. (The CPSC has an excellent Web site at www.cpsc.gov, or they can be reached by telephone at 800-638-2772.)

Much of what we have suggested regarding winterization is not required (or recommended) for pools located in mild climates. Instead of closing the pool, chemical treatment and filtration can be scaled back if you don't plan to use the pool during the winter months. Simply keep the water balanced, as discussed earlier in this chapter, and reduce the equipment time clock to run about half the time that it would during normal swim season.

It is still a good idea to do all of the cleaning steps and the pool can be covered. However, an automatic pool cleaner will continue to keep the pool spotless in the winter provided it is used frequently — making the cover optional.

For those areas where the mercury dips below freezing only a few times a year, run the filter pump continuously to avoid damage from freezing. Some modern automation devices have a temperature sensor that turns the filter pump on automatically to avoid damage from freezing.

Consult your local pool water professional or maintenance specialist for specific recommendations regarding winterizing your pool.

Ready, Set, Swim!

Whether or not a pool is shut down during the winter, the beginning of swim season is one of the most critical times for pool maintenance.

If the pool is located in a colder climate and the equipment has been shut down for the winter, drain plugs at the solar system, pump, and heater will need to be replaced. Also, the skimmer expansion plug must be removed.

For pools that are covered, any water that has collected on top of the cover should be pumped out using a small submersible pump. Use the leaf net on the end of an extension pole to remove leaves and other large clusters of debris.

Use this opportunity to clean the cover before storing it. Rinse the cover with fresh water while using the pool brush on an extension pole to work loose debris that may be clinging to the cover.

Get the equipment running by first restoring the prime to the pump. Before starting the pump, the valve from the main drain should be completely open. Water should be added to the pump pot — where the strainer basket is located at the pump. Use a garden hose rather than a bucket since you'll be filling the main drain line as well as the pump pot. The pump pot should be filled until it runs over. Replace the lid at the pump pot hand tight. Add a little Teflon or silicone lubricant to the O-ring or gasket material to keep it supple and avoid a leak. It also keeps seals pliable underwater and keeps them from drying out when the system is drained.

You can now safely start the pump motor. Air might blow out of the pool inlet lines causing bubbling at the surface of the water in the pool. This should quickly disappear as water fills the lines and makes its way into the pool.

If the pump should lose its prime, refill the strainer basket and repeat the process. Once the pump is running at capacity, excess air should be bled from the filter by opening the drain cock at the top of the filter.

With the equipment running, it is an excellent time to check the system for leaks. Check the strainer basket, valves and plugs, plumbing and equipment fittings, and at the compression rings which hold the filter and separation tank lids in place. The most common repairs for leaks include gasket and O-ring lubrication or replacement, and valve or plumbing fitting repair or replacement.

Always start out the season with a clean filter.

Pool Water — It's a Balancing Act

Properly balanced water not only provides a safe and healthy swimming environment, it also preserves the integrity of the pool and equipment.

At the beginning of the swim season, an opening "shock treatment" is the first order of business. This extra dose of sanitizer kills bacteria and other organic contaminants and is the first line of defense for keeping algae from getting started.

Total alkalinity (TA) should be maintained in the range of 60 to 100 parts per million (ppm). Low TA causes fluctuating pH and excessive corrosion and staining of equipment. And speaking of pH, it should be adjusted to the ideal range of 7.2 to 7.6. The calcium hardness should be maintained at a minimum of 200 ppm. Once the water is conditioned, maintain free available chlorine in the range of 1.0 to 3.0 ppm.

Pool water must be tested regularly, especially when the pool is being used heavily, to ensure that the water is properly balanced. Green water is a frequent problem. This is a sign that the pH needs to be adjusted and the pool water needs to be "shocked."

Algae, which looks like green or brown stains on the interior of the pool, is probably the most common threat to pool owners. It can also cause the water to turn color and pool surfaces to feel slippery. Reducing the pH to 7.2 to 7.6 and the total alkalinity to 80 to 100 parts per million (ppm) combats the condition. Also, the pool water may need to be diluted with tap water. This is done simply by draining approximately one quarter of the water in the pool and replacing it with water from the tap.

Bleached hair and bathing suits are a sure sign of excess available chlorine. Adding sodium sulfite or sodium bisulfite or sodium thiosulfate can typically treat this. Once the water is conditioned, maintain free available chlorine in the range of 1.0 to 3.0 ppm.

For more information on how to care for your pool, contact the National Spa and Pool Institute at 2111 Eisenhower Avenue, Alexandria, Virginia, 22314. Their telephone number is 703-838-0083. Or you can visit their Web site at www.nspi.org.

Chapter 8

Landscape Irrigation

• •

In This Chapter

▶ Cleaning sprinkler heads

▶ Replacing a riser

▶ Repairing a pipe

▶ Cleaning and maintaining an anti-siphon valve

▶ Maintaining the controller

▶ Cleaning a wiring connection

▶ Winterizing the system

• •

*W*hen we were kids, it was our job to care for the garden. One week we would turn all the soil. The next week we would trim the hedge. The following week it would be time to prune the lilies or the hydrangeas. Yep, we had to pick the peaches, too. There was always something to do.

No matter what else had to be done, there was always watering. Dad made sure that we watered at least twice a week. The carnations, the roses, everything had to be watered. It was our job for over 14 years. Can you imagine how many times we watered our parents' garden in 14 years? By hand, no less. Nope, there wasn't a sprinkler system at the old homestead. But you can rest assured that we both have complete irrigation systems now.

If you want to really appreciate the value of your irrigation system, try watering your lawn and garden by hand for a week or two. You will gain a new respect for built-in sprinklers and sprayers. So, it goes without saying that it makes good sense to keep your irrigation system in tip-top condition. Here's how.

Raindrops (Should) Keep Falling from Your Sprinkler Head

Your landscape irrigation system may include several types of sprinklers depending on the layout of your yard and types of plants that need watering. Shrubs, flowerbeds, and small lawns use sprinkler heads commonly called *spray heads*. Larger lawns typically use *impact* or *rotary sprinkler heads*.

Spray heads

Spray heads have *water ports* (nozzles) in a variety of arc patterns, including full, half, and quarter, circle, and variable. A slot cut in the edge of the head allows water to flow out in the arc pattern.

Another kind of spray head, a *bubbler,* discharges water in a 360-degree circle, but instead of spraying, it lets out a gentle flow of water up to 3 feet from the head. Bubblers are used for smaller jobs, like watering shrubs and plants. Often bubblers are dedicated to only one plant or tree.

Spray heads can be attached to fixed risers or to popup canisters that are buried in the ground.

No matter what kind of sprinkler head you have, it most certainly contains a filter (or has one attached). Filters catch large pieces of debris that can easily clog a sprinkler head. Every several years, you need to clean or replace these filters. Just unscrew the sprinkler head, pull the filter out of the riser, clean it, and then replace the sprinkler head. As easy as you please.

Brown spots in your lawn can mean bad sprinkler head coverage, which is a good indication that a filter (or a head) is clogged and needs cleaning.

Cleaning the head

If you notice that one of your sprinklers is discharging water in an irregular pattern, it could mean that the head needs cleaning. Dirt can get into the head through a broken filter. In the case of popup units that reside at ground level (or slightly below), dirt or vegetable matter can get lodged into the port from the outside. Slightly raising the canister (above dirt level) can often reduce this problem.

Cleaning the head is simple. With the water on, gently probe the opening with a large needle or fine stiff wire. The needle or wire dislodges the blockage, while the water pressure clears the dislodged matter. Instantly, the head will begin to spray properly. Hey, you may get a little wet, but the satisfaction of successful maintenance more than makes up for damp tootsies.

You can "floss" the port of a sprinkler head by holding a piece of fishing line in both hands and sliding it into the slot while the water is flowing (see Figure 8-1).

Figure 8-1:
"Flossing" a
sprinkler
head.

If you can't unclog the head in place, it has to be removed. Soak the head in water to soften stuck-on debris. Next, use a bristle brush to scrub it clean. Use a pocket knife or a screwdriver to scrape off hard-to-remove material.

Blowing through the head immediately tells you whether it is sufficiently clean. If not, you can use compressed air to remove any final bit of debris. Most gas stations have compressed air available. Ask to use a spray nozzle instead of their tire-filling tip.

A screw mounted in the top of the head adjusts the water pressure to the head and the resultant area that the spray of water covers. Sometimes just opening this screw to allow full flow removes fine dirt that may be plugging the port.

Cleaning the filter

An erratic spray or a reduced spray, a brown spot on a lawn, or a dry spot in the garden all indicate that water has ceased to flow properly. In some instances, the problem is a clogged sprinkler head. But when the head is cleaned and the problem continues, you can be sure that a filter needs cleaning or replacement. Here's all you have to do:

1. **Remove the spray head.**

2. **Look for the filter inserted into the bottom of the head or in the top of the riser assembly.**

3. **Remove the filter and clean it with water or compressed air.**

   A toothbrush is a great tool for this task.

4. **Replace broken filters or those that are too difficult to clean.**

   A filter only costs a few pennies.

If the filter is extremely dirty, it indicates that dirt has gotten into the water line at some point. With the spray head removed, turn on the water supply to allow any remaining dirt to escape.

Impact sprinkler heads

Impact sprinklers spray single streams of water over great distances — like those used at golf courses and schools where the lawns are really big. As the stream of water passes through the head, it hits a built-in hinged drive arm that causes the head to rotate from side to side. First, one way, and then the other. As the water repeatedly hits the arm, you hear a "tick, tick, tick" sound.

Impact sprinklers fit on the top of fixed risers or in canisters that allow the sprinkler to pop up. The latter are commonly used for lawn watering because they are flush with the ground and remain out of the way for mowing.

Impact sprinklers are far more complex than a simple spray head. Unless you have a fatal failure, maintenance usually consists of cleaning dirt and grass from the canister and filter.

Keeping grass clipped around the canister minimizes cleaning chores. Spreading grasses tend to grow into the canister because they find a ready source of water in the canister. To remove grass, lift the lid and cut the grass even with the canister; then remove clippings from the tank and the operating mechanism.

Dirt gets into sprinklers that are located near public streets and dirt or gravel drives; the salt and sand used for winter snow and ice removal often finds its way into your sprinklers. To remove dirt from the canister, you need the special wrench used to remove the sprinkler mechanism. Our friends at the local irrigation supply store tell us that everyone refers to the "wrench" in question as a roto-wrench. The roto-wrench is capable of reaching into the base of the canister so that the head can be disconnected without disturbing the base.

Clean out as much dirt as possible with your hand. If it is sticky clay, you may need a garden trowel to remove it. While the sprinkler is out, turn on the water and flush out the line. It may take more than one cleaning to remove all the dirt.

While the sprinkler is removed, check the filter located in the bottom of the stem. If it's dirty, remove and clean it.

Don't use oil, grease, or pipe dope on an impact sprinkler; it is water lubricated. If the sprinkler fails to operate, check the nozzle for obstructions.

In cold climates, you should purge your irrigation system to prevent damage from freezing. (See "Winterizing the System" later in this chapter.)

Rotary sprinkler heads

A rotary sprinkler (sometimes referred to as an orbital sprinkler) is almost identical to a conventional popup spray head except that it rotates when water passes through it. Both the conventional spray popup and the rotary popup are sealed; the head is mounted on a riser that slides up and down through a snug seal in the top of the canister. Nothing can get in or out of the canister except the riser. This configuration prevents dirt from getting into the canister when the head pops up (a major advantage over impact sprinklers).

As with other kinds of sprinklers, keeping your rotary clean is your primary maintenance task. To clean this kind of head, simply follow the instruction earlier in this chapter in the section entitled "Cleaning the head."

Rising above It All

The *riser* is a vertical pipe that connects the underground water supply line to the sprinkler head, or in the case of a popup, to the canister. Risers are made of metal, plastic (PVC), or polyethylene, with plastic and polyethylene being the most common. Both types of material are inexpensive and easy to work with.

Because risers are located near the surface or above the ground, and because they are commonly plastic, they're pretty easy to break. Shoveling, roto-tilling, and raking take their toll on risers. Lawn tractors and misguided automobiles don't help either. If water comes gushing up from beneath the ground more often than not, the problem is a broken riser.

Risers should always be installed into a threaded fitting so they can be removed.

To access the riser, you need to remove the soil from around it. We remove only enough dirt to completely expose the riser and the supply line to which it is connected. You only need a little bit of room to work. Dig carefully, so that you don't damage the supply pipe. Use a damp cloth to clean the fitting so that dirt and foliage don't fall into the supply line as the riser is being removed.

To remove the riser, simply use a pair of pliers to unscrew it from the supply line. If the riser is broken off inside the supply line, you won't be able to grip it with a pair of pliers. Here, you need a special tool known as an *easy-out* to remove the riser. Unlike pliers, an easy-out removes pipe by gripping it from the inside. An easy-out is a tapered tool that is inserted into the inside of a piece of threaded pipe allowing the pipe to be gripped from within. Turning the tool unscrews the broken riser from the fitting.

To install a new riser, wrap Teflon tape around the threads and screw it in hand tight. Then give it another half-turn or so with pliers until the connection begins to feel snug. Don't overtighten.

Sometimes you can't get a riser to stand straight. Here's a neat trick that will definitely solve the problem. First, you'll need to purchase two plastic *street 90's* (90-degree street-elbow or ell). A street 90 is nothing more than a 90-degree connector with female threads on one end and male threads on the opposite end. With the riser removed and the 90's in hand, follow this procedure:

1. **Screw the two 90's together.**

   This can be done only one way (the male end of one into the female end of the other). This leaves one male end and one female end.

2. **Screw the male end of the pair of 90's into the female supply line fitting.**

   With the 90's in place, the female end of one of the 90's will be unused.

3. **Screw your riser into the female end that's left.**

You end up with is a hinge joint that turns laterally on the threaded connections in two directions (forward to backward and left to right). With this kind of versatility, you can radically tilt the riser in whatever direction needed to get it absolutely straight — without breaking the pipe. What a deal!

Making Good Connections with the Pipes

Eighty percent of the pipes used in residential in-ground irrigation supply are made out of PVC. Polyethylene or polybutylene plastic pipe (poly pipes) is also used because it's easier to work with, less expensive, and less likely to crack during a winter freeze. PVC is a rigid plastic and is the strongest of the three; it should always be used at the main water supply to the sprinkler system.

PVC water lines are laid out in straight lines with 90- or 45-degree joints and in yards that are relatively flat. In hilly areas, or where a lot of twists or turns in the supply line are necessary, poly supply pipes are often used. Poly piping is easily curved using fewer fittings than PVC. Poly pipes are held in place with metal clamps.

A properly installed sprinkler line should last years without developing a leak. But human activity and earth movement can cause joints to fail and pipes to be cut or punctured. The first indication of a leak is low pressure somewhere in the irrigation system. Another good indication is a flooded yard. Would you believe a water fountain gushing up from nowhere?

Finding the leak

Big leaks that spray into the air are easy to locate. If the leak is small and the only indication is less water coming from the sprinkler heads, you may have to search to find it. Look for obvious wet spots near underground lines.

To find a slow leak, turn off all the sprinkler heads. This forces more water through the leak and may expose its location. You shut off most heads by turning the adjusting screw to the full off position (turn the screw clockwise until it stops turning). For heads that can't be turned off, remove the sprinkler from the riser and place a cap on the riser. Eventually, the leak shows itself.

Repairing poly pipe

Polyethylene and polybutylene pipes (tubing) are repaired using polyethylene insert couplings and stainless-steel worm-drive hose clamps. This process is a bit easier than a PVC maintenance because the pipe is highly flexible and only a small length needs to be unearthed before tubing movement can be achieved.

A coupling is nothing more than a short piece of rigid tubing that fits snugly within the flexible tubing being repaired.

Half of the length of the coupling fits into one piece of tubing, while the other half slides into another piece of tubing. The clamps are fitted around the outside of the tubing being repaired. As the circular clamp is tightened, it seals the connection between the rigid coupling and the softer tubing. Essentially, the soft tubing is squeezed against the hard coupling as the diameter of the metal clamp is screwed tighter and tighter. When cutting out a damaged piece of tubing, two connections must be made. Here's what to do:

1. **Cut out the damaged section of the pipe.**

   Two pieces are left in the hole.

2. **Slip clamps loosely over the ends of the pipes in the hole.**

3. **Insert couplings into each of the pipes as far as they will go.**

   You may have to tap the coupling into the pipe using a hammer with a rubber or plastic head. A regular hammer and a wooden tapping block works just fine.

4. **Tighten the clamps to secure the couplings to the pipes in the hole.**

   Cut a piece of tubing to fit the gap created when you cut out the damaged pipe. You'll need a new piece.

   Use the technique mentioned in the previous section. Take the damaged section to the store with you.

5. **Slide two clamps onto the repair tubing. Leave them loose; then force the new piece of tubing over the couplings that reside in each end of the two pipes in the hole.**

6. **Tighten the two clamps with a screwdriver or nut driver.**

To get a tighter fit of the pipe and coupling, lightly heat and soften the pipe with a propane torch; then tighten the clamp. Be careful — overheating the pipe melts it, and you get to start over.

Repairing galvanized pipe

If you have galvanized pipe in your outdoor irrigation system, the system is probably ancient. If you find a leak, we suggest you fix it with a pipe clamp (see Figure 8-2).

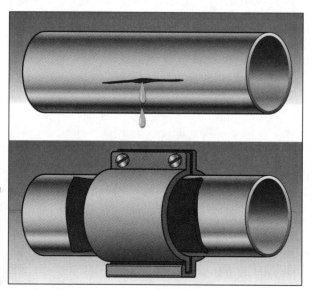

Figure 8-2:
Repairing galvanized pipe with a clamp.

Admittedly, this is a temporary fix, but trying to remove a piece of galvanized pipe that has been in the ground for 30 years or more invites problems you have never even dreamed of.

If you have repeated leaks in your galvanized pipe, you may want to consider replacing it with plastic.

The Anti-Siphon Valve Needs Attention, Too

An anti-siphon valve is a control devise that prevents contaminated water from flowing backwards from the irrigation system into the household water supply. In most homes the landscape irrigation system and the potable water system are one and the same — there is no separation. Here's where the danger comes in. Sprinkler lines lay in gardens and lawns that are often sprinkled with weed killer, pesticides, and other poisons. Irrigation systems occasionally draw water inward (backwards). This phenomenon is known as a *siphon* or *backflow*. Backflow can result in contaminated water at a tap inside the home. Is there any wonder why the building code requires that all outside irrigation lines have some sort of anti-siphon protection?

An anti-siphon valve must be installed at least 6 inches above the highest sprinkler head. Fortunately, the anti-siphon valve can be located anywhere in the water line as long as it is between the sprinkler valve and the inlet pipe to the house. This makes it easy to hide it behind a shrub or a bush. Most sprinkler valves are sold with an integral anti-siphon valve. By the way, a sprinkler valve is the faucet that is used to turn the sprinklers on and off. Some sprinkler valves are operated by hand and others are controlled electronically. One valve can control several sprinklers and one electric timer can control several valves. Imagine the possibilities.

Back to our anti-siphon valve. An anti-siphon valve has no moving parts, therefore maintenance requirements are minimal. As we said, many folks construct their sprinkler systems so that the valves are hidden behind shrubs. This works when it comes to esthetics, but can be a bear if leaves and debris get clogged in the open top of the valve. It's a good idea to occasionally check each anti-siphon valve to ensure that its open top is clean and free of debris.

Cleaning and maintenance

As with the other parts of a landscape irrigation system, eventually one or more of your sprinkler valves ends up needing some kind of cleaning or repair. We just hope that it doesn't happen while you're on vacation. Can you imagine? You return home after 10 days in the tropics to find that your garden looks a lot like the Mojave Desert. Not the cactus part — the sand part. If your entire garden died, you could be pretty sure that the electronic timer failed. An electronic timer controls all of the valves. If it fails, no water goes anywhere. If only one section of the yard became toast, chances are only a single sprinkler valve failed. Got it? Each sprinkler valve controls only a part of the sprinklers. You'll be glad to know that valve failure can be minimized via a sound maintenance program.

A sprinkler valve contains a rubber diaphragm and a spring. Basically, two moving parts. Although it is rare to see the spring fail, the diaphragm often wears out. Here's how to keep your valve is in good condition:

1. **Shut off the water at the main valve or at the meter.**

2. **Remove the screws that hold the top of the valve in place (there are four).**

   With the top removed, you can see the diaphragm. It's a thin round rubber disk that looks like a skinny pancake with holes in it. The holes are normal if they align with holes in the valve. Remove the diaphragm and inspect it for tears, gouges, or discoloration (it should be solid black).

3. **Check the rest of the valve to be sure that it is clean and free of debris.**

4. **Install a new diaphragm if necessary.**

   Don't forget to replace the spring — even if it seems to be in good condition. Some replacement diaphragms are all-in-one design. Here, the spring and diaphragm come as one piece. Be sure the holes in the diaphragm line up with the holes in the valve.

5. **Replace the top and reconnect it using the four screws. They should be snug.**

Be sure to pressure test the valve to ensure that it doesn't leak. If the valve leaks, there is a very good chance that the diaphragm is improperly installed. Remove the top and try again. And next time you go on vacation, have someone keep a close eye on your sprinkler system.

Backflow preventers

Most irrigation systems are equipped with manual or automatic sprinkler valves that incorporate an anti-siphon valve.

Some municipalities don't allow the use of anti-siphon valves with drip irrigation systems. An anti-siphon valve uses an air chamber to prevent the siphoning action that allows water to backflow. Because of problems with improper installation, poor maintenance and increased awareness surrounding dangerous garden chemicals, many states and cities now require a more sophisticated (and more expensive) contraption known as a backflow prevention device (backflow preventer).

Almost everywhere, local authorities dictate what type of backflow preventer must be used (or can't be used). Some authorities require that a licensed professional install the backflow preventer. Some even require that the backflow preventer be replaced at regular intervals. This may be overkill, but better safe than sorry.

If your system is not equipped with backflow preventer or anti-siphon valves, it should be. Check with your local authorities to determine their requirements.

An anti-siphon valve must be installed 6 inches higher than the highest sprinkler head, and there must be no other control valves between it and the sprinklers or drip emitters.

Sprinkler timers

A sprinkler timer is the electric device that is used to automatically turn the sprinkler valves on and off. If the timer is located inside the house, it won't require much maintenance — other than battery replacement (if applicable) from time to time. When the timer is located outdoors and is relatively unprotected, it needs to be checked monthly to be sure operating parts are clean and insect nests are removed. Check exposed wiring to ensure connections are secure and dry. All you have to do is open the door and take a quick look inside. Here, clean is good.

Most sprinkler timers have dual controls. They can be operated manually (the sprinklers can by turned on by the flick of a switch) and automatically (with house power or batteries). The timer can be either mechanical or electronic (digital). Typically, electronic timers are electrically operated and use a backup battery to retain the programming. The battery won't operate the timer. Other timers are operated by battery power alone. They're used in places where electric power is not available.

The batteries used to maintain memory in electronic timers should be replaced annually or as often as recommended in the operating instructions. Typically, the timer retains memory as long as external power is on.

Be sure you have the replacement battery in hand before you remove the old one.

Some timers use rechargeable batteries. Be sure you use the type of rechargeable battery called for in the instructions.

Winterizing the System

If you live in an area where it never freezes, you can skip this section. But even if it only freezes in the morning, you need to protect your irrigation system to some degree.

Winterizing your irrigation system consists of these steps:

1. **Turn off the water to the irrigation system at the main irrigation shut-off valve.**

   Most irrigation systems have a single valve that can be used to disconnect the entire sprinkler system from the water system. This is important if you need to repair a sprinkler valve and want to leave the water on in the house. Liken this main valve to the one under your sink that turns the water off (at that location) so that the faucet can be repaired without turning off the water to the rest of the house.

2. **If the main irrigation shut-off valve isn't in a heated room, use pipe insulation to insulate it, or use heat tape to prevent freezing.**

3. **Turn on each of the sprinkler valves for a few moments to release pressure in the pipes.**

4. **Set the automatic irrigation controller to the rain/off setting.**

5. **Drain all of the water out of any irrigation components that might freeze.**

   In temperate climates, underground valves and sprinklers are generally safe. But if the temperature remains below freezing for days at a time, these components can be severely damaged if the water isn't drained out of them.

Landscape irrigation maintenance companies use compressed air to remove the water from a sprinkler system. A special air compressor is used. They're special because they produce a different pressure and volume than the type of compressors most of us are used to seeing in the home and shop. Too much pressure can destroy the valves, pipes, and sprinklers. You may want to hire a professional for this job.

If you have a backflow prevention device that is exposed to the weather, it must be drained and protected from freezing. Once drained, wrap it with two or three layers of foam insulation. Some agencies recommend removing it altogether and storing it in a heated area during the winter. We agree!

Chapter 9

Ornamental Iron

· ·

In This Chapter

▶ All about ornamental iron's #1 enemy — rust

▶ Preventing rust

▶ A few simple rust-removal techniques

· ·

Rust is a reddish-brown crust that forms on materials that contain iron. Rust is caused by low-temperature oxidation in the presence of water.

Unlike maintenance to plastic, rust can be removed from metal year after year, layer after layer, without causing appreciable damage to the structural value of the metal. This is the main reason why metal is such a good buy in the long run. Simply put, metal can be maintained over very long periods of time. All you have to do is control rust.

Note that we didn't say "completely prevent rust" because it can't be prevented, entirely. We can't tell you how to absolutely prevent rust, but we sure can show you how to slow it down. We can also tell you how to remove that layer of rust, should it appear.

And Then There Was Rust

Barbecues, patio furniture, hand rails, lawn and garden equipment, steel window frames, rain gutters, and downspouts are just a few of the many metal finishes around the home that are susceptible to damage by rust. Even though this chapter refers to exterior maintenance, the problems and solutions apply to interior ornamental iron as well.

Aside from its ugly appearance, left untreated, rust can bring any of these finishes to an early demise and lead to other damage. For example, a rain gutter with a rusted joint can leak and allow water to travel along the wood trim at the roof line, or, perhaps down the wood siding, ultimately resulting in rot which might cost hundreds, or even thousands, of dollars to repair.

Another example is a rusted window frame. Water could enter through the window frame and leak down into the wall framing until the wall must literally be removed and replaced with new framing, siding, and plaster or wallboard. That ain't cheap!

Rust also presents a safety issue. A rusted-out screw in a hand-rail or the rust-ravaged leg of a garden chair could send an unsuspecting guest flying to a nasty fall. Rusty outdoor power equipment leaves the operator particularly vulnerable because a rusted bolt could act as a projectile. Remember Superman and that speeding bullet? That could be you if you let rust have the upper hand.

Shielding Your Metals with a Protective Coat

Paint and oil are two types of coatings that can be relied upon to shield a metal surface, and, therefore, prevent oxygen and water from doing their damage.

Priming the surface

A good paint job always begins with a high-quality primer. In this case, the primer should be made specifically for metal. Certain pigments contained in paint, such as zinc and iron oxide, adhere to metal much more effectively than other types. Ask the person at the paint store for primer and paint specifically designed for use with metal.

Applying the topcoat

Whichever primer you decide to use, you must choose a topcoat that is compatible with the primer. In general, an oil-base finish coat is the most compatible with an oil-base primer. It also offers the greatest abrasion and weather resistance.

There are, of course, exceptions to the oil-base topcoat rule. For example, the architecture of gutters and downspouts should be considered. A flat-luster, acrylic, water-base topcoat produces a low sheen that tends to hide certain flaws, such as dents and joints. Furthermore, due to the inaccessibility of gutters and downspouts, the more abrasion-resistant oil-base paint becomes unnecessary.

Grills, fireplaces, wood or coal stoves, heaters, and furnaces generate heat that exceeds 200 degrees Fahrenheit. These fixtures should be topcoated with high-heat enamel paint specifically designed for use with items that are "too hot to touch."

Most paints emit a harmless odor the first time that they are heated.

One coat each of a high-quality primer and a high-quality oil-base topcoat is all that should be required. The primer and topcoat can be applied using a brush, roller, paint-pad, or sprayer.

When brushing an oil-base paint, use a natural-bristle brush. Synthetic brushes made from nylon or polyester work well with latex paints. However, they are too stiff for use with oil-base paints, often causing brush marks to remain in the finished product — not to mention loose bristles.

Spray painting using canned aerosol spray paint or a do-it-yourself spray rig poses several advantages. Spray painting works well on intricate designs and is smoother (no brush marks). There are several precautions that should be taken when spray painting:

- Employ the necessary safety precautions. Be sure to wear eye protection and a respirator. And never spray paint in an area where flames or sparks could ignite volatile vapors.

- Use a tip that is compatible with the paint to avoid putting too much paint on at once. Tip sizes vary in accordance with the type of paint being used (oil base, water base, lacquer, and so on). Each type of paint has a different viscosity and therefore must be sprayed through a different size tip. It really is hard to tell the various tips apart. Once you have purchased one for a specific use, you must either remember which type of paint that it works with or mark it so that you won't have to depend on your memory.

- Avoid paint runs by applying several thin coats rather than one heavy one.

- Mask off surrounding areas with plastic, paper, or canvas to avoid damage by overspray. This is not a project that should be attempted on a windy day unless, of course, your neighbor's car needs a paint job. Just be sure she's pleased with the color.

Protecting your metal with paint helps prevent rust as much as it can be prevented. However, as paint is chipped or scratched, and as it oxidizes with time and the elements, its effectiveness as a rust barrier diminishes. Eventually, moisture can make its way through to the paint to the metal's surface, and rust results. To extend the life of your paint job and your ornamental iron, it's a good idea to touch up chipped and scratched areas immediately. We keep a container of touch up paint in the garage for each color in our home.

Do you have nerves for steel?

It's an age-old decision — whether to purchase an item made of steel that is strong, solid, and durable — or to use a lighter, less expensive material that may be easier to maintain — like aluminum or plastic. Think about it. Would you rather sit on a plastic patio chair or one made of steel?

Many products made of steel, when properly maintained, far outlast most other materials. The bad news is that, in the short run, products made of steel are more expensive than the alternatives. Remember, we said in the short term. Factoring together the initial cost, the maintenance cost, and how long an item ultimately lasts is the only way to accurately measure the overall cost of anything.

In some cases, you must use steel for its strength and longevity, despite the short-term cost. Remember that some of the oldest standing structures in America were built from steel and continue to stand tall and beautiful after decades of existence. Can you imagine how long the Golden Gate Bridge would have lasted if it were made of wood? Would you want to chance a drive across it if it was made of plastic?

Some folks think that plastic is the solution to rust. We don't. In our opinion, plastic is not the last-forever wonder-material that many believe it to be. Plastic simply deteriorates differently than steel. Plastic doesn't rust; instead, it gives off something known as "free chlorides." This process begins the day the plastic is manufactured. As free chlorides are given off, the plastic becomes more and more brittle.

Rust is unsightly, constantly reminding you that metal is capable of deteriorating. With plastic, the process of becoming brittle isn't so apparent, but it does happen, and the deterioration that occurs is just as damaging. When plastic becomes inflexible, it doesn't spring back. Instead, it cracks. And unlike steel, "oxidized" plastic can't be repaired.

Don't be misled when people tell you that plastic won't disintegrate. It will. And there isn't anything that you can do to prevent it. Fortunately, it can be recycled, but so can steel. We aren't anti-plastic. We both have plastic and steel products in our homes. However, there is so much hype about plastic, we thought we would try to set the record straight.

Giving Rust a Vacation

The real secret to dealing with rust is to remove as much of it as possible before attempting to apply a new finish. (You can read about applying a new finish in the preceding section.) Depending upon the configuration of the item in question, removing rust can be a tedious process that requires lots of elbow grease. In the final analysis, the rust must be removed down to bare metal.

Stripping off rust

There are various methods (and tools) which can be used to remove rust. Sandpaper, sanding tape, flexible sanding sponges, steel wool, and nylon scouring pads all work well and can be especially useful when working on tubing or twisted and curved material.

Sanding cord (industrial strength dental floss) is a must when working around hard-to-access decorative elements, such as those you might find on a railing. As with sandpaper, sanding cord is available in a variety of grits.

In those situations where there is more rust than elbow grease can handle, we recommend the addition of a little power. A wire brush or wire wheel attached to an electric drill can make simple work of stripping rust. A bit of fine finishing with sandpaper or steel wool helps remove any residue that may remain.

Whichever method you should choose, be sure to wear protective gloves and safety goggles. These prevent metal splinters and eye injuries caused by flying metal particles.

Using chemical removers

Not all rust is created equal. Some rust simply can't be sanded or scraped without resulting in damage to the fixture. When dealing with this kind of rust, use a chemical rust remover or "dissolver" (see Figure 9-1).

Figure 9-1:
Dissolving rust with rust dissolver.

Rust removal products containing gelled phosphoric acid work best. The gel can be brushed on (with a cheap paint brush) or sprayed onto the surface and should then remain there for 15 to 30 minutes for best results. Then, simply rinse the chemical off with fresh water.

More than one application may be required depending upon the severity of the rust. Again, safety first. Make sure to wear rubber gloves, safety goggles, and have plenty of fresh ventilation.

Quick, thorough drying is a must. Raw, wet steel begins to rust in minutes.

Dealing with rusted fasteners

Remove any rusted screws and fasteners when stripping a fixture of rust. Rust-free replacements should be installed after surrounding rust has been eliminated and the object has been refinished.

If you have trouble removing a rusted-out fastener, first saturate it with cutting oil. The cutting oil helps dissolve a small amount of the rust and acts as a lubricant to help free up some frozen connections. In combination with a screwdriver, pliers or a wrench, cutting oil can be a favorable ally.

Heat is another viable alternative for removing a stuck fastener. A heat gun or propane torch causes a stubborn nut to expand and break loose from the bolt. If you plan to use heat to remove a fastener, be sure to wipe off any lubricant or cutting oil first because the combination can cause a fire.

When all else fails, a drill and a hacksaw usually does the trick.

Difficult-to-find replacement fasteners can usually be acquired at machine shops. They will either have the items in inventory or can fabricate a match.

There are different grades of nuts and bolts. Some are much stronger, and therefore safer to use. Be sure to specify your use to the sales clerk to be sure that you get one that is strong enough for the task at hand.

Don't count on using penetrating oil to remove rust. Penetrating oil breaks down a certain amount of rust, but it isn't considered a good rust remover.

Converting rust

While we recommend removing rust, there may be areas where this is impossible. If you can't dissolve or scrape off rust, then you have another alternative — you can convert it.

Rust converters are applied directly over rust in the same way as you might apply a coat of primer. The converter combines with the rust changing the rust to an inert by-product. Once the converter has cured (it doesn't actually dry hard like paint, so industry types call the combining and drying process "curing"), a fresh coat of paint can be applied directly over the converter.

One major disadvantage in using a converter in lieu of removing the rust is the likelihood of an uneven finish. The best way to guarantee a top-notch finish is to scrape, grind, and sand the rust until it's smooth.

Repairing damage to the surface

Badly pitted areas can be filled with a patching compound in the same manner that wood is repaired. The difference with metal is that the patching compound must be specifically made for use with metal. Metal expands and contracts at a much different rate than wood does. A metal patch is designed to expand and contract the same way that metal does. That's why it's more likely to stay in place once you apply it.

Making good time

After the rust has been removed, the metal should be dried and then primed within 24 hours to avoid the formation of new rust. (See the section earlier in this chapter for tips on priming and finishing a metal surface.)

Chapter 10

Walkways, Patios, and Driveways

. . . .

In This Chapter

▶ Keeping concrete drives, paths, and patios clean and looking good

▶ Repairing concrete steps

▶ Painting and staining concrete

▶ Cleaning masonry and stone

. . . .

*W*ord has it that Jimmy Hoffa's career ended abruptly one evening while wearing cement-toed slippers. And because he hasn't popped-up since, we assume that the team who mixed the concrete knew exactly what they were doing — either that or they just got lucky. But then again, they weren't terribly worried about cracks caused by ground movement — and that's what damages most concrete.

Although concrete gets the lion's share of traffic around most homes, masonry (brick and stone) is often used in lieu of or in addition to concrete for paths, patios, and walkways. When not used on the ground, brick or stone can almost always be found as a decorative element on most homes. Moreover, because concrete, brick, and stone are similar in composition, the materials and techniques that are used to clean one can, more often than not, be used to clean and preserve the others.

No matter if you carport is concrete or your backyard brick, cleaning, repair, and sealing makes them look good and last a long time. You'll see.

Cementing Your Relationship with Concrete

This may come as a surprise to you: Your sidewalk, driveway, patio, and paths are not made of cement. Rather, they are made of concrete — which contains cement — Portland Cement to be exact. (See the sidebar "Cement has a not-so-rocky past" for more information on Portland Cement.)

Cement has a not-so-rocky past

Although Portland Cement was purportedly invented by Joseph Aspdin, a builder in Leeds, England, who obtained a patent for it in 1824, the use of cementing materials goes back to the ancient Egyptians and Romans. It is said to have been dubbed "Portland Cement" due to its resemblance to limestone found on the Isle of Portland, England.

Basic concrete is a mixture of rock, sand, and cement. In combination with the oxygen in water, the three dry elements bond together to make good old fashioned concrete. You know — the stuff in your yard that usually has cracks in it that you're always trying to patch.

Cleaning Concrete with No Fuss

If your driveway looks like an Indy 500 pit stop, a good cleaning makes the concrete look better and does wonders to improve the curb appeal of your home. By keeping your concrete clean, you also significantly reduce the risk of falls.

Cleaning off grease and oil stains

A garage, carport, or driveway are the areas where most of us allow our tired vehicles to rest between each use. More often than not, and depending upon the mechanical condition of the vehicle, oil and grease spots begin to decorate the concrete in these areas like litter on lawn. If this sounds familiar, you'll be pleased to know that we have a formula for you. A couple of formulas actually, depending upon the severity of the stains. In either case, wait until the area is shaded to prevent the cleaning solution from drying out too quickly.

This first formula may cause your neighbors to wonder whether you're playing with a full deck. However, you'll soon be the envy of the neighborhood when you have the cleanest driveway on the block. We recommend this formula first, because it is safer than our second cleaning formula, which is more powerful and designed for more severe stains. You need the following items.

- A small bag of cat litter
- A few cans of a cola beverage (diet or regular)
- A nylon brush or stiff bristle broom
- A mixing bucket
- Powdered laundry detergent
- Liquid chlorine bleach

‣ Eye protection and rubber gloves

‣ A garden hose and running water

Then follow these steps:

1. **Completely cover the grease or oil with a thin layer of the cat litter and grind it in using the soles of your shoes.**

2. **Sweep up the cat litter and pour on enough cola beverage to cover the entire area.**

   The oil and grease-laden cat litter should be properly disposed of. Don't just throw it in the garbage can — dispose of it as you would used motor oil, paint, or other potentially hazardous chemicals. If you're not sure how to dispose of such materials, call your local waste management company for advice about the rules in your area.

3. **Work the cola into the affected area with a scrub brush or bristle broom, making sure to keep the entire area damp with cola.**

   Leave the cola on for about 20 minutes or until it has stopped fizzing, but don't permit it to dry.

4. **Rinse off the cola with fresh water.**

   You should see a gray stain.

5. **Scrub the gray stain with a solution of 1 cup liquid chlorine bleach, 1 cup powdered laundry detergent, and 1 gallon of very hot water.**

If formula one doesn't do the trick, then it's time to bring out the big guns — muriatic acid. Make a solution of 1 part muriatic acid to 9 parts water, adding the acid to the water (not the other way around).

Working with muriatic acid is dangerous! Wear eye protection, put on rubber gloves to protect your hands and arms, and make certain that there is plenty of ventilation. This project should not be attempted when there are children or small animals present.

After you mix the acid solution, follow these steps:

1. **Pour the solution over the area and work it in using a nylon scrub brush or stiff bristle broom.**

   Be careful not to splash to avoid damaging the surrounding area.

2. **Flush the entire area with fresh water after the solution has stopped fizzing — about 10 minutes.**

   More than one treatment may be necessary for those stains that only professional race car drivers can appreciate.

Once your concrete is clean, it would be the perfect time to get that leaky engine fixed!

Cleaning off efflorescence

Another unsightly substance that can often be found on concrete is a white powdery substance known as *efflorescence.* This condition results when mineral salts in the concrete come to the surface.

While efflorescence is not particularly destructive, it is unattractive, and, in some cases, can result in spauling or minor deterioration of the surface.

A 50/50 percent solution of vinegar and water is all that is generally needed to remove efflorescence. Stubborn or more extensive areas can be cleaned using a wire brush along with a light acid washing (try a 10 percent solution of muriatic acid and water).

After you remove the majority of the efflorescence with a wire brush, apply the vinegar or acid solution using a nylon brush. Allow the solution to stand for 10 to 15 minutes, but don't let it dry. The area should then be thoroughly rinsed with fresh water. Here again, more than one application may be required to achieve the desired result. Unless the soil in your area is particularly alkaline, efflorescence will usually cease to exist after the concrete or mortar is a couple of years old. If, however, the efflorescence continues to rear its ugly head, you can usually solve the problem by sealing the concrete, masonry, or stone with a penetrating concrete sealer. See the section on sealers later in this chapter.

Cleaning up mildew: No slip slidin' away

Mildew is a fungus that grows as a surface mold on virtually any material (inside and outside of the home). Dormant mildew spores are in the air almost everywhere, and all they need to develop and prosper is a warm damp environment, which they often find on your concrete.

We think that Paul Simon must have been thinking about mildew on the concrete around his home when he wrote and recorded the song *Slip Slidin' Away.* Even if he wasn't, the song perfectly describes what can happen to an unsuspecting pedestrian when he sets foot on a patch of moist, mildew-covered concrete surface.

In addition to its potential for causing falls, its unsightly appearance, and its often fierce odor, recent medical studies have shown that mildew can cause a variety of physical ailments as well. In 1989 the British Medical Journal reported that "Scottish doctors who surveyed 597 families in London, Edinburgh, and Glasgow found that those who lived in damp, moldy houses — about half the number studied — suffered a much higher incidence of respiratory problems, headaches, nausea, fevers, backaches, high blood pressure, and fatigue."

Many years ago, we discovered a full-proof formula to clean up mildew on all kinds of surfaces. This formula was developed by the same agency that gave us the $750 toilet seat — the U.S. Government! Actually, credit should go to the U.S. Department of Agriculture's Forest Products Laboratory. While this formula has no problem zapping mildew on concrete, it can also be used on any (non-colorfast) painted or washable surface — inside or outside. You need the following items:

- ⅓ cup powdered laundry detergent
- 1 quart liquid chlorine bleach
- 3 quarts warm water
- 1 mixing bucket
- Safety goggles
- Rubber gloves
- 1 stiff bristle broom
- 1 garden hose and running water

Then follow these steps:

1. **Add the bleach to the water first, then the detergent.**

   Even though this solution is mild, make certain to wear safety goggles, rubber gloves, and have plenty of ventilation.

   Never mix bleach with ammonia since the combination of the two creates a lethal gas similar to mustard gas.

2. **Apply the solution to the affected areas using the broom.**

   Leave the mixture on long enough for the black or green stains to turn white, but don't allow it to dry — 15 minutes should be long enough.

3. **Rinse the entire area with fresh water.**

To prevent the return of mildew, make sure that you have good drainage off of your concrete surfaces. Ponding water is a primary source of mildew. Sunlight is another major enemy to mildew. Prune and thin trees and shrubbery that shelter concrete surfaces. Proper cleaning helps fight the battle against mildew, while taking the preventative steps helps win the war!

Turning up the pressure clean

When tough stains aren't the issue, and you just want to give your concrete a good once-over cleaning, use a pressure washer to eliminate almost all the elbow grease. A pressure washer produces a jet of water from a wand with a trigger — similar to what you might find at a do-it-yourself car wash.

You can clean just about anything with a pressure washer, including roofing, siding, window screens, decking, fencing, cars, boats, even concrete! You name it — it can be cleaned effectively and easily using a pressure washer.

In the past, a pressure washer could only be found at tool rental stores (as they still can be) or for sale for $1,000 or more dollars. Not anymore! Today, most home-improvement retailers stock a full line of pressure washers that range from what we classify as "toys" to heavy-duty, industrial strength models. And while the $1,000 models can still be had, a few hundred dollars

will get you all the power you need to blast away all the grit and grime you can muster up around your house.

When shopping for a pressure washer, the first consideration is the means by which the tool is powered — either by gas or electricity. While each has its advantages, we prefer the freedom that the gas models offer; they eliminate the need to string electrical cords, especially when working in the back forty pressure washing a fence. The disadvantage of a gas model is that you do need to fuss with gasoline and oil.

After you decide on the power source, consider how powerful a unit you want. Pressure washers are rated in "cleaning units," or CU's. The higher the cleaning units, the more powerful machine. 2000 to 9000 cleaning units are ample for virtually any do-it-yourself household-cleaning task.

Patching Cracks in Concrete

Aside from sprucing up the exterior appearance of your house, repairing cracks and holes in concrete also prevents water damage and improves safety. Cracks in concrete can allow water to travel into areas where it isn't invited — like a crawlspace of your basement, which can wreak havoc. Furthermore, cracks, potholes, and uneven concrete are notorious causes of nasty falls. Did you ever stop to think that a little concrete maintenance could keep you out of court as the defendant in a personal injury case?

Frequently, extensive or severe cracks in concrete are the result of a soil condition that needs attention. For example, an inordinate amount of water may exist in the soil beside or below a path or foundation, causing the soil to expand and the concrete to crack. All of the cosmetic crack repairs in the world won't correct a drainage problem that could conceivably result in more severe damage if left uncorrected. Address excessive moisture due to overwatering or poor drainage before making any crack repairs. Standing water, mold and mildew-laden walls and siding, cracks in walks and walls, and difficult to open doors and windows are telltale signs of poor drainage.

Only banana peels should cause slips and falls on concrete

If your concrete is clean, but is still slippery when wet, the surface should be slightly etched using a 25-percent solution of muriatic acid. The acid removes a very thin layer of cement, which exposes the sand in the concrete creating a rougher surface. The finish is a similar medium to fine grit sandpaper.

Simply pour the solution onto the concrete and let it stand for approximately 15 minutes before flushing the entire area with water. Allow the concrete to dry to determine if the new finish meets your expectations. More than one application may be required to achieve a coarser surface.

On steps, consider installing peel-and-stick, non-skid tread tape. You can purchase the tape by the foot in various widths at most home-improvement retailers. If the non-skid tread tape doesn't appeal to you, consider the newest kid on the block — a non-skid material that can be painted onto a surface. The result is essentially the same. The basic difference is that you can customize the size by using masking tape and applying the material within the perimeter of the tape.

After you take care of any long-standing drainage needs, turn to the section "Being Wise about Cracks" in Chapter 3 for instructions on patching concrete using one of our favorite tools — vinyl concrete patch.

Concrete childhood lessons

Like many children, we walked to and from school. Unlike our parents, we didn't have to walk ten miles a day through sleet, snow, and what have you. However, we did have a good honest mile in either direction.

Walking to and from school was one of our most favorite parts of the day. We went from store to store along the main street in our little town greeting each shopkeeper and admiring his wares. Because candy and toys were our favorites, we allowed extra time for the toy store and the corner drug store. Believe it or not, we even found time to pop into the local hardware store, although it was off the beaten path. You see, our fascination with tools and building "stuff" began at a tender age.

Aside from window shopping, one of our favorite diversions was a game that involved the lines and cracks in the concrete sidewalk and how to avoid stepping on them — at all costs. If we stepped on a line, it would break our mother's spine, and if we stepped on a crack, it would surely break her back. Fortunately, although we set foot on many a line and crack, mom's back never suffered in the least.

As adults, we've learned that cracks in concrete don't break your mother's back, but they can be the cause of a nasty fall. Yikes! A little concrete maintenance from time to time can save big time on repair bills and perhaps even doctor bills.

Grinding high spots in concrete

We received the following letter from a home owner in San Francisco many years ago. The problem: a section of sidewalk lifted by tree roots, a very common tale.

She wrote: "A city inspector sent us a notice that requires us to replace about 20 square-feet of concrete sidewalk in front of our house because that particular section has raised about ¼ to ½ inch. We spoke with the inspector and asked if we could make a small repair by ramping up to the raised section with a patching or repair compound. She said that she didn't feel that such a small patch would hold up, but she agreed to let us try it anyway — with the proviso that she might not accept it. Would you have any other thoughts or recommendations?

Our response: "We have to agree with the inspector. Small patches that go from zero thickness to ½ inch won't hold for very long. This is not the same as patching a crack where the patching material or caulking would be held in between two solid surfaces — one on either side. Since the problem is so slight, why not simply grind down the high spot? This is more expensive than the method you want to try, but is far more permanent. And it's a lot less expensive than replacement. Rub cement mixed with water and lime over the ground surface to hide the irregular pattern that will appear as you grind off the top surface. Grinders can be rented at local tool rental outlets."

Using a masonry drill and a tube of clear or gray silicone caulk, you can easily mix up a concrete patching compound that leaves the crack virtually invisible. Find an out-of-the-way spot in your cracked patio or step, such as just below the grade. Using a masonry drill bit, drill a hole in the hidden area and collect the dust coming out of the hole (just place a small flat metal pan under the hole). Next, apply a bead of caulk to the top of the crack. While it's still fresh, sprinkle the masonry dust over the crack and work it into the caulk with your finger. After you're done, sweep away the excess dust and violá — no more crack!

The Steps for Repairing Steps

Patching crumbling concrete steps enhances the appearance and safety of your home, all for a fraction of the cost of new stairs. And the best part is that it's a task that most do-it-yourselfers can handle with ease.

As the weakest point of construction, the step's edge is most vulnerable to damage. Expansive soil, freeze and thaw cycles, efflorescence, and deterioration from salt and disruptive traffic are a few of the major causes of crumbling concrete stairs.

Crumbling steps frequently result from what were once small cracks that were not tended to. A majority of the damage to steps can be prevented by caulking, which allows the concrete to expand and contract yet prevents moisture from entering the area.

Isn't it just like a home fix-it expert to suggest breaking it the rest of the way as the first step in making a repair? Well, that's it! To repair a concrete stair — or anything else made of concrete — you must first completely remove all loose pieces and make sure that what remains is solid.

Start the repair process by removing the loose and crumbling concrete with a sledgehammer and cold chisel. Be sure to wear safety goggles! Sweep up all of the debris and clean the area with the strong spray of a garden hose.

After you have a clean, solid foundation, assemble the following:

- 1 mixing container
- 1 shovel
- 1 garden hose
- 1 concrete finishing trowel
- 1 wooden float (a wooden trowel used to tamp and work the concrete into place)
- 1 small piece of ¾ quarter-inch plywood to act as a form board (scrap pieces of plywood can be obtained from most home centers or lumber yards)
- Concrete bonding agent
- Ready-to-mix concrete patch material (or epoxy patch material)
- 1 tarp or plastic sheeting
- 1 quart of clean motor oil or concrete form release oil
- At least 4 bricks (more may be needed)

Follow these steps to get your steps feet-worthy:

1. **Paint the raw patch area with a concrete bonding agent.**

   The bonding agent is a glue that helps the new patch material adhere to the old cured concrete. Allow it to set up for about 15 minutes before installing the patch material.

2. **Use a circular or hand saw to cut the scrap piece of plywood to act as the form board that will be set flush against the face of the step to hold the concrete patch material into place until it is fully cured.**

   The form board should be cut equal to the height of the step and a few inches longer at either end than the damaged area.

3. **Apply a light coat of clean motor oil or form release oil on the surface of the form board facing the concrete to prevent the form from sticking and damaging the patch when removed.**

4. **Place the form flush against the face of the steps for a smooth patch.**

   The bottom of the form board should fit flat against the top of the step below.

5. **Use several bricks to hold the form boards firmly in place (see Figure 10-1).**

Figure: 10-1:
Propping up
the board
with some
bricks.

6. **Mix the concrete patch material.**

   Vinyl concrete patch or polymer cement are the most popular concrete patching products because they are easy to use and blend well with the old material. Though more expensive, epoxy patch material is the best money can buy. It is stronger and holds better — the result of a chemical reaction among the ingredients of the adhesive.

   Pack the material into the area with a wood float. The butt end of the float works great for this. The consistency of the patch material should be loose, but not runny. The material must be firmly packed into the orifice, eliminating any air pockets for a solid connection.

7. **Remove excess patch material with a wooden float and finish the patch to match the surrounding concrete with a metal concrete trowel.**

8. **When the material starts to set up (in approximately 10 to 30 minutes), cover it with a tarp or sheet of plastic.**

   Doing so holds moisture in. If the material dries too fast, it may crack or not adhere securely.

9. **Until the concrete has completely dried (which could take up to a week), remove the cover once a day and spray the patch with a fine mist of water. Then replace the cover.**

   Leave the form board in place during the drying process to reduce the prospect of damage resulting from form removal or foot traffic. Complete the job by carefully removing the form boards, stakes, and bricks.

Most exterior concrete surfaces have a slightly rough finish to prevent slipping when wet. The most common finish is the broom finish. After the concrete has had a chance to become firm, it is brushed with a broom. A similar look can be achieved for a small patch by using a stiff paintbrush instead of a broom.

Your Very Own Trained Sealer

Concrete is quite porous and acts like a sponge. When temperatures drop and concrete is wet, it can freeze, causing cracking and spalling or chipping. You can minimize this damage by periodically sealing the concrete with an acrylic or silicone-based concrete and masonry sealer.

A liquid concrete sealer prevents water absorption by filling the pores of the concrete. Generally clear, a concrete sealer lasts for six months to a year depending upon the quality of the material, surface preparation, and the climate.

Inexpensive "water seals" don't offer the level of protection that some of the more pricey products do. Moreover, poor-quality sealers need to be applied more frequently and can end up costing more money in the long run.

Concrete sealers can be applied with a brush, roller, or by using a pump garden sprayer (see Figure 10-2). Before you begin, the concrete should be clean. (See "Cleaning Concrete with No Fuss" in this chapter for some tips.)

Figure 10-2:
Applying
sealer.

 Rock salt used to melt snow is another primary source of deterioration of concrete. Sealer can also help protect the concrete from salt damage. After the snow melts, rinse the area with hot water to remove the majority of salt.

Polishing Concrete with Paint

Paint remains a popular finish for concrete porches, patios, paths, garages, carports, and basements.

Preparing the surface

Don't be in a hurry to paint freshly poured concrete. For best adhesion, the concrete should cure for 60 to 90 days before painting. In any case, the concrete should be free of surface grit, grease, oil, and other contaminants that could inhibit the paint from sticking. Thus, cleaning is the first step. (See "Cleaning Concrete with No Fuss" in this chapter for the details.)

After a thorough cleaning, the surface of the concrete should be lightly etched using a 25-percent solution of muriatic acid to get the paint to stick better. (See the sidebar "Only banana peels should cause slips and falls on concrete" for more information on working with this acid.)

You need to paint soon after cleaning the concrete to avoid future contamination of the surface that could flourish under the new coat of paint. For further protection, look for paint that contains a mildewcide. A mildewcide is a pesticide that prevents mildew and fungus from occurring on painted surfaces. Although it is added to many paints during manufacturing, it can be added after the fact.

If you have rust stains on your concrete, try using a concrete cleaner that contains phosphoric acid. It can be purchased in liquid form or as a jelly.

Flaking, peeling paint on previously painted surfaces should be removed using a chemical remover, sandblaster, or a mechanical abrader. Once the paint has been removed, follow the cleaning and etching steps noted earlier in this section.

Choosing your paint

There are three basic types of paint for concrete: latex, oil, and epoxy.

Of the three, latex is the most widely used. It has excellent adhesion properties, allows water vapor to escape (prohibiting delamination), and is the most user-friendly to apply because it cleans up with water. Most latex concrete floor paints are designed to be applied directly to raw concrete. The first coat serves as a primer, and a second coat offers a full and uniform finish. Use a medium-to-long nap roller cover to apply concrete floor paints. Edges can be cut in using a nylon/polyester brush or paint pad.

Oil-base paints are still a favorite for porches and patios. They offer a harder, shinier, and more abrasion-resistant finish. Unlike latex, oil-base paint should be applied over a coat of oil-base concrete or masonry filler/primer. After the primer dries, the finish coat can then be applied. Application is similar to latex, although mineral spirits must be used for clean up.

Thin the primer slightly using mineral spirits to enhance the penetration and improve the bond.

Oil paints can be applied over an existing oil finish provided it is clean and has been deglossed with tri-sodium-phosphate (TSP) or a similar liquid paint deglosser. Chipping, peeling paint should be scraped, sanded, and filled with a patching compound.

The cream de la cream of concrete paint is epoxy — it's the most durable and longest lasting. Epoxy is especially popular in basements as a means of controlling dampness. They generally consist of two parts which, when combined, create a chemical reaction that results in an above-average bond and highly abrasion-resistant finish.

Unfortunately, man has yet to develop a paint that will not eventually sustain damage generated by the hot tires of vehicular traffic. Over time, all types of concrete paint bubble, peel, or chip when subjected to constant exposure to car tires.

Besides concrete floor paints, there also exist concrete stains. To its benefit, concrete stain is much thinner than paint, thus penetrating the surface more thoroughly for better adhesion. When dry, it highly resembles pigmented concrete rather than a painted finish. On the other hand, because it is so thin, it is not nearly as abrasion-resistant as concrete paints and must, therefore, be applied more frequently. Oops! As with painting prep, the concrete should be cleaned and lightly acid washed for maximum penetration. You then mix the stain in a five-gallon bucket and mop or roll it onto the concrete.

Memories and more on our little red porch

We grew up in a home built around the turn of the century by our boat-builder-turned-contractor grandfather. Several generations were raised in that home. It boasted traditional Mediterranean architecture, a reflection of our grandfather's European roots.

Much to our chagrin, our old family home is no longer. It was sacrificed in the name of progress. Our city called it "urban renewal." Out with the old, and in with the new. After all, "new" was synonymous with better. A significant piece of the hearts and souls of each of the members of our family died the day that our old family home fell prey to the ravenous jaws of the indiscriminate bulldozer. All that remains some 25 years later are memories, fond memories.

Our home stood proud among those in our neighborhood. It consisted of a towering (from the eyes of children) two stories with a large basement. The building had a beige dashed plaster exterior, a red S-shaped tile roof, and vast archways flanked by stately sculpted columns. There were lots of windows, a multi-lite radius-top entry door, generous architectural ornamentation, two spacious verandas at the second floor, and an ample front porch that was first to greet each visitor to our home.

Some of the most vivid memories of our old home took place on that front porch. Many a family gathering was held there. Although the arid climate necessitated it, air conditioning was something reserved for more modern homes. Instead, we sought refuge from the sweltering heat ambling to and fro on the canvas-clad bench swing.

The porch, located a half dozen steps above the street, was constructed of concrete and finished with a deep red paint. It was that porch wherein we had our first experience with house painting. It needed a fresh coat every few years. How rewarding it was to admire our workmanship and to be the objects of praise from the family.

We'll never forget that handsome red porch at our old family home. It's been 30 years since its last painting, and, in our minds, it's as bright and fresh looking as the day it was last painted.

For the Love of Masonry

One of our favorite children's stories is "The Three Little Pigs." In fact, we credit, to some degree, our early interest in construction to that book. After all, the story is about three pigs that delve into construction as owner-builders. And like most construction projects, they had their share of headaches. Enter the Big Bad Wolf — he tried to destroy each of their homes with expectations of a delectable ham dinner.

Sadly, he was successful in demolishing the first two homes constructed of straw and wood, respectively. However, the third little pig used brick to build his home, which foiled the wolf. Huff and puff all he might, he couldn't blow down the house built of bricks. And he wouldn't have been any more successful with a home made of stone. Although reinforced brick is structural, stone is primarily decorative. However, when it comes to cleaning, repairing and sealing, the techniques and materials used for brick and stone are the same.

We have yet to see a wolf attempt to blow a house down; however, efflorescence, salt air, stress cracks, and severe weathering can be as big a threat. If efflorescence is the problem, see "Cleaning off efflorescence" earlier in this chapter.

Stress cracks typically occur in mortar joints rather than within the brick or stone itself. If stress cracks in mortar are the problem, see "A Few Pointers on Brick and Block Foundations" in Chapter 3 for the lowdown on repointing.

If the problem is a cracked or broken stone or brick, it can be removed by chiseling out the mortar surrounding it. With the mortar out of the way, the brick or stone will have room to expand and can be easily broken up using a cold chisel along with a small sledgehammer. A new brick or stone can be inserted into the hole to replace the one removed. The brick or stone should be surrounded with mortar for a solid fit.

Applying a sealer can minimize brick or stone damage from salt air and severe weathering. It can even work to prevent efflorescence. However, just as with concrete, brick and stone should be thoroughly cleaned before applying a sealer.

If you've come up against a stone wall trying to clean brick or stone in patios, walkways, walls, or a chimney, then you really should read on. The three most common masonry-cleaning problems are:

✔ **Fungus, moss, and mildew:** One quart of household liquid bleach mixed into 1 gallon of warm water applied with a stiff bristle brush usually takes care of these guys. (Don't forget to rinse the solution off with clean water.) However, sodium hypochlorite, the active ingredient in bleach, might not dissolve large masses of these types of growths. In such cases, scrape off as much of the crud as you can with a broad-bladed putty knife (or wire brush). Then, scrub on the killer mixture.

When trying to eliminate fungus, it's the bleach that does the job — not the elbow grease. Make sure you give the bleach plenty of time to work before scrubbing and rinsing away. If not, fungus spores will remain and can grow back quickly.

✔ **Oils, soot, and mineral residue:** Oils, soot, and white, powdery mineral residue pose a slightly more difficult problem. Characteristically, they are embedded more deeply into the pores of the masonry than moss and mildew. You need a solution of 1 part muriatic acid to 9 parts water to get rid of these unwanted guests. Add the acid to the water and apply the solution – allowing it to set for about 15 minutes. Then use a bristle brush to clean the affected area and rinse with fresh water.

If soot is the problem, see "A major fireplace-cleaning Advanage" sidebar in Chapter 15.

✔ **Paint:** Sandblasting, wash-away or peel-off paint removers, hand or electric wire brushing, muriatic acid washing, and power washing are just a few of the ways that you can remove paint from masonry. Sandblasting or wire brushing is hard, messy work, and paint removers sometimes create more mess than they eliminate. Instead, we recommend power washing. A commercial power washer can be rented for about $50 per day. It's easy to operate, mess is kept to a minimum, and you don't have to be a chemist to make it work. A power washer might work fine on the outside of your home, but all of that water could wreak havoc on the inside of your house. Therefore, when it comes to removing paint from brick or stone, your best bet is a chemical stripper such as Peel Away. See "Removing paint on a brick fireplace face" in Chapter 15.

In addition to cleaning your masonry, you need to repoint the brick mortar from time to time as it shows signs of deterioration. See "A Few Pointers on Brick and Block Foundations" in Chapter 3 for the lowdown on repointing.

When a new mortar patch dries and doesn't match the existing shade or color, have a small amount of latex paint color matched to the existing mortar. Use an artist's brush to paint the new mortar joints. No one will ever know where the existing material ends and the new work begins — including you!

Part III:
Interior
Maintenance

The 5th Wave   By Rich Tennant

"To preserve the beauty and durability of the dental molding, we put fluoride in the trim paint."

In this part . . .

We figure that you have to do something with your spare time when it's too cold or wet to work outside. So we came up with an entire part of maintenance tasks that you can perform inside your home while you wait for Mother Nature to ease up a bit. In this part, we help you care for the floor, walls, ceiling, and everything in between. Granted it's a lot of ground to cover, but hey, it's not like you don't have the whole winter.

Chapter 11

The Plumbing System

More than any other system in a home, the plumbing system has the greatest impact on a family's comfort and health. In particular, the water pipes deliver fresh water for drinking and food preparation, for washing clothes and dishes, and for bathing and waste disposal. They work in harmony with other components of a residential plumbing system — fixtures and fittings, the drain, waste, and vent system, and the gas meter and supply lines.

Part of this chapter is devoted to the water delivery system — the water pipes, if you will. They are the thin pipes that run through the walls, basement, and attic, carrying water in and out. In contrast, drain, waste, and vent pipes are fatter and are not pressurized — filled with water under pressure. Gas lines sometimes resemble water lines — they are thin and often made of the same material, but they travel from the gas main to fuel-burning appliances such as a water heater, range, furnace, and gas-powered dryer. We also tell you about getting the most out of your water heater and water softener.

Types of Pipes

When it comes to plumbing, lead is a dirty word. Millions of American homes are equipped with water pipes that contain lead. Studies performed by the Centers for Disease Control and the Environmental Protection Agency have shown that lead can be a health hazard.

Galvanized iron pipe has its drawbacks, too. Just ask anyone who owns a home that is 30-plus years old. Mineral buildup and corrosion within the pipe can result in a significant drop in water pressure and ultimately can be the cause of leaks.

Water's come a long way, baby

We are a spoiled society. For most of us, whenever we need water, we simply turn on a faucet at one of several locations in or around our homes. It wasn't always that way.

Not long ago, people had to gather urns of water from a nearby river or pump it from a community well. What's more, hot water had to be heated over an open fire. And an indoor toilet was a luxury reserved for royalty or the rich and famous. Most folks "took care of business" in a little shed out back, appropriately called an *outhouse.*

Life around the house in those days was like camping 365 days per year.

Homebuilders began using copper pipes for residential water systems in the late 1950s. Unfortunately, even copper systems have their health drawbacks. Until the late 1970s, solder — the material used to weld the connections — was comprised of 50 percent tin and 50 percent lead; lead at soldered connections can leach into the water system. A whole-house water softening system can magnify this problem, because it can be corrosive and further break down the solder.

 To minimize exposure to lead from drinking pipes, follow these simple precautions. Never drink water straight out of the faucet. Let the water run for a few minutes first. Second, never use hot water out of the faucet for cooking. Hot water tends to draw more lead out of pipes and lead solder than cold water. If you need to heat water, always start with cold water first.

Today, solder consists of 95 percent tin and only 5 percent lead. This makes copper piping one of the safest and most cost-effective choices for residential water systems.

Plastic piping has overtaken copper for residential water systems in some parts of the country. But it only accounts for a fraction of the systems nationally. Moreover, many municipalities don't yet permit its use.

Replacing a Damaged Section of Threaded Pipe

Replacing a section of threaded pipe (pipe that is screwed onto a fitting) is not nearly as difficult as you might imagine thanks to the wide assortment of threaded sections of pipe that are now standard inventory at most hardware stores or home-improvement centers. These "pre-fab" sections come in various diameters and lengths. Furthermore, many stores custom cut and thread a section of pipe in the event a stock item is not available. This prevents the do-it-yourselfer from having to rent or purchase a costly set of iron pipe cutting and threading tools.

Removing the old pipe

The first step in replacing a section of damaged water pipe is to turn off the main water shutoff valve so that no water flows into your home. The shutoff valve is located where the water supply enters the house — at an outside wall, in the basement, or at the water main. (See "Turning off Your Water Main" later in this chapter.) Open a faucet at the lowest point in the home to allow the line to empty. Next, cut through the damaged section using a hacksaw or a reciprocating saw. This allows each of the two pieces that remain to be unscrewed from its adjacent fitting.

Removing the existing pipe from the fittings to which it is attached may prove difficult. Over time, these connections can "freeze" in place, making them virtually impossible to separate. Using two medium pipe wrenches in opposing directions (one gripping the pipe and the other the fitting) enhances the leverage needed to break the connection.

If at first you don't succeed in loosening the connection, spray the area with a penetrating oil or lubricant, such as WD-40. This breaks down some of the rust and corrosion that prevents the pipe from budging.

Once the pipes have been removed, spray the threads within the fittings with more of the penetrating oil. Allow the oil to sit for approximately 15 minutes and use a small wire bottle brush to remove any residue and prepare the area for a new leak-free connection.

Picking up the pieces

To put things back together, you need two sections of pipe and a union. The total length of the two pieces of pipe and the union must equal the length of the damaged pipe.

When calculating the overall length of material needed, measure from the face of one fitting to the face of the opposite fitting and add 1 inch. This accounts for ½ inch of threads at either end, which overlap into the fittings.

The *union* is a fitting that consists of three components: two union nuts and a ring nut. The union nuts attach to the replacement sections of pipe where they are to join. The ring nut is inserted over one of the sections of pipe and acts to join the two pieces together.

Prior to assembling the pipes, apply a pipe joint compound to the threaded ends and the threads in the fittings. Press the compound into the threads with a fingertip. Screw each of the two sections of pipe into their respective fittings (where the previously damaged sections were removed). Make sure that the union ring nut is inserted over one of the sections of pipe because you won't be able to slip it over the union nuts. Tighten both sections of pipe and then the ring nut. Just as with the removal process, using two pipe wrenches makes reassembly easier and safer. Complete the process by turning the main water supply on and checking for leaks. Your iron pipe will be as good as new — that is until the next leak!

Preventing Freezing Water Pipes

The old saying, "an ounce of prevention is worth a pound of cure" is especially true when it comes to cold temperatures, water, and the pipes that transport it. The following tips reduce the chance of freezing and help keep water running in your pipes all winter long.

A faucet left dripping at the fixture farthest from the main water inlet allows just enough warm water movement within the pipes to reduce the chance of a freeze. Even though it is cold, during the winter, the water coming in from deep below ground is usually warmer than the water above ground. This warmer cold water moving in the pipes makes it much more difficult for old Mother Nature to freeze things up.

Insulating pipes that are above ground (those that are most susceptible to freezing) prevents them from freezing during most moderate-to-medium chills — even when faucets are off. This includes pipes in the subarea or basement and especially any that might be in the attic. (See Chapter 5 for more information on insulating pipes.)

If your kitchen or bathroom sink faucets are prone to freezing, leave the cabinet doors open at night. This allows warm air to circulate in the cabinet and warm the cold pipes.

Temporary Pipe Leak Fixes

Being prepared to defend your home's plumbing system against a sudden burst pipe can save you thousands of dollars in damage. Think of these quick, easy fixes as plumbing first aid. They slow or stop a leak long enough to give you time to enlist the services of a qualified plumber during regular working hours. Remember: Plumbers charge double time nights and weekends. Where do you think they get the money to buy all of those gold chains?

To temporarily stop a pinhole leak, you need to apply pressure to the opening. If you were strong enough, you could simply grab the pipe and hold on. Not very practical though. Can you imagine all the good TV shows that you would miss? Instead, wrap duct tape around the pipe. No kidding. In many instances duct tape supplies the necessary pressure.

Unfortunately, duct tape doesn't always give you enough pressure. Another neat trick enlists the use of a C-clamp, a block of wood, and a piece of rubber. The rubber is used as a gasket. The block of wood applies pressure over a wider area than the end of the C-clamp, and the C-clamp holds the gasket and the wood block in place. Because the block of wood is flat, it can only be used to create pressure along a very narrow area of the pipe. Here's how to do it:

1. **Turn the water off at the main shutoff valve.**

2. **Place a piece of rubber over the area where the pipe is leaking.**

3. **Put the block of wood on top of the piece of rubber.**

4. **Open the C-clamp wide enough to surround the pipe, gasket material, and the block of wood.**

5. **Place the stationary part of the opening of the C-clamp against the pipe (opposite the location of the leak) and the screw part of the C-clamp against the block of wood. Tighten the screw clamp until it is snug.**

When you have several pinholes traversing around the pipe, we suggest a hose clamp and a piece of rubber. A single universal hose clamp fits every water pipe in your home. Boy, how often can you find a home fixup where one size fits all?

Simply wrap the damaged section of pipe with the rubber and surround the rubber with the hose clamp. You'll need to use a screwdriver to fully open the hose clamp so that it is free to be wrapped around the pipe. Once it is around the pipe use the screwdriver to tighten the clamp snuggly around the rubber wrapped pipe. You can even use side-by-side clamps to quell larger leaks.

Junkyards are filled with rubber that can be had for pennies. Old automotive radiator and heater hoses are just what the doctor ordered. A friend who works on cars will probably be glad to give you all you need.

A sleeve clamp stops everything from pinhole leaks to larger leaks. (Forget searching out a piece of rubber for this one — it comes with its own gasket.) A sleeve clamp consists of two semicircular pieces of metal that, when put together, completely surround the pipe — hence the name sleeve. The clamp is about three inches long, but must be purchased for use with a specific pipe size. That is, a sleeve clamp made to repair ½-inch pipe is a different size than one needed to repair ¾-inch pipe.

Using your water meter to detect hidden leaks

If you are on a public water system, you have a water meter somewhere on or near your property. Besides telling you how much water you are using, it can also help you detect leaks.

Water meters look a little like either an analog or odometer. Subtract the first reading from the second reading to find out how many cubic feet of water you have used in any given timeframe. A cubic foot contains 7½ gallons of water.

You can use your water meter to detect a hidden leak. Take a meter reading, and then turn off every plumbing fixture in your house for a couple of hours. (Don't forget to turn off the built-in icemaker or other water-consuming appliances.) After everything is off, take another meter reading. If the reading changes, you have a leak.

Here's how it works:

1. **Wrap the damaged section of pipe with the gasket material provided.**

2. **Surround the gasket-wrapped pipe with the two semicircular clamps.**

3. **Tighten down the screws that connect the two halves of the sleeve clamp.**

In the case of both the hose clamp and the sleeve clamp, only a screwdriver is needed for installation. Not too complicated.

No one relishes the ideas of spending money on plumbing repair items on the off chance that they might be needed. But if you think about it, things like hose clamps, C-clamps, duct tape, and rubber are pretty cheap, especially when you consider how much money they can save you if your pipes do spring a leak. These simple items are good junk to have in your workshop.

Quieting Noisy Water Pipes

Did you ever turn off a faucet only to experience sounds and vibrations similar to those produced by a three-point earthquake?

Imagine a fast moving stream of water traveling down a narrow pipe. Suddenly and unexpectedly, the water finds a closed valve in place of what, moments earlier, was an escape point. All of a sudden, the water has nowhere to go, and water doesn't compress. As it comes to an abrupt stop, a loud thud results that can be heard throughout the entire house. This deafening sound is known as a *water hammer*. The hammering action that creates the horrible racket is actually capable of damaging joints and connections in the pipe.

Why doesn't your plumbing system make a loud noise each and every time a fixture is turned off? First of all, not every water valve closes quickly. In fact, most valves close slowly enough to prevent water hammer. However, as gaskets in a faucet get old and brittle, they can cause the faucet to close more quickly — and a water hammer can result.

Combating water hammer with air chambers

An *air chamber* is a vertical pipe located in the wall cavity at the point near a faucet or valve where the water supply pipe exits the wall. Air chambers are added to the plumbing system when it is first installed to act as cushions to prevent water from slamming against the piping. Because air compresses, it absorbs the shock of the fast-moving water before it has a chance to slam against the end of the pipe.

The pipe that makes up the actual air chamber usually ends about 12 inches above the point where the supply pipe exits the wall. Although they remain concealed in the wall, air chambers are close enough to the fixture to properly cushion the water.

Many household plumbing systems have air chambers built into them at critical locations — like the clothes washer and dishwasher — where electric shutoff valves close rapidly. In some homes, air chambers exist at every location where water is turned on and off — even the toilet.

In copper systems, a one-piece pipe called a *closed nipple* is used to make air chambers. Their one-piece construction means no place for the air leak; thus these are the most dependable kind. In older systems that use threaded pipe, the air chamber is made from a *capped nipple.* Here, there is the chance that air can leak from the cap, allowing the air chamber to fill, rendering it useless and making a once quiet, functional water supply system noisy and prone to damage.

Getting rid of water hammer

To eliminate a water hammer, you need to replenish all the air chambers with air. You can't inspect the air chambers, so this procedure is a must whenever you notice a faint noise in the pipe. Here is how to do it:

1. **Shut off your home's main water supply valve.**

2. **Open the highest faucet inside your house.**

3. **Find the lowest faucet on the property — it's usually outside. Turn it on to completely drain all water from the pipes.**

   As the water is drained from the pipes, it is automatically replaced by air — this includes the air chambers.

4. **The moment the water is completely drained from the piping, the lowest faucet should be turned off and the main valve reopened.**

   Air pushes out of the horizontal and open vertical water lines, sputtering as it exits the faucets inside. However, air remains in the air chambers, eliminating water hammer.

Sometimes a water hammer can occur when there is a loose pipe-mounting strap. These straps consist of metal plumbers tape or the vinyl-coated nail in hooks and hangers that attach pipes to roof, wall, and floor framing. A loose pipe strap allows the pipe to freely vibrate against framing members as water is turned on and off. This can happen even if all the air chambers are in good shape. Check all accessible pipes to ensure that they are properly and tightly connected.

Another reason for banging pipes is excessively high water pressure. Water pressure can be adjusted with a water pressure regulator or pressure-reducing valve. Most modern homes have one mounted at the location where the main water supply enters the home.

You can test the water pressure yourself using a water pressure gauge that screws onto a hose bib or, in most communities, the water department will make the test at no charge. This is an important test regardless of whether you have a pressure regulator or not. High water pressure is not only wasteful; it can damage dishwashers, icemakers, washing machines, and other water-supplied automatic appliances. In fact, many appliance warranties are voided when water pressure exceeds 100 psi.

A professionally installed pressure regulator can cost several hundred dollars, but is a good investment in the long run. If you already have a regulator, adjust it using a screwdriver or a wrench so that the pressure does not exceed 50 pounds per square inch (psi) (see Figure 11-1). Normal water pressures runs between 30 and 55 psi. Most water pressure regulators have a small adjusting nut or screw that can be turned using a wrench or screwdriver.

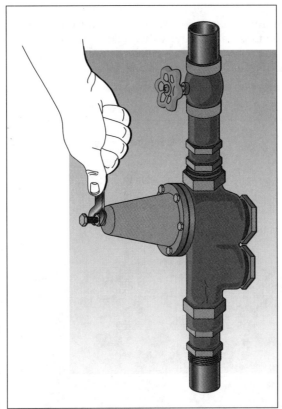

Figure 11-1:
Adjusting
the water
pressure.

Turning off Your Water Main

If you don't already know where your water main is, read this section, and then put down this book and go out and find it. Don't wait until an emergency to hunt for it where the consequences could be catastrophic.

The water main is typically located in a precast concrete vault in the front yard near the curb. Often, the water main is located below the sidewalk in front of a home. In either case there is a concrete or metal lid that must be removed to access the main water valve.

Turning off the main water valve can sometimes be quite a chore. (Periodically turn the valve on and off to prevent it from becoming difficult to operate.) Although most main water valves can be turned using an adjustable crescent wrench (also known among friends as a "knuckle buster"), it is easier, more effective, and safer to use a special water main wrench (see Figure 11-2).

Water main wrench

Figure 11-2:
Using a
water main
wrench.

This tool is constructed of steel dowels, stands about 3 feet high, and looks like the letter "T." It has a slot at the base that fits snuggly over the lug on the valve. The tool should always be kept handy in case of an emergency.

Some Like It Hot: The Water Heater

It's been a while since our modern civilized society heated water for daily use over an open flame — thanks to the water heater (see Figure 11-3). Instead, the dilemma facing most folks is one of short showers and high utility bills. If this sounds familiar, it's time to take action! A bit of preventative maintenance on the water heater can provide hot water longer, result in energy savings, and even extend the life of the water heater.

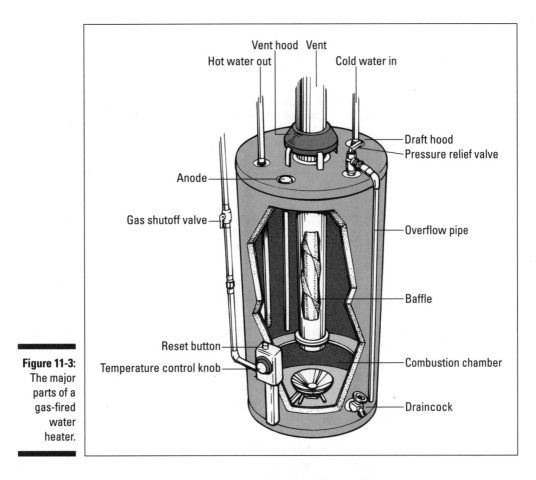

Vent hood   Vent

Hot water out   Cold water in

Draft hood
Pressure relief valve

Anode

Gas shutoff valve

Overflow pipe

Baffle

Reset button

Temperature control knob

Combustion chamber

Draincock

Figure 11-3:
The major
parts of a
gas-fired
water
heater.

Improving your heater's efficiency

An insulation blanket makes a water heater more energy efficient. However, a blanket is not recommended for a water heater that is located where its lost heat could be felt. Also, if you have a new water heater that is factory insulated with R-16 or better, a blanket isn't necessary. The manufacturer's label will tell you how much insulation your water heater contains. The factory installed insulation is located between the metal shell and the tank, so don't freak if you can't see it.

If, on the other hand, your water heater is located in unconditioned space (a garage or basement) or you don't want added heat, install a heavy blanket — R-11 or better. The R value relates to the thickness of the blanket; the higher the R value, the thicker the blanket the more insulating horse power.

A water heater insulation blanket is purchased as a kit based on the size of the heater — 30, 40, 50 gallons, and so on. The kit contains the blanket that is finished with white vinyl on the outside and raw insulation on the inside and enough adhesive tape to finish the seams.

Gas water heaters should be completely wrapped all the way around and from the top to just below the controller. Don't worry if it seems a bit short. Remember, the bottom of the tank is several inches above the very bottom of the water heater — a couple of inches below the drain valve. Don't wrap the top since the insulation could catch fire from the heat being exhausted. Also, the blanket should not cover the controller, the anode, or the pressure and temperature relief valve.

In addition to the sides, the top of an electric heater can also be insulated since there is no exhaust. However, access panels for elements should not be covered to prevent electrical components from overheating.

Keeping your heater clean

If the bottom of your water heater fills with sludge, blanket or not, the heater won't operate at peak performance. If you don't clean your water heater, you can probably compare it to a large Thermos bottle filled with coffee that hasn't been emptied or cleaned for a year. Assuming you don't have strange taste buds, the coffee would not be drinkable, and the Thermos liner would be a stained, sludge-filled mess. Need we say more about the importance of cleaning a water heater?

A water heater has three basic parts: the enclosure, the water tank assembly, and the burner and control assembly. The enclosure holds everything together and protects the tank and other fragile parts from damage. The water tank stores water that arrives cold and leaves heated. The burner and control assembly are responsible for heating the water, discharging combustion gases and adjusting the temperature. An electric water heater varies slightly. It has an enclosure and a tank, but instead of a burner, it contains one or two electric elements that heat the water. Consequently, there is no need for a flue to exhaust combustion gases. Aside from these fundamental differences, gas and electric water heaters function essentially the same and require the same tender loving care.

Cleaning the enclosure

There really isn't much you can do to maintain the enclosure, except that regular cleaning could improve its appearance. Use a mild solution of soap and hot water along with a sponge.

Additional sentiments about sediments

Aside from being a breeding ground for bacteria, sediment at the base of a tank significantly diminishes the efficiency of a gas water heater and can cause it to sound like the Chattanooga Choo Choo.

Sediment buildup causes the water at the base of the tank to super heat and, thus, turn from a liquid into a gas — steam. This conversion process causes mini-explosions that blast small amounts of sediment off the bottom of the tank. The rumbling and banging that keeps you awake at night begins at your water heater and radiates wherever hot water pipes travel throughout your home.

Cleaning and caring for the tank assembly

Because the tank has no inspection ports, it's hard to tell when it's dirty or beginning to rust. Actually, tank rust usually isn't discovered until after a leak occurs — and then it's too late.

Most tanks are made of glass-lined steel. If water gets through imperfections in the glass, then you can count on rust and eventually a leak.

A special rod called a *cathodic anode* (or *sacrificial anode*) is built into the tank assembly to prevent rust. As long as the rod is in good condition, deterioration of the tank is drastically reduced.

Unfortunately, there is no way to determine the condition of the anode by just looking over your water heater. This must be done by turning off the power and water to the water heater and removing the anode with a wrench. Checking the anode at least twice a year will give you an idea of how long it will last. You can then include its replacement in your maintenance schedule accordingly.

To prevent damage to the tank, simply replace the cathodic anode, a $15 item that takes about 30 minutes to install. Cathodic anodes are not readily available in hardware stores. You'll probably have to obtain one from a plumbing supply company. Since anodes come in all shapes and sizes, be prepared to give them the make and model of your water heater so that you get the right one. You can find this information on a label located on the water heater housing.

The cathodic anode is about 5 feet long, about ¾ inch in diameter, and has a hex bolt welded onto one end. The hex bolt screws into the top of the tank, holding the rod in place inside the tank, and, when tightened down, the nut also makes a watertight seal at the same time.

Before unscrewing the rod, make sure that the cold-water inlet valve at the top of the water heater and power to the water heater are both turned off.

While the water is off and the rod is removed, use the open hole to clean and flush the tank. Pour in a citric-acid-based cleaner, and wait about 8 hours for the acid to dissolve the minerals at the bottom of the tank.

One such citric-acid-based cleaning product is called Mag-Erad. Mag-Erad is a one-of-a-kind product; it can sometimes be hard to find at your local plumbing supply store. If you have trouble finding it, call its manufacturer, Tri Brothers Chemical Corporation in Morton Grove, IL at (312) 564-2320, or A.O. Smith Distributors at 1-800-845-1108 or 1-800-527-1953.

After the cleaning agent has had time to work, the tank should be flushed. To do this, connect a garden hose to the drain valve located at the bottom of the water heater and run the hose out into the garden. Open the drain valve and then turn on the cold water supply to the water heater. The cloudy water and sediment that comes out of the end of the hose will amaze you.

When the water runs clear, close the drain valve, remove the hose, and bleed air from the system by turning on the hot water faucet farthest from the water heater. When water runs from this faucet, turn it off and repeat this process at other faucets throughout the house to permit any trapped air to escape. The power can then be restored to the water heater and, hopefully, you'll be in hot water.

The burner: just an old flame

On a gas water heater, the burner assembly is located at the bottom of the unit below the tank. When the water temperature in the tank drops below the desired temperature, a thermostat activates the burner. The same process occurs with an electric water heater, however instead of a burner, electric heating elements are activated.

The burner should periodically be inspected to make sure that it is burning safely and efficiently. A dirty burner chamber can cause a fire and can make the burner less efficient. (If your burner is operating at peak efficiency, you will see a blue flame. If, on the other hand, the flame is orange, adjust the shutter until it turns blue.)

To clean the burner, first turn off the gas shutoff valve (located on the gas supply to the water heater), remove the access panel, and vacuum the burner and chamber. A stiff wire and a wire brush clears clogged burner ports and removes rust. If you are not successful in getting a blue flame, it's time to call in a service rep from your utility company or a plumber or heating specialist.

Caring for your electric water heater

If your water heater is electric, you can perform all of the maintenance steps mentioned in the previous sections with the exception of cleaning burners — there are none. An electric water heater contains one or two heating elements similar to what you might find in your oven, except that they are short and narrow.

These electric elements can become laden with lime and mineral deposits that reduce their effectiveness or cause them to overheat and short out.

Hard water and an electric water heater are a disastrous combination. You will forever be cleaning and replacing electric elements. We suggest that you consider installing a water softener if you have an electric water heater.

Electric elements can be cleaned. The tank needs to be drained as follows in order to do this. Start by turning off the power and the cold-water valve at the top of the water heater. Attach a garden hose to the drain valve at the base of the water heater, open the drain valve, and open a hot water faucet somewhere in the home to facilitate draining. After the water heater empties, and depending upon the number of elements, one or more access panels can be removed using a screwdriver.

You may need to move a piece of insulation to expose the element. Elements are generally attached with a series of bolts, or they have a threaded base that screws directly into the tank. Electrical wires that power the element need to be removed and replaced using a screwdriver. Each wire is fastened to the terminals on the element with a screw.

Once the element has been removed, it can be cleaned in a solution of vinegar and water or sodium carbonate and water along with a scouring pad. Use 2 tablespoons of vinegar or 2 tablespoons of sodium carbonate in 1 quart of hot water.

An element that has begun to corrode should be replaced with a new one. Many different element types and styles are widely available; simply take the old one to the hardware store and find a match. Cooler than normal water, sporadic hot water, and a short supply of hot water are all telltale signs of a corroded element.

After you have cleaned or replaced the heating element, reconnect the wires and refill the water heater. To do this, close the drain valve and turn the cold water supply valve on, making sure that the hot water faucet farthest from the water heater is left open to express all of the air from the system.

Don't reinstall the insulation and access panels until the water heater is full. This allows you to check for leaks around the elements.

After you are sure that there are no leaks, replace the insulation and access panels and turn on the power.

If you perform this ritual and still have a problem getting hot water out of your electric heater, it may be due to a defective thermostat or a tripped or defective high-temperature limit switch. The limit switch cuts off power to the element when the water temperature exceeds a certain limit — usually 190 degrees. A tripped high-temperature limit switch can be reset with the push of a button behind the access panel.

If the switch continues to trip, it may be due to either a defective limit switch or element. In either case, one or both need to be replaced. To replace a thermostat, remove the access panel and insulation as described previously, turn off the water and power to the water heater, and use a screwdriver to remove the wires from the thermostat. Loosen the bracket bolts that hold the thermostat in place and slide the thermostat out. Slide the new thermostat into place, tighten down the bolts, reconnect the wires, press the reset button, reinstall the insulation and access panel, and turn on the water and power.

When things get too hot

Water temperature is another important factor in controlling out-of-control energy costs and extending a water heater's life span.

Water heater manufacturers recommend a lower water temperature setting whenever possible — 130 degrees or less. Modest settings economize on utility bills, extend the service life of the unit, and provide some margin of safety for the very young and the elderly.

On a gas water heater, the temperature is adjusted by turning the dial located on the front of the controller. On an electric model, the thermostat is located behind an access panel adjacent to a heating element.

A temperature setting less than 120 degrees could allow potentially fatal bacteria to propagate within the tank.

Testing the temperature and pressure relief valve

The temperature and pressure relief valve (TPR valve) opens to release pressure buildup in the water heater when the temperature or the pressure get dangerously high, thus preventing a possible explosion.

When we talk about the TPR valve, we always think of an interesting, and insightful, experience that we had on our talk-radio show. Doing talk-radio is interesting to say the least. Our callers ask their questions in a minute or so, and we must formulate and clearly articulate an accurate answer in an equally brief period of time. As with our newspaper column, we do an incredible amount of research to ensure that the information we provide over the air is not only correct, but timely, as well.

In any event, a recent caller had a question about a water heater. As an adjunct to our answer we suggested that she toggle the lever on the TPR valve every six months or so to make sure that it was operating freely. She thanked us and the program continued.

About 20 minutes later, a caller wanted to scold us for advising our listeners to test TPR valves. When he came on the line, he stated that he worked for a water heater company, and that they recommended never testing a TPR valve. According to the caller, "testing could cause the valve to leak and would most certainly damage the spring within the valve."

We were stopped in our tracks and stumped. We knew that our research was correct, but neither one of us could put our fingers on the literature that was the basis for our recommendation. We thanked the caller for his comments, advising him that we would go over our research. And we did! What we discovered was newsworthy, to say the least. We knew that regularly checking the operation of the TPR valve was important, but we had forgotten just how important.

We contacted the folks at Watts Regulator Company in North Andover, Massachusetts, a firm that manufactures TPR valves. We spoke to one of their technical service representatives, Linda Hopkins, who advised us that Watts Regulator Company recommends an annual check of their TPR valves. Mineral salt, rust, and corrosion buildup can cause a TPR valve to freeze up and become non-operational, which, Hopkins says, can lead to a water heater explosion. She said that when a water heater explodes, the force generated is equal to that caused by one stick of dynamite (other sources say two pounds of dynamite for a 30-gallon unit). To make your water heater as safe as it can be, make darned sure that the TPR valve is operating freely.

By the way, if the valve wasn't supposed to be tested, all TPR valves wouldn't have a lever designed specifically for that purpose, and appropriately named by the manufacturer, the "test" lever. To test the valve, simply raise and lower the test lever several times so it lifts the brass stem it is fastened to (see Figure 11-4). Hot water should rush out of the end of the drainpipe. If no water flows through the pipe or you get just a trickle, replace the valve.

Some water heater experts recommend testing every six months. More frequent testing can reduce the chance of a leak caused by mineral and corrosion buildup. However, if a leak results immediately after a test, simply operate the test lever several times to free lodged debris that may be preventing the valve from seating properly. If the valve is doing its job and hot water is dripping or spewing out of the TPR drain valve, turn down the temperature on the water heater controller and/or turn down the water pressure, as discussed earlier in this chapter, if necessary.

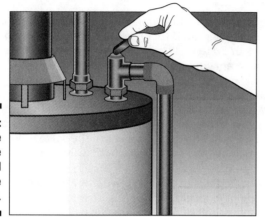

Figure 11-4:
Testing the
temperature
and
pressure
relief valve.

Also, the pipe leaving the relief valve should be the same diameter as the exhaust port of the valve — usually ¾ inch. Moreover, the pipe should be made of a material that is not adversely affected by heat, such as copper. If the pipe is undersized or not heat-resistant, replace it with copper or have a plumber do it for you.

The TPR drainpipe should travel in a slightly downhill direction from the valve to the point where it terminates. It should end outside the house at 6 to 24 inches above the ground. If the drainpipe moves uphill and then downhill, water could get trapped against the outlet of the valve and corrode it shut. If the drain line had a trap or a low spot, water could freeze. And even if the valve works, pressure would be captured and an explosion might occur. If the drainpipe isn't properly configured, call in a plumber to correct it.

Caring for the dip tube

When the hot water in your shower suddenly turns ice cold, you have the right to be frustrated and confused. (That is, if the hot water supply hasn't been drained due to recent use.)

If you receive this rude wake-up call, you may have a broken *dip tube*. The dip tube consists of a plastic pipe that travels vertically within the water heater tank from the cold-water inlet to within a few inches of the bottom of the tank. The dip tube brings cold water into the bottom of the tank where is can be heated.

If we remember anything from high school physics — and we don't remember much — it's that heat rises. The same holds true for hot water in your water heater. The hot water rises to the top where it can be fed or forced through a pipe at the top to various locations throughout your home. When water is introduced into a water heater at the top, it cools the already heated water until the water becomes cold — resulting in your unwelcome early-morning shock. When this condition arises, a cracked or broken dip tube is usually to blame.

Changing a dip tube is easy. As always, the first step is to turn off the power to the water heater. Then turn the cold-water inlet valve off and use a wrench to disconnect the cold-water supply line at the top of the water heater. The nipple — a short piece of pipe threaded at both ends — also needs to be removed. This exposes the top of the dip tube, which can be removed by inserting a screwdriver at an angle and using friction to pry the tube out of the opening.

Drop a new tube into the opening and replace the nipple and supply line, and then turn on the water and restore power to the unit.

Nipples — a sensitive subject

Nipples are short pieces of pipe that are threaded on both ends. They come in various lengths and diameters and are made of a host of materials. Most water heaters have two nipples that are used to connect the cold-water supply line and hot-water outlet line at the top of the water heater. These nipples are subject to corrosion and a buildup of solids at the interior that can bring your supply of hot water to a screeching halt.

This problem can be solved by installing galvanized iron nipples that are lined with plastic or PVC. The PVC prevents mineral buildup, and the galvanized finish helps prevent rust.

Use Teflon tape on the threads for a leak-free seal. Also, make sure to use dielectric connectors between dissimilar metals to prevent electrolysis — a deterioration that occurs when unlike metals come into contact with one another.

The cold-water shutoff valve

If you discover rust at the top of your water heater — aside from the nipples — it may be due to a leaking pipe fitting or a leak at the cold-water shutoff valve. If all the fittings are in good shape, and the valve is the culprit, try to stop the leak by tightening the packing nut using a wrench.

The thermocouple

If you have a gas water heater with a pilot light that won't stay lit, it is probably due to a blockage in the tiny tube that supplies gas to the pilot, or the thermocouple has failed. If it is the former, inserting a thin piece of wire or blowing air through the tube can generally clear the tiny tube. Make sure that the gas controller is in the off position before attempting this repair.

If your pilot light won't stay lit, the thermocouple probably needs to be replaced. The thermocouple is a thermoelectric device that shuts off the gas if the pilot light goes out. In simple terms, it is a short piece of tubing that runs from the gas controller to the pilot. The pilot end of the thermocouple and the pilot are held side by side in a bracket that is anchored to the burner.

To replace the thermocouple, first turn off the gas supply and, using a couple of small wrenches, remove the thermocouple from where it attaches to the bracket at the burner and at the other end where it connects to the controller. It may be necessary to remove the entire burner assembly to replace the thermocouple.

Since not all thermocouples are alike, buy a replacement model designed especially for your water heater. Install the new one the same way that you removed the old one. Turn the gas back on and follow the lighting instructions on the water heater.

The controller: the brains of the operation

The controller is the device you use to light the pilot and turn the unit off and on. It is also used to adjust the temperature setting.

The controller is usually pretty reliable and doesn't require much maintenance other than an occasional dusting. However, if you have too little hot water, water that is not hot enough, or water that is excessively hot, it may be time to replace the controller. This is a job best left to a pro.

The venting system

A gas water heater has one — an electric one doesn't. A flue runs up the center of the water heater from the burners, out the top of the water heater, and through the rooftop to vent deadly gases created by combustion.

At least twice each year, the venting system should be inspected to ensure that it is properly aligned at the top of the water heater and that the connections are secure.

Here's a quick test you can use to see if your gas water heater is venting properly. With the water heater running, hold a match near the draft diverter (that's the opening at the top of the water heater where the vent pipe connects to the unit). If the flame on the match leans in towards the vent pipe, your draft is good. But if it leans back towards the room, or worse yet, if it blows out the flame, your unit may be "back-drafting," a potentially dangerous situation. If this happens, turn the unit off immediately and call the gas company for assistance. Chances are your vent pipe of chimney is blocked somewhere, and your house may be filling with deadly combustion gases.

Disaster safety

A water heater thrown over during an earthquake or other disaster can cause both broken gas lines and broken water lines. This can be prevented if the water heater is securely strapped to an adjacent wall.

Metal straps around the belly of the heater can be screwed to the housing and then anchored to wall framing (see Figure 11-5). You can also install a special anchor that attaches to the water pipes at the top and to wall framing. In either case, your best bet is to check with your local building department for recommendations and a diagram on how best to anchor your water heater.

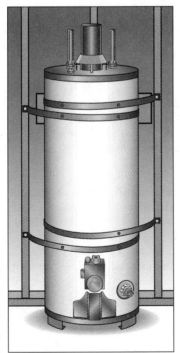

Figure 11-5:
Securing
your water
heater.

Softening Your Water

Excessive levels of calcium or magnesium in water cause hard water. Hard water causes buildup in water heaters, produces unsightly water stains in bathtubs and fixtures, and leaves behind soapy scum in the shower and on your skin.

The minerals in hard water gradually settle, forming a hard scale surface. This scale eventually clogs pipes and diminishes the efficiency of toilets, water heaters, clothes washers, and automatic dishwashers.

The negative effects of hard water can be reversed through the use of a water softener. There are three basic types of water softeners: automatic, demand initiated regeneration (DIR), and portable exchange.

An automatic water softener is equipped with a timer, which starts the softening process at preset intervals. The intervals are generally based on a calculation of water hardness, unit capacity, and estimated water use.

In contrast to an automatic system, DIR units use either a meter, which monitors water usage, or a sensor, which monitors a change in water hardness. Because they adjust to actual usage or change in water quality, DIR units consume up to 50 percent less sodium or potassium chloride and water than present automatic softening units.

A portable exchange unit has an exchangeable resin tank. When the resin material in the tank runs out, a fresh tank is delivered and the used tank is returned to a central plant for regeneration.

With the exception of adding salt to the brine tank on a regular basis, a water softening system is reasonably maintenance-free. Every now and then, the brine solution becomes clogged at the base of the brine tank, which prevents the solution from being siphoned into the resin tank. You know that this is the case if your brine tank is full of salt, yet your water doesn't have that "slick" feel of softened water.

This problem can be corrected by removing all of the salt from the brine tank and flushing the bottom of the tank with a garden hose and water. Before replacing the salt in the brine tank, the unit should then be manually cycled to ensure that it is operating properly. Individual units will have either a lever or a button that, when pressed, will manually cycle the system. Check your owner's manual to determine where the manual cycle button is on your water softener.

Wishing Your Well Is Working Well

If you don't get your water from a municipal water source, it probably comes from a private well. A basic well includes a water source — typically at least 100 feet deep to prevent contaminated drinking water; a casing pipe that is 4 to 6 inches in diameter lines the interior of the well. The casing extends out of the ground at least 12 inches and is capped to prevent contamination. Water is pumped from the source with a submersible pump that is usually about 10 feet from the bottom of the well to a pressure tank in or near the house. The tank, in turn, feeds the water supply lines.

In a standard pressure tank, incoming water forces air into the upper third of the tank, where it forms a spring-like cushion. When the air pressure reaches a preset level — usually between 50 and 60 pounds per square inch (psi) — the spring action of the compressed air triggers a pressure switch, which shuts off the pump. As water is drawn from the tank, pressure diminishes. When it reaches a preset level — 30 to 40 psi — the switch turns the pump on again.

When the pressure tank loses too much air pressure, it can become "waterlogged." This causes the pump to switch on and off frequently. This problem can be solved by turning off the power to the pump and attaching a garden hose to the drain valve at the bottom of the tank. The valve should be opened and remain open until there in no more pressure in the tank. A faucet must then be opened in the house to drain all of the water out of the tank. After the tank is empty, turn off the faucet, close the drain valve on the tank, remove the hose, and turn the pump back on.

A leaking tank is another prevalent problem. If a leak develops, it usually appears first as an oozing rusty blemish. Although tank plugs are available, they are only a temporary measure. The tank should be replaced as soon as possible.

Occasionally, the pump may stop working. If this is the case, first check for a blown fuse or tripped breaker. A loose wire may also be the source of the problem. If all of these check out, your best bet is to call in a well service technician.

Chapter 12

Plumbing Fixtures

*I*n this chapter, we tell you how to keep your plumbing fixtures in tip-top shape, which will definitely prolong their lifespans.

Easy Surface Maintenance of Fixtures

A home dweller eventually becomes intimately familiar with the various plumbing fixtures in a home — the sinks, tubs, toilets, and shower pans. It's no fun when these fixtures become tattered and worn out looking. In many situations, cleaning is all it takes to make a worn-out fixture look brand spanking new!

Vitreous china fixtures

Vitreous china is used primarily for bathroom sinks, toilets, and bidets. Vitreous china is a smooth form of baked clay with a shiny or glassy look. While strong, it can be chipped or broken if hit with a hard object, such as a tool. The bottom-line: Be careful around vitreous china, especially during repairs and maintenance.

China also is easily scratched, so for most cleaning, leave your scouring powder and abrasive pads in the cupboard.

For lime deposits try a pumice stick dipped in turpentine. Pumice is an extremely fine abrasive used for polishing. It comes in four grades with 4/0 being the finest. Don't use hand cleaners; the grade of pumice used in them is too coarse.

Remove tea or coffee stains with a solution of 2 tablespoons chlorine bleach per 1 quart of water; soak for just a minute or two; then rinse promptly. (Never mix bleach with a solution containing ammonia. The combination can release a poisonous gas.)

A variety of commercial products claim to clean china without causing damage, but proceed with caution. Abrasive cleaners slowly wear down its brilliant surface. The process can take years. Make sure that the cleaner you select states that it is non-abrasive.

Porcelain on steel or cast iron fixtures

Porcelain looks an awful lot like vitreous china. However, there are differences. Rather than a clay base, porcelain is a hard, glass-like coating melted onto a steel or cast iron base. The base material makes porcelain fixtures much stronger. Of the two bases, cast iron is superior.

Porcelain on steel or cast iron are both used primarily for kitchen sinks, laundry sinks, and bathtubs. Although the stronger base makes porcelain fixtures generally more durable, they do chip, and the finish is every bit as easy to scratch as vitreous china.

When porcelain is new its surface gleams and glistens, but over time, it can lose its luster, especially if abrasives are used for cleaning. If you drop a heavy object onto a porcelain fixture, you may not shatter it, but you might chip the enamel. Fortunately, there are companies that specialize in making such repairs. Look in the yellow pages under plumbing fixture refinishing. A chip can be repaired for about $50 to $75. Sorry, but there aren't any D-I-Y repairs that we can recommend. Chip-touch-up kits are available at your local home center or hardware store, but we think they're useless. They don't last, and the finished result usually looks terrible.

Reglazing porcelain

Porcelain and ceramic sinks, tubs, and other bathroom fixtures that are badly scratched, chipped, and have lost their luster can be *reglazed* (refinished) by a professional porcelain refinisher. (Reglazing a porcelain fixture isn't worth the cost or effort unless it is a valuable antique or a family heirloom. Reglazing is very expensive. Compared to reglazing, replacement is far less expensive.)

Refinishing porcelain

Reglazing is expensive, but refinishing — a paint-like process — is a far less costly alternative that can be performed with varying degrees of durability.

The least durable refinishing method involves paints or epoxies similar to what you can buy in a home improvement store. Applied directly to the ceramic surface, they quickly fail due to lack of proper adhesion and abrasion resistance.

The best materials are the industrial systems designed specifically for ceramic refinishing. These consist of a number of various catalyzed (chemically hardened) materials. The topcoats are acrylic, urethane, or polyurethane products.

The refinishing process takes time, typically as much as two days, due to drying time. Make sure to ask the refinisher how long your sink, faucet, or tub will be out of commission.

Anything less than a five-year guarantee makes this process a bad bet. Some companies offer ten-year guarantees.

Stainless steel fixtures

Vitreous china and porcelain fixtures are great, but when it comes to sinks, one made of high-quality stainless steel wins hands down. Stainless steel sinks are light and easy to install, they don't chip, and they are easy to keep clean.

Although we believe high-quality stainless steel is a real winner, cheaper stainless steel sinks are a drag. You can buy a stainless sink for less than $100 or more than $500. In general, you get what you pay for. The cheapest sinks are made of thinner, poorer-quality steel. They're easy to dent, noisy (they vibrate especially loudly when the disposal operates), and they are difficult to keep clean because of the low quality of the finish.

To clean a stainless steel surface, use a mild detergent, baking soda, or vinegar diluted in water. Clean and then dry with a soft cloth. For tougher cleaning tasks, look for a commercial stainless steel cleaning product that contains oxalic acid. Regardless of the cleaner, a nylon scrubbing pad will help.

When caring for stainless steel, follow these two simple rules:

- ✔ Never use steel wool. Steel wool fibers can lodge in the surface of the stainless steel and eventually rust, giving the appearance that the stainless steel is rusting. What a mess that can be.

- ✔ Don't use abrasive cleaners. They can scratch the surface over time.

Fiberglass fixtures

Fiberglass fixtures are popular because they are competitively priced. Fiberglass has been around for a long time and is used most commonly in tubs and shower pans. Fiberglass fixtures aren't as durable as other types of fixtures and must be treated with care. However, given such care, they will last as long as any other. A stained fiberglass tub or shower pan is a breeze to clean. Here's how:

1. **Wet the entire surface to be cleaned with water.**

2. **Sprinkle on a layer of automatic dishwashing powder.**

3. **Let it sit for about an hour while keeping the surface wet by spraying with clear water.**

4. **Use a nylon bristle brush to scrub stains away.**

A paste made of turpentine and salt is another alternative:

1. **Mix 2 or 3 tablespoons of turpentine into ¼ cup of regular table salt to make the cleaning compound.**

2. **Use a nylon bristle brush to apply the cleaner and scrub stains away.**

3. **Wipe up the excess cleaner with a paper towel.**

4. **Use mild detergent and water followed by a fresh water rinse to finish the job.**

Composite fixtures

Composite fixtures are long lasting and far more durable than fiberglass. However, they aren't as damage resistant as stainless steel.

Ordinary spills on composite require only a damp cloth for clean up. Tougher stains can be eliminated with a paste made of turpentine and salt (see the previous section about cleaning fiberglass).

While fiberglass is a resin painted onto a backing, composite fixtures are great thick hulks of plastic. Therefore, what you see on the surface goes all the way through to the other side of the fixture. This can be a blessing in the case of a burn or some other surface damage.

If a composite sink ever becomes really grungy, try filling the sink with a solution of bleach and water. The bleach works very well and will bring back the sink's original color.

Because the finished look of a composite fixture goes all the way through, light sanding can remove burns, stains, or minor scratches. Polish the sanded area with fine 400- to 600-grit wet-dry sandpaper lubricated with turpentine to restore the surface to its original beauty. Wipe the excess turpentine up with a paper towel and finish the job by cleaning with a mild detergent and a fresh water rinse.

Cleaning Your Faucet Works

When a faucet becomes dull, it makes an otherwise bright and shiny decorating accessory look tattered and worn. It isn't worn out — it's just dirty. The bad thing is that dirt that has built up for a long period of time can be difficult to remove. The good thing is that it can be removed without damaging the faucet if you know a few tricks. Cleaning a faucet is a two-part operation:

- ✔ Cleaning the aerator
- ✔ Cleaning and polishing the exterior finish

Cleaning the aerator

No matter how clean you keep the outside of your faucet, there is one part that only gets dirty from the inside. If the water flow from your faucet is slow, or if the water sprays out in random streams, or if a once smooth flow has become sporadic and now sputters, then you probably have a clogged *aerator*.

The aerator is a thimble-size accessory that screws into the end of a faucet spout. When operating normally, it causes the water coming out of the spout to travel in a smooth, gentle, even flow. It does this by mixing the water with air and by controlling the amount of flow.

The aerator consists of a very small disk filled with tiny holes. Because they are so small, they are easily clogged. Sediment in water, rust that works its way loose from piping, and mineral deposits can clog an aerator.

Cleaning the aerator is really easy. Here's all you have to do:

1. **Unscrew the aerator from the spout by turning it counterclockwise.**

2. **Disassemble the aerator parts.**

   They simply sit one atop another inside the aerator housing.

3. **Use an old toothbrush and a toothpick and some vinegar to clean each part.**

   If lime deposit build-up can't be easily removed, soak the parts in straight vinegar overnight. Then scrub them clean.

4. **Reassemble the aerator and reinstall it.**

As you disassemble the aerator, note exactly how the parts are assembled. If you make a mistake during reassembly, the aerator won't work.

Cleaning and polishing the outside of a faucet

To keep a faucet clean, regularly wipe it down with a damp cloth followed by a clean, dry towel.

Built-up debris is a bit more difficult — especially when it's a thick layer of lime deposits. There are several different cleaners that can be used to remove hard water stains and other mineral deposit buildup:

- Pure sodium carbonate (also known as washing soda or soda ash). Soda ash is available at swimming-pool supply stores.
- A paste made of white vinegar and baking soda
- 1 teaspoon of Calgon in 1 gallon of hot water
- Plain vinegar

Don't use abrasive cleaners on a faucet. Liquid cleaners work best without damaging the finish. It's always a good idea to test a cleaner on an out-of-the-way spot to ensure it doesn't remove or damage the paint.

Pure sodium carbonate

Pure sodium carbonate is nothing more than laundry detergent. No fillers, no anti-bubbling agents, no odor eaters, nothing except pure cleaning power. Here's how to use it:

1. **Mix ½ cup sodium carbonate with a few drops of warm water.**

2. **Use a soft clean cloth to rub the paste onto the faucet surface.**

3. **Rub until it shines.**

4. **Rinse with fresh water and towel dry.**

White vinegar and baking soda

To use this foamy cleaner, just follow these steps:

1. **Mix equal parts of baking soda and white vinegar.**

2. **Wipe the concoction onto the surface of the faucet with a clean soft cloth.**

3. **Rub until the surface is clean and shiny.**

4. **Rinse with clear water and towel dry.**

Calgon

Calgon is a common household product that acts as a really neat faucet-cleaning agent. Here's how to use it:

1. **Mix 1 teaspoon of Calgon into 1 gallon of hot water.**

2. **Soak a rag in the concoction and very gently wring it out.**

   You want the rag to be really soaked.

3. **Place the soaked rag onto the faucet and press the rag against all parts of the faucet.**

4. **Cover the rag with plastic food wrap so that it doesn't dry out.**

5. **Come back in 1 hour, remove the rag, and use it to briskly wipe away the mineral buildup.**

   For long-time buildup, the rag may have to be re-soaked in the solution and placed back onto the faucet several times.

6. **Rinse the Calgon away with fresh water and pat dry with a soft clean cloth.**

Plain vinegar

Plain vinegar is great for removing a major mineral salt buildup. You won't believe how easy it is to use:

1. **Fill a bowl with plain vinegar.**

2. **Soak a rag in the vinegar and very gently wring it out.**

3. **Place the soaked rag onto the faucet and press the rag against all of the parts that need cleaning.**

4. **Cover the rag with plastic food wrap so that it doesn't dry out (see Figure 12-1).**

5. **After an hour, remove the rag and use it to briskly wipe away the mineral buildup.**

6. **Rinse the vinegar away with fresh water and pat dry with a soft clean cloth.**

Figure 12-1:
Letting the
vinegar sit
and do its
job.

Removing copper residue

If your plumbing pipes are made of copper, or if the faucet entrails are made of copper, then there is a very good chance that a dark green cast will appear at the faucet spout. The patina color indicates oxidation of copper. If left unattended, this condition will destroy the finish on a polished brass faucet in no time.

If you see green at the tip of your faucet, reach for a metal cleaner such as Brasso or Flitz. Both products are used in the same way:

1. **Pour a small amount of the cleaner on a soft, dry cloth.**

2. **Rub the cleaner onto the corroded area. Keep rubbing until the ultra fine polishing compound eats away at the bad finish.**

3. **Let the remaining compound form a white haze and use another soft clean cloth to wipe away the last remnants of the polish.**

Toilet Training 101

What follows is a bit of toiletology that we hope will bring you and your family even closer to your bathroom and specifically your toilet.

Some of the problems associated with toilets also apply to bidets, including slow water flow and mineral deposits. Obviously, a bidet doesn't have a tank, but the bowls are similar, so if the problem fits, so does the solution.

Preventing a sweaty tank

A toilet tank sweats when the cold water inside chills the tank in a warm bathroom. The result is condensation and a wet tank. One way to reduce sweating is to make sure that the water entering the tank isn't cold. Having a plumber add a mixing valve at the tank inlet can accomplish this. It introduces warm water into the tank. Unfortunately, this is a relatively expensive fix.

You can also fit sheets of polystyrene or foam rubber against the inside of the tank walls. Use a kit or cut the liners to fit the bottom of the tank and the walls. Glue the liners in place with silicone cement and let the adhesive dry for at least 24 hours before filling the tank (see Figure 12-2). Hopefully, you have a second bathroom to use while the adhesive dries.

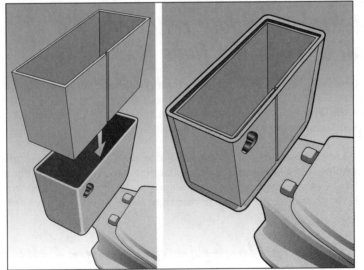

Figure 12-2:
Lining the
inside of
your tank.

Cloth tank liners are supposed to insulate the tank and reduce the chance for condensation. However, if the temperature difference is great enough, a certain amount of condensation will occur. This can be a problem. If the cloth liners gets wet, mold and mildew can result. Yuck! We never did like those cloth covers anyway.

Preventing plugged toilets

A clogged toilet is always an accident. No one ever intends to cause the disgusting mess associated with a toilet backup.

Quite simply, to avoid the hassle of a plugged toilet, you need to make sure that only proper materials are flushed down it. That includes feminine hygiene products and, if you have children in the house, toys. Mom should know that a sanitary napkin should never go down the toilet. Kids should be given guidance about how toys can cause a clog.

When an overflow occurs, everyone in the family should see the result. The experience is memorable.

If you do experience a blockage, try clearing the obstruction with a plumber's helper (a plunger). If that doesn't work, cut a coat hanger and bend a hook in one end. Force the coat hanger into the neck of the toilet and try to hook the blockage. If you're not successful, it's time to use a closet auger (plumber's snake) or call the plumber.

Making sure your toilet doesn't fall through the floor

A toilet isn't supposed to be loose enough to rock you to sleep. If it isn't secure, it means that there isn't adequate support below. It's usually a sign that the floor is rotted from a water leak or that the floor was not properly supported when the toilet was originally installed.

Rot is a serious issue and should be addressed by a qualified technician. To determine whether rot exists, you must first remove the toilet. Then, use a blunt object such as a screwdriver to poke into the suspect flooring. If it is soft and easy to pierce, get on the phone right away. Rot can spread like wildfire.

Looking for leaks in and around the toilet

A little earlier we talked about internal toilet leaks. Now it's time to talk about the ones that occur outside the toilet. If the floor is wet around the toilet, you obviously have a leak. There are several places to look:

✔ First, check the shut-off valve at the wall. Use a towel to dry the floor around the toilet. Next, lay a piece of toilet paper on the floor beneath the valve. Wait for about 15 minutes. If the toilet paper is wet, the shut-off valve (or the supply tube connected to it) leaks. Try tightening the valve fittings. If that doesn't work, the valve and supply line should be replaced.

✔ Use a small clump of toilet paper to wipe the bottom of the tank where the supply tube connects. If it is wet, the leak is there. Tighten the nut and the supply line at that location. If that doesn't work, replace the supply line.

✔ Check the area beneath the bowl where the tank connects. You will find two bolts that hold the tank to the bowl. If either of them leak try tightening them slightly. Don't over-tighten, you can crack the toilet. If this doesn't work, replace the rubber gasket that is on either bolt within the tank. Empty the tank, remove the bolts, replace the gaskets, and reinstall the bolts.

✔ Check the entire exterior surface of the toilet for hairline cracks. If you find any, the toilet needs to be replaced.

✔ If water is seeping out between the base of the toilet and the floor then the wax ring (sewer line to toilet seal) has failed. Remove the toilet, replace the seal, and reinstall it.

Even if the floor is dry, if you have access to the area beneath the toilet, it is a good idea to occasionally check to see if the toiled has developed a hidden leak. (Like in the basement or crawlspace.) Check for damp wood or evidence of dripping water. If you find telltale evidence, the wax ring should be replaced.

Cleaning the toilet

Toilets that aren't cleaned regularly can become a mess, and toilet bowl cleaners don't always do the job. The strong ones can be dangerous to work with, and the others aren't always strong enough to get things really clean.

Because bacteria love to live in toilets, pour 1 cup of bleach into the tank and mix it into the water. Let it set for a few minutes, then flush the toilet a few times. You have just sanitized your toilet.

Cleaning the siphon jets

The siphon jets are the small openings under the rim of the bowl. If these jets become clogged, your toilet won't flush properly.

Flush the toilet and watch how the water flows. It should swirl. If it comes straight down, the holes are probably plugged. Discolored vertical lines in the bowl are another good sign that the holes need cleaning.

Inspect the rim openings with a pocket mirror. It they're clogged with mineral deposits, first empty the tank and the bowl using the following procedure:

1. **Turn off the water to the tank (at the wall valve) and flush the toilet.**

   This empties the tank. With the wall valve off, the tank will not refill.

2. **Fill a large container with 1 gallon of water.**

3. **Pour the water into the toilet bowl.**

   The bowl should empty.

Until you turn the water on and flush the toilet, the bowl and tank will remain empty. Your toilet is now ready to be cleaned.

Use a hanger as a "pipe cleaner" to ream out the holes at the rim (see Figure 12-3). If the scale that exists is too hard to remove, try this trick to soften things up:

1. **Use a towel to completely dry the underside of the rim.**

2. **Apply a layer of duct tape to the underside of the rim.**

   If it doesn't stick the rim is wet.

3. **Fill the tank with 1 gallon of pure vinegar (any kind).**

4. **Flush the toilet.**

   The vinegar travels from the tank into the rim of the toilet. Let it sit there for as long as possible. Twenty-four hours is super.

5. **Remove the tape, scrub away the softened scale, turn the water back on, and flush the toilet.**

   It should work beautifully.

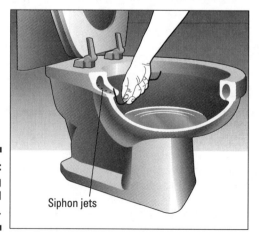

Figure 12-3:
Clearing
clogged
siphon jets.

Siphon jets

Removing a ring around the bowl

If a white or brown ring forms in the bowl, place a couple of denture tablets in the bowl. The tablets will effervesce in the water and dissolve. Let the mixture set over night. (We recommend a separate container for your dentures.) The next morning, just flush the toilet and easily wipe away the softened buildup.

If some of the stains remain, clean them with a pumice stick and turpentine. You'll love this one:

1. **Empty the bowl using the procedure listed in the preceding section.**

2. **Dip a pumice stick (looks like a large dark gray piece of chalk) into some turpentine and scrub.**

Turpentine is a great cleaning agent, and the pumice is a super-fine abrasive. Together they make cleaning a breeze. However, pumice is abrasive — don't use a pumice stick on chrome or painted finishes.

A nylon scrubbing pad can be used in place of the pumice for lighter buildup.

Maintaining Tubs and Showers

Most of us make at least one trip a day to the tub or shower. We don't know anyone who wants to perform their morning scrub-down in a mildew-lined fixture with a dangerously slippery floor. Our tub and shower tips show you how to easily maintain these fixtures so that your movie called *Showering and Bathing* will be a love story — not a horror film.

Cleaning

To minimize major cleaning problems at tubs and showers, after each use, squeegee wet surfaces or wipe them dry with a towel. It only takes a moment.

Squeegeeing a dirty surface doesn't work. So, if you'd like to implement the procedure in the preceding tip, you must first ensure that your tub or shower is absolutely clean.

A porcelain tub is cleaned using the same methods described for cleaning vitreous surfaces (see the section "Vitreous china fixtures" earlier in this chapter). You can also remove soap scum and dirt using automatic dishwasher detergent and hot water. Rinse with fresh water and towel dry.

To clean fiberglass, use a mixture of ¼ cup of salt mixed with 2 to 3 tablespoons of turpentine. Scrub the concoction onto the surface with a nylon bristle brush. Wipe up the excess with paper towels. Follow by washing with a mild detergent. Rinse with fresh water and towel dry.

Towel drying prevents mineral salts from remaining on the surface. Towel drying is a "must do" final step in most cleaning processes.

You can apply either a coat of lemon oil or a coat of car polish (not both) to your tub, shower walls, and shower door. These products reduce surface tension and cause water and soap residue to drain off instead of sticking to a surface.

Caulking

If you have tile shower walls, there is a very good possibility that a leak could develop between the tile and the tub. As the house moves (a natural process that occurs in every home), a hairline crack can occur that allows water to get into the joint. Once water gets in, there is no telling how much damage can be done. That's why it's important to annually caulk the connection between your shower walls and the tub or shower pan. It is always best to remove what exists and caulk from scratch.

There's another good reason to re-caulk. If you've tried to remove the black mildew stains from caulk, you know it's sometimes hopeless. That's because the stains are often behind the caulk — between the caulk and the wall. The answer, of course, is to remove the caulk, kill the mildew, and then replace the caulk.

Removing the caulk isn't as hard as it appears. One company makes a product called Caulk-Be-Gone and another makes an Adhesive & Caulk Remover, two commercial products that can assist you in the job. These products are specially formulated to soften caulk for easy removal.

After the caulk has softened (it may take a few hours), remove it with a plastic putty knife. Clean the joint with paint thinner and wipe the area dry with a clean rag.

Then clean the joint with our famous mildew cleaner:

1. **Add 1 quart of liquid chlorine bleach to 3 quarts of warm water.**

2. **Add ⅛ cup of powdered laundry detergent.**

3. **Mix thoroughly and place in a spray bottle.**

4. **Spray the mixture onto the mildewed area. Let it sit until the black mildew turns white. Rinse with fresh water.**

Although this mixture is mild, don't forget to wear gloves and eye protection and make sure the area is well ventilated. Make sure the detergent you use is ammonia free. Mixing bleach with a solution containing ammonia can release a dangerous gas harmful to your lungs.

Immediately after eradicating the mildew, use a hair dryer or a hot air gun to thoroughly dry out the area. The joint can now be re-caulked.

Use a roll of blue painter's masking tape for a professional-looking job. Apply the tape to the tub ⅛ inch from the joint. Next, apply another strip of tape along the wall, ⅛ inch from the joint. Now the caulking will go between the two pieces of tape, making straight, smooth lines.

Apply tub and tile caulk into the joint and smooth it with your finger, an old teaspoon, or a caulking spreader. Immediately remove the tape by pulling it out and away from the freshly caulked joint. Be careful not to touch the caulk. Let it dry. You simply won't believe how beautiful your job will look.

Decorative non-skid pads

These pads look nice when they're first installed, but as they are regularly exposed to dirty tub or shower water, they can become disgustingly ugly. Sandy feet and daily activity eventually wear out your non-skid pads.

If your pads are simply worn out, you can easily replace them. You need a hair dryer and a plastic or wood scraper (metal can scratch the tub or shower pan).

Heat the pad until it becomes soft, and then use the scraper to lift it from the surface (see Figure 12-4). Wear gloves to protect your hands when handling the hot pads. Remove the leftover adhesive with a commercial, spray-on adhesive-remover, paint thinner or naphtha. Be sure to leave a window open to remove the fumes. Then apply new pads according to the manufacturer's instructions.

Before you go to your favorite discount store to buy replacement pads, consider this alternative. Companies that refinish plumbing fixtures can also apply a clear anti-skid material. It's basically invisible, covers the bottom of the tub or shower, and has excellent anti-skid properties.

Figure 12-4:
Heating the
pad to
remove it.

Avoiding overflow leaks

The tub overflow is the device located at the end of the tub just above the drain. It derives its name from the purpose it serves: preventing a tub from overflowing.

Sinks also have overflows (a hole beneath the front edge), but with sinks, the overflow is built in — no hardware is attached that can fail and leak.

What you see when you look at a tub overflow is a decorative metal cover. Sometimes the overflow assembly holds the lever for a built-in drain stopper. There is a gasket behind the cover and on the outside surface of the tub. Beyond the gasket is the pipe that is used to direct overflow into the sewer system. The two screws located in the overflow plate hold together the decorative cover plate, the overflow gasket, and the overflow pipe. When the screws become loose the gasket can leak.

You should check the screws every year or two to ensure that they are snug. If you overfill the tub and the gasket is not tight, it can leak behind the tub, causing problems that can be hard to detect.

Chapter 13

The Drain, Waste, and Vent System

● ●

In This Chapter

▶ Getting to know your sewer system

▶ Keeping your sewer system running clog-free

▶ Eliminating the most common clogs

● ●

*T*aking the time to read this chapter and follow the advice that we give you about maintaining this important system will save you untold headaches. Do yourself a favor — kick back and read this one page-for-page, if you can.

Sewer System Basics

Every plumbing fixture in your home is joined by the same drainpipe, including the kitchen sink, the dishwasher, the clothes washer, the toilets, and so on. The waste from each of these fixtures exits the house through this one drainpipe. A problem caused by one fixture can easily become a problem for all the other fixtures.

Your common, everyday household sanitary sewer system consists of three basic elements (see Figure 13-1):

✓ **The waste lines and drainpipe:** The waste lines carry sewage from each of the fixtures in your home down through the walls and under the floor then outside the home to either a public sewer system beneath the street or a septic tank somewhere below ground on your property. A clog in any of these pipes stops waste from reaching its destination away from your home — and it can back up into your home.

✓ **The vent pipes:** Vent pipes travel from each plumbing fixture (or group of plumbing fixtures), upward (inside walls) and out through the roof. These are the black pipes on top of your roof. The vents allow air into the sewer lines so that they drain freely. A clogged vent pipe can be a serious problem, preventing good drainage of the waste.

The p-traps: You have one of these traps in every fixture: sink, toilet, washing machine, you name it. If the fixture drains into the sewer system, the water or waste first travels through a p-trap. The trap allows water and waste to enter the sewer system while at the same time preventing sewer gases from backing up into the house. A clogged p-trap can inhibit the flow of waste from the home and can allow stinky gases to back up into the home through the fixtures.

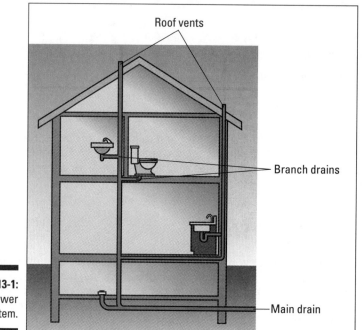

Roof vents

Branch drains

Main drain

Figure 13-1:
Your sewer
system.

Keeping Your System Clog-Free

One of the single best ways to prevent slow or clogged drains is by being careful about what you put into them. Daaahhhh!

Cooking grease, coffee grounds, hair, and soap scum are four of a drain's biggest enemies. Great caution should be taken to avoid introducing any of these into a drain:

Taking your sewer system off the roller coaster ride

If you repeatedly have drainage problems, and you have determined that all waste lines, vents, and traps are clean and clear, then the fall, or actually the lack of fall, of your pipes could be the problem.

One thing you don't want is a sewer system that looks like a set of roller coaster tracks — up and down, up and down. Sewers work best when the waste lines slope downhill. In fact, they don't really work very well at all, otherwise.

The National Plumbing Code requires sewer lines to fall (slope downward) at a rate of ⅛ inch per foot (which equals 1 inch every 8 feet). We think the minimum should be twice as much. There is no maximum fall. The more the better.

If fall is an issue, you probably ought to call a plumber in to correct the problem. We don't recommend major sewer work as a D-I-Y project.

- ✔ Save cooking grease in an old coffee can or cardboard milk container.

- ✔ Throw coffee grounds away in the garbage or add them to your mulch pile.

- ✔ Avoid the majority of problems with hair and soap scum with a screen or drain-grate covering (and protecting) the drain's opening. Stop by your local plumbing supply store to study the choices that relate to your particular fixture. Take a picture of the drain system along to better explain your needs. Most filters and screens can be simply laid in place.

Regular cleaning also has its merits. To keep sink drains in your home running freely — and absent of odor — try these methods:

- ✔ Run hot water through the sink after each use.

- ✔ Throw a handful of baking soda into the drain and follow it with hot water.

- ✔ Pour 1 cup of vinegar and let it sit for ½ hour. Then chase it down with very hot water.

For sinks with garbage disposals, you can also try this trick:

1. **Fill an ice-cube tray half full with vinegar and top it off with clear water.**

   Vinegar alone won't freeze well. Be sure to mark the tray clearly — you wouldn't want an unsuspecting family member to end up with a mouthful of vinegar. Can you imagine how that martini would taste?

2. Turn the disposal on and then throw in the cubes.

Vinegar is a mild acid that cleans the disposal and the drain while the ice literally chills and scrapes grease off its walls (see Figure 13-2). If you don't like the smell of vinegar, you can chase the cubes with one sliced lemon. Your disposal and your kitchen will smell great!

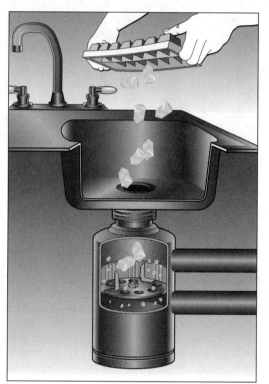

Figure 13-2: Cleaning your disposal with ice and vinegar.

If clogging is a regular problem at your place, try this one out for size. It works on drains in sinks, showers, and tubs. You need ½ cup each of baking soda, salt, and vinegar and a couple of quarts of boiling water. Just before going to bed, do the following:

1. Pour the salt and the baking soda into the drain.

2. Add the vinegar and let the concoction foam for a minute or two.

3. Chase with at least 2 quarts of boiling water.

For additional tips on cleaning your sink, toilet, tub, and shower, turn to Chapter 12.

Using commercial drain cleaners

Lye is the active ingredient in most popular store-bought drain cleaners. It dissolves soap scum and hair in a heartbeat. All you have to do is pour some down the drain, chase with a small amount of water, and wait for the chemical to do its job.

Small amounts of lye are reasonably safe. But too much of a good thing could suddenly turn nasty. Strong drain cleaners aren't safe when used in large quantities. Make sure to follow the directions on the label to the letter.

The waste lines

The clean-out system in your sewer provides access to the waste lines for easy cleaning, which can save you hundreds of dollars in plumber's bills.

A clean-out is a port with a removable cover that provides access to the inside of the sewer line. Clean-outs can be found under sinks, sticking out of exterior walls, and randomly in the area beneath the floor. The National Plumbing Code requires clean-outs to be placed in your waste lines at least every 100-linear-feet of horizontal travel. Clean-outs must be even closer together when the total angle of all bends in the horizontal sections of line exceed 135 degrees.

Use a device that measures angles to determine the angle of each bend in a horizontal waste line and then combine the total of all of the bends to see if they exceed 135 degrees. If so, call a plumber and add a clean-out.

Once you know where all of your clean-outs are, you can use that knowledge to keep your sewer clean on your own. And you can give your plumber a rest — at home, not in Tahiti with your money!

The cover to a clean-out is a flat, threaded disk fitted with a hexagonal pro-trusion at its center. This allows it to be easily removed (or replaced) with a wrench or a pair of pliers.

With the clean-out cover removed, a plumber's auger or "snake" can be sent down the line to clear a clog at the first sign of a drainage problem (see Figure 13-3). Most good do-it-yourselfers own a small version of a plumber's auger. A small auger is not only inexpensive; it is easy to store as well.

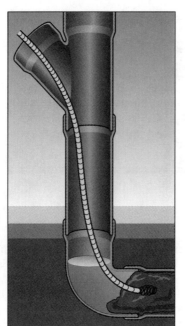

The vents

When a vent becomes clogged, it shows up within the home as everything from "ghost flushes" at the toilet to sinks that simply won't drain properly.

When a sink isn't draining properly, and the waste line isn't clogged, you may need to take a look upward to find the culprit. Up toward the vent system. You know, the black plumbing pipes that stick up out of your roof.

One or more of the following can collect in a vent line and completely clog it up. Here are a few things that we've found:

- ✔ Birds (usually deceased, but sometimes nesting)
- ✔ Rodent carcasses (once we found just the skeleton)
- ✔ Leaves, trash, and other rubbish, which are sometimes almost impossible to remove
- ✔ Tennis balls and baseballs (we're still waiting for our first water balloon)

ANECDOTE

Is your ghost flush friendly?

About five years ago, we were on the air doing our radio show. A caller phoned in with a most unusual question. "My toilet flushes all by itself," she said. She went on to explain that no one was near the toilet when it flushed. It did it all by itself. "Do I have ghosts," she asked? Naturally, we decided to run with it. We excitedly told her that Casper the Friendly Ghost was on a toilet-flushing rampage and, well, you can probably figure out the rest.

After a few moments of horsing around, we returned to serious diagnosing. The flush that our caller described was not a conventional one. The flush-lever never moved — not once. And water wasn't released from the tank. Each time, the tank remained full and undisturbed. But the toilet was flushing. Every once in a while, the water in the bottom of the toilet bowl would simply be sucked right down the drain! Fllluuuusssshhh!

As we continued to diagnose, we found out that each time that the toilet had flushed, someone was taking a shower. We surmised that the shower and toilet were connected to the same vent pipe and that the vent had clogged. (Often, two or more plumbing fixtures are connected to a single vent pipe.)

When the shower drained, the water moving down the sewer line acted like a piston, causing suction. Apparently, air could not be drawn in from the clogged vent to offset the increasing negative pressure, so the next best place — the toilet — became the ventilation intake port. Casper really had nothing at all to do with it.

The p-traps

The p-trap is that strangely curved pipe that you see beneath any sink in your home. Actually, a p-trap can be found at every single plumbing fixture — whether you can see it or not. If you can't see it, you can be sure it is either inside the fixture (a toilet), beneath the floor (showers and tubs), or inside the wall (washing machine drains).

The name of this special piece of drain comes from the letter of the alphabet that it resembles, and also from the fact that it actually traps water. Essentially, the trap holds enough water in its curved base to act as a "water door," preventing unpleasant waste and sewer gases from backing up into the home.

Unfortunately, the trap's water-trapping ability extends to hair, grease, debris, and soap scum. This makes a p-trap the number-one location of clogs in the sewer system. If the p-trap becomes only slightly clogged, then you experience slow drainage in the fixture. Oh, you say the toilet is the place where all the clogs occur at your house. The toilet has the largest p-trap of any fixture in the home. Had to pull out any toys of yours lately?

You can prevent drain clogs by being careful about what you put in and by performing monthly preventive cleaning. (See the beginning of this chapter for more info.)

If you experience slow draining in your fixture, try cleaning the p-trap to avoid a full-blown blockage. You need:

- ✔ 1 small plastic bucket
- ✔ 1 rag
- ✔ 1 large pair of pliers or a pipe wrench
- ✔ 1 portable light

Before beginning, remove all of the junk from under the sink so that you have ample room to work. Then follow these steps:

1. **Position the plastic bucket directly under the p-trap.**

2. **Using the pliers, remove the two coupling nuts that attach the trap to the sink tailpiece and to the adjacent wall fitting.**

   If these nuts won't budge, or simply fall apart when you try to move them, it's time to purchase a replacement trap.

3. **Clean the interior of the trap with a straightened wire coat hanger or a large nylon bottle brush.**

   Make certain that all the parts are completely clean inside and out. A piece of debris lodged between a drain washer and the drainpipe can cause a leak.

   Use the cleaning as an opportunity to inspect all of the washers — they should be soft and supple. (Don't you just love that description? Go to the hardware store or home center and ask for "soft, supple, drain washers.") If they aren't soft, you need to replace them.

   If you discover that the trap is clean and clear (and not the reason for the clog or slow draining), then use a small retractable drain snake. The snake can be inserted directly into the drain or, in the case where the p-trap has been removed, directly into the pipe in the wall. Work the snake in and out while rotating the handle clockwise.

4. **Reassemble the trap.**

   Make sure that each washer is properly seated. Twisting can be a real problem. Don't over-tighten the connections. At first, the coupling nuts should be no more than hand tight. If a leak persists, continue to tighten a little at a time until the leak disappears. If increased tightening doesn't do the trick, chances are the washers are dirty, twisted, or defective. Try again!

If cleaning doesn't solve your p-trap problems, pick up the telephone and call a plumber or sewer and drain specialist who has the expertise and proper tools to get things flowing freely.

If all of the drains in the home are running slowly, the main sewer line may be the problem. Skip all of the steps above and go straight to the plumber.

Chapter 14

The Heating, Ventilating, and Cooling Systems

In This Chapter

▶ Keeping your furnace and boiler happy

▶ Keeping your air conditioning cool

▶ Ventilating your home from top to bottom

*I*t's there in a dark corner of the basement, amid a tangle of pipes and ducts. It roars, is silent, then roars again. You can see flames burning brightly inside, behind its door. Is it possibly the entrance to hell? Heck, no. It's your furnace (or boiler).

Most grown-ups would never admit it, but their furnaces frighten them. It's a big, mysterious piece of machinery. Plus, as every kid knows, monsters live behind it.

We're here to tell you that there's nothing to be afraid of. A furnace is less mysterious than you think. And according to our 5-year-old nephew, you can keep the monsters away by turning on all the lights and loudly humming the theme from *The Lion King*.

Your heating system simply heats up air or water, and then moves that heated air or water (or steam) around the house. It's really that simple. However, the technology behind this process is pretty complicated, which means that a professional must perform most maintenance tasks associated with your heating system.

The maintenance that can be done by a do-it-yourselfer is easy and non-threatening — we're confident you can do it without any difficulty (or monster trouble).

If you ask ten people what that thing in their basement is that's used to heat the house, most will say "a furnace." Truth is, it may not be. Here's how to tell. If your home is heated by air, it's a furnace. But if it's heated by water, it's a boiler. Furnaces heat air, but boilers heat water!

Making Friends with the Heat Monster in the Basement

Because most people don't know diddley about their heating systems, here's a quick look at the most common types:

- **Forced-air systems:** Heats air as it passes through the furnace. A blower and a system of ducts take the warm air throughout the house, and then back to the furnace.

- **Hot-water (hydronic) systems:** Water gets heated in the boiler and is then circulated through pipes to radiators or convectors. The water then returns to the boiler to be reheated and begins the journey again. The water can be circulated either mechanically through the use of circulator motors (pumps) or via gravity, as is common in older homes.

- **Steam systems:** These resemble hot-water systems, except that the water in the boiler is heated until it becomes steam and can travel under its own pressure through the pipes to radiators. Steam radiators get much hotter than water radiators and are therefore smaller. They should be covered to prevent burn injuries.

- **Electric systems:** Use electrical resistance to generate radiant heat in baseboard units, or in cables embedded in the ceiling or floor.

Forced-air systems

Have a qualified, licensed heating contractor inspect and service your forced-air system every year before the heating season begins. This is not optional. Sure, you could save $75 by not doing it. But a dirty, inefficient furnace costs you ten times that much in wasted fuel. Even more important, a cracked heat exchanger or dislodged flue could fill your house with deadly carbon monoxide gas. We think you would agree that you and your family are worth more than what it costs to make sure the furnace is functional and safe.

When the furnace serviceperson does your annual service, dozens of maintenance tasks are performed (lubrication, burner adjustment, and so on) that help maintain (and even improve) your furnace's efficiency and keep it running year after year. Frankly, these aren't the kinds of things the typical home owner can do, so we think it's best to let a pro do the job.

If you do decide to do your own maintenance, take heed. Certain parts of your furnace may be difficult to locate. They all don't look like the illustrations in this book. For specifics, refer to your owner's manual. In some instances, the local public utility or the building department offer no-charge assistance in these matters.

Replacing the furnace filter

Of the maintenance tasks you can do yourself, the easiest is replacing the furnace filter. It should be replaced every month during the heating season. If an air-conditioning system is part of the same system, the filter should be changed every month year round.

The filter takes dust, dirt, pollen, carpet fibers, and pet dander out of the air, which keeps the house cleaner and helps keep allergies at bay. Without all that stuff in the airflow, the blower motor lasts longer, too. The filter also prevents compressor coils (hidden within the system) from becoming clogged.

It may seem silly to replace the filter so often, but you would be surprised by how much airborne crud gets into your house. As a result, the filter gets clogged quickly, which makes the furnace work harder (it's like trying to breathe through a straw). And anyway, filters only cost a couple of bucks apiece.

Don't buy filters one at a time — get a whole case. They're cheaper by the dozen. What's more, the box reminds you to make a change, you see when you've missed a change, and you never skip a change because you don't have a filter on hand. As soon as you get home with the filters, open the box and label each one with the date you intend to install it. You can't go wrong.

You usually find the filter near where the cool air enters the furnace — in the cold-air return duct, or at the entrance to the blower chamber, or sometimes in both locations (see Figure 14-1).

After you find the filter, slide it out and replace it with a new one. Make sure the airflow arrows on the side are pointing the right way (toward the blower and away from the cold air).

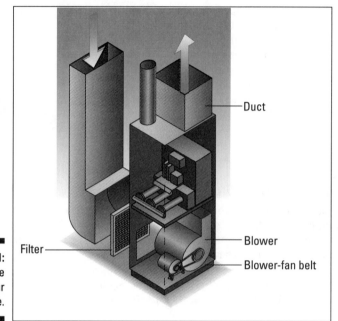

Figure 14-1:
The inside
of your
furnace.

Duct

Filter

Blower

Blower-fan belt

Cleaning the blower compartment

Before you put a new filter in, take a minute to clean the *blower compartment* (see Figure 14-1).

First, turn off the power to the furnace at the emergency switch. The switch may be mounted on or near the furnace itself. If you can't find the switch, turn the power off at the circuit breaker or fuse box before sticking your hands anywhere near the inside of the unit.

Next, open the hatch on the front (if it isn't already open to change the filter), and use a vacuum cleaner with the upholstery brush attachment on it to remove any dirt, lint, and dust bunnies you find.

If you're feeling extra-handy, you can clean the *burner compartment,* too. Moisture from the air can cause the burners to rust. Use a wire brush to clean them. Then, use your vacuum's small snoot or the end of the hose. Don't get too ambitious — just carefully suck up the loosened rust, lint and debris lying around in the compartment and on the burner elements. Make sure the furnace is turned off and has had a chance to cool down before you start.

Be careful not to disturb any of the small wires inside the furnace area. Most heating systems have low voltage controls and if you were to inadvertently disturb a control wire, the system may not come back on.

Checking on the blower-fan belt

As long as you have the hatch off, check the condition and adjustment of the *blower-fan belt* (if you have one). A worn, wimpy belt isn't dangerous, but it makes a squealing noise that drives you crazy, and, more important, costs you money. You see, if the belt isn't tight enough, it slips, and the fan won't turn like it should. You get less hot air for your money.

If the belt is frayed or looks worn, it must be replaced. Loosen the adjusting bolt on the motor enough to get some slack, then slip the belt off the pulleys. Take the old belt with you when you go to the store to make sure you end up with the right one. When you get back home about four hours later, put the belt back on the pulleys, then tighten the adjustment bolt until you have a ½ inch or so of give when you press on the belt with your finger.

When you buy a new blower-fan belt, buy two. Keep the extra one in a plastic bag on a nail by the furnace. That way, you have an extra on hand when you have a middle-of-the-night, all-the-stores-are-closed, the-house-is-freezing, blown-fan-belt emergency.

If the belt looks fine, but seems to have more than ½ inch of give either way (1 inch total), tighten it by taking up the extra slack using the motor adjusting bolt. Make sure you don't go too far — a too-tight belt damages the motor and fan bearings, and makes a big, expensive mess of things.

While you're in there fooling with the belt, check the pulley alignment by placing a ruler against the pulley faces. The pulleys should line up perfectly, and the belt should travel between them without twisting even a little. If that isn't what you see, loosen the motor pulley mounting bolts and make an adjustment.

Put the hatch back on before you decide to try to fix or adjust anything else!

Checking the ducts for leaks

Take a step back from your furnace, and check the ducts for leaks. The ducts are used to distribute warmed air to various locations throughout the house. A furnace with ducting is known as a central heating system.

If you see fuzz or feel warm air coming out through the joints between duct segments, seal them with metal tape (a new type of duct tape). Yes, for once you'll be using duct tape on ducts!

If you don't already have a carbon monoxide detector, you need to install one. It could give you important early warning of a potentially deadly leak.

Hot-water systems

As with forced-air systems, routine annual inspection and cleaning by a qualified, licensed heating contractor keeps your hot-water system running for many years without trouble. Don't be penny wise and pound foolish. A dirty, inefficient boiler costs you far more than the service call. The serviceman catches little problems before they become big trouble. And a neglected system fails years sooner than a well-maintained one.

Annual service keeps the system running properly and heads off most problems. You should also keep an eye on the system to make sure that all is well between inspections.

Gauging the pressure

Most hot-water systems have only a single gauge, which measures three things: pressure, temperature, and altitude (the height of the water in the system).

It's important to monitor the pressure. Most boilers run with only 12 to 15 pounds of pressure. The boiler can become seriously damaged and even dangerous if the pressure exceeds 30 pounds.

Monitoring the pressure on a regular basis is probably all you ever need to do to maintain your system. The majority of the maintenance tasks should be left to a heating professional. However, if the pressure is abnormally high, you may have a waterlogged expansion tank that can be drained. Before calling in a repairperson attempt to resolve the problem by draining the expansion tank.

Located overhead near the boiler, a conventional expansion tank is cylindrical and has a drain valve at one end. To drain excess water, turn off the power, turn off the water supply to the boiler, and let the tank cool. Attach a garden hose to the valve, open it, and let water out until the levels of the pressure gauges on the boiler and the expansion tank match. Don't forget to close the valve, turn the power back on, and re-open the water supply.

If you have a diaphragm expansion tank, the pressure problem is not too much water — it's too little air. You need to recharge the expansion tank. Use an ordinary tire pressure gauge to check the air pressure. If it is lower than the recommended psi (look on the tank for the correct reading), use a bicycle pump to juice it back up.

Check with a representative from your local building department or public utility to determine which type of expansion tank you have.

Once the expansion tank has been drained or the diaphragm tank refilled, restart the system and monitor it carefully. If the pressure goes back up, turn the system off and call for a professional. You've done all you can do, and it's time to call the experts!

Boilers must have a proper pressure-relief valve, located at the top, which opens when the pressure reaches 30 pounds, to prevent the boiler from exploding.

If you ever see water draining out of the relief valve, chances are the system is operating under excessively high pressure and should be checked by a professional.

Bleeding the radiators

Bleeding radiators is sometimes necessary in even the best of systems. If you have a radiator in your system that just won't heat, chances are it's air-logged. Bleeding the air out of the radiator relieves the pressure and allows the system to fill normally.

To bleed the radiators, just turn the bleed valve about a quarter-turn counter-clockwise and keep the screwdriver or radiator key in the valve. If you hear a hissing sound, that's good — it's air escaping. As soon as the hissing stops and you see a dribble of water come out, close the valve.

Don't open the valve more than is necessary; hot water will come rushing out before you can close it. At the very least, you'll make a wet mess. At the very worst, you could be scalded.

Steam systems

Again, as with forced-air and hot-water systems, it pays to have a professional, licensed heating contractor check your steam system every year. Not only will you save money in the long run through greater efficiency, you'll also have peace of mind, knowing that your system is operating safely. We can't emphasize this enough.

Most adjustments to your steam boiler should be performed by a pro. But there are three important things you can do by yourself:

- ✔ **Check the steam gauge on a regular basis.** Make sure it is within the normal range. If it isn't, shut the system down immediately and call for service.

- ✔ **Check the safety valve every month.** Located on the top of the boiler, this important valve vents excess pressure if the boiler goes crazy and exceeds safe levels. When the system is hot, push down on the handle to see if steam comes out. Make sure to stand away from the outlet — the steam is boiling hot. If no steam comes out, call a serviceman to replace the valve immediately.

✔ **Check the water level once a month.** The water-level gauge has valves on each side. Open them both and make sure the water level is in the middle, and then close the valves. If you didn't see any water, shut off the boiler, let it cool down, and add water.

Because steam systems occasionally need water added, it's better, and more convenient, to have an automatic water valve added to the system. The valve will monitor water levels and add water ever so slowly to avoid damaging the boiler if the system needs it.

You also can do a few things to keep your radiators working well:

✔ **Make sure every radiator slopes slightly toward the steam inlet pipe (that comes out of the wall or floor).** If one doesn't, slip a little ¼-inch-thick rectangle of wood under the feet at the vent end. This prevents those irritating knocking and clanging noises.

✔ **Check the vents to make sure they are not blocked.** Corrosion and paint can keep the vent from venting, and then air trapped in the radiator prevents steam from entering the radiator. If your vent is blocked, replace it. Your local hardware store probably carries them (yours is not the only house in the area with steam heat), and they simply screw off and on.

✔ **Check the position of the inlet valves.** They should be either all the way closed or all the way open. A partially open/shut valve does nothing to regulate the heat, and it causes knocking and clanging.

Got an inlet valve that's leaking? Chances are it's actually leaking at the cap-nuts (the big nuts at the vertical and horizontal connections). Luckily, a leak there can be cured with a little retightening. Get two wrenches — use one to hold the valve and the other to tighten the capnut. If the leak seems to be coming from under the valve handle, take off the valve head and tighten the topmost nut, which (amusingly) is called the *gland nut.*

If neither of those solutions fixes the leak, the valve adapter — the double-ended/double-threaded clunk of brass that connects the valve to the radiator — is probably the culprit. Once again, you need two wrenches to remove the valve, remove the adapter, and install a replacement. After you refill the system, check for leaks and tighten everything again.

Electric systems

Installations of electric heating systems hit their peak in the 1960s, when electric rates were low. But now, at least in areas of the country not adjacent to a hydroelectric dam, the cost of electricity makes these systems very, very expensive to operate. If you have one, you're probably paying twice as much to heat your house as a neighbor with a gas-fired furnace or boiler.

ANECDOTE

A sad story about radiator valve connections

A Chicago friend of ours bought a newly rehabbed condo in an old building with steam heat. He moved in in June, and everything was fine until the first cold night in October, when he was awakened at 4:00 a.m. by a deafening hiss. Finding his bedroom filled with a warm fog, he stumbled naked through his foggy hallway and living room toward the source of the noise and steam — his home office.

When he flipped on the light, he saw a jet of steam roaring out of the radiator's valve/valve adapter connection. The room was filled top-to-bottom with steam, and big drops of condensation fell like rain from the ceiling. Rivulets of water were running down the freshly painted plaster walls, across the vintage moldings, and onto the refinished oak floor. Drops of condensation were falling from the wood sash windows and pooling on the inside sills. The desk chair and area rug were soaking wet, his computer monitor and keyboard were filled with water (the CPU and laser printer were beneath the desk,

luckily), and everything on the desktop was sopping wet.

After he closed the inlet valve (and put on some clothes), he discovered that the valve adapter capnut was screwed on but had not engaged the threads of the valve. And because the contractor hadn't fired up the system and checked all the newly installed radiators for leaks, the misconnection went unnoticed until the first time the heat came on, with terrible results.

Our friend mopped up the best he could, but everything was ruined. The walls, ceiling, windows, and doors had to be repainted (after being washed to remove mineral deposits left by the steam). And all the office furnishings and wet computer equipment had to be replaced. What a mess! But at least he had his contractor to blame — and pay for the damage. You won't have that opportunity if you fail to check your own connections.

That's the bad news. The good news is that electric heating, whether delivered via baseboard convectors or radiant floor or ceiling systems, requires you to do virtually nothing to maintain it. The only two things you have to do:

- ✔ Vacuum the convectors once a month (if you have them).
- ✔ Pay the electricity bill.

Big or Small, an Air Conditioner Cools Y'all

Window units (which also can be installed through the wall), are refrigeration-type air conditioners. Central systems typically are refrigeration units too, but in hot/dry areas, evaporation units (sometimes informally called "swamp coolers") are popular.

Window units: Buy smart and live in cool comfort

Got a 10-year-old window air conditioner? Throw it out! A new unit will be 25 percent more energy efficient. But don't buy just any air conditioner; get one that works efficiently and does all it can to help you keep your electric bill reasonable:

- ✔ Buy the right capacity unit. Measure the room you want to cool and bring the width, length, and height measurements to the store so that the salesperson can help you choose a unit that's efficient for the space.

- ✔ Get a unit with an energy-saving thermostat that cycles the unit on and off.

- ✔ Make sure you get a three-speed fan (high to cool the room quickly and medium or low to maintain the temperature).

- ✔ Choose a model with a timer to turn the unit on before you get home.

As for maintenance, there's not much to do:

- ✔ **Clean the filter on the interior face every month.** Unplug the unit. Pull off the front panel and remove the filter, or slide the filter out the side. Then wash the filter gently in mild detergent, rinse, and dry.

- ✔ **Clean the condenser coil fins on the exterior face at least once a year.** Gently vacuum or brush the fins and then straighten any bent fins with a comb.

Don't ever remove the cover and clean inside the unit. You could get a shock (even when it's unplugged), and all you can do is bend or break something. If you goof up something inside, all you'll have is an ugly doorstop.

Central systems: Let an A/C pro handle maintenance

Maintenance-wise, just change the furnace filters monthly, hose off the exterior unit periodically to remove dust and debris, and most importantly, call a licensed heating/cooling contractor every spring for a thorough inspection and comprehensive maintenance.

If your air conditioner seems dead, or if it is blowing only hot air, check the circuit breakers before you call for service. Nothing makes you feel more stupid than paying a serviceman $75 to flip the breaker back on.

Ventilation: Letting You and Your House Breathe

When we talk about ventilation, we actually are talking about two different things: interior ventilation and structural ventilation.

Proper interior ventilation is vital to the health and comfort of your family. It helps your home rid itself of moisture, smoke, cooking odors, and indoor pollutants. Structural ventilation controls heat levels in the attic, moderates dampness in the crawlspace and basement, and keeps moisture out of uninsulated walls.

Interior ventilation

Kitchens, bathrooms, and laundries are the biggest sources of moisture and odors. The secret to having a non-stinky home is to have three key exhaust units: an exterior-venting range hood and bathroom and laundry exhaust fans.

Many kitchens have a range hood that doesn't actually vent anything — it just "filters" and recycles stovetop air. It's much better to get rid of the greasy, smoky, steamy air, and that requires ductwork to an exterior vent.

If your kitchen is perpetually stinky, and the walls are covered with a thin film of grease, you need to stop eating so much fried food, and you need an exterior-venting exhaust fan. Your favorite appliance retailer can make it happen for you.

Airborne grease makes exhaust fans sticky, which in turn attracts dirt and dust. Clean the grill and fan blades twice a year, or whenever they start to look bad. The filters in recycling range hoods need cleaning every couple of months or so (depending on how/what you cook), and the fan and housing need a good cleaning every six months. If the filters have charcoal pellets inside, they need to be replaced annually. We clean our range hood filter in the dishwasher. Works great. For the grill and fan blades use a spray-on degreaser. (Test the degreaser to make sure it won't remove paint.) Follow with a mild soap and water wash. Finally, flush with fresh water and towel dry.

Bathrooms generate huge amounts of moisture and some unpleasant odors — especially at my brother's house. If you've got incurable mildew in the shower, paint peeling off the walls, or a lingering funky smell, you need to either install an exhaust fan or get a bigger, higher-capacity fan. Exhaust fans can be installed to vent the bad air through the wall or through the ceiling and attic. Call an electrical contractor to do the work, not your brother-in-law.

Steamy air, hairspray, and other grooming products create a tacky surface that attracts dust, dirt, and fuzz at an alarming rate. Clean the housing, grill, and fan at least twice a year. Use the same techniques for cleaning that we suggested in the preceding section.

Structural ventilation

To keep heat and moisture from roasting and rotting your home over time, it's important to have adequate ventilation in the attic and the crawlspace (and the basement if it is unfinished).

In the attic, the idea is to create an upward flow of air. Cool air flows in through vents in the eaves and out through vent(s) nearer to, or at the peak of, the roof. In the crawlspace, cross-ventilation is utilized.

If insulation, crud, or dead squirrels block the vents, or if there are not enough vents, the attic and subarea can become tropical. Rot can develop. Condensed water can soak insulation, making it ineffective. Condensation from above and below can make its way into the house, ruining ceiling, floor, and wall finishes, and short-circuiting electrical wiring. If you notice that your vents are clogged, clear them immediately.

Building codes specify how much ventilation you need. As a general rule, have 1 square foot of vent area for every 150 square feet of attic area or crawlspace. We think more is better.

Roof ventilation

If your attic space is hot and humid in the summer, you may need to install additional vents at the eaves and at the ridge of the roof. Assuming you're not a trained carpenter, we think it's best to leave this kind of work to a professional, someone who knows his way around the roof structure and knows how to install leak-free roof penetrations.

Yep, even venting must be maintained. Make sure that each vent and screen is painted (to prevent deterioration) and that the screens are secure to the frame of the vent. Animals, baseballs, and other common household missiles have a way of dislodging vent screens. Badly damaged vents should be replaced. Solid vent screens prevent varmints of all sorts from settling in your attic.

Cardboard baffles can be stapled to the rafters inside the attic adjacent to the vents. The baffles prevent insulation from being blown into piles, leaving bare spots.

Moist air can cause rot in the crawlspace too, attacking your home from below. Just like the attic space, crawlspaces need a good flow of fresh air. If your crawlspace is always overly damp, or you see mildew on the walls or structure, you may need better ventilation.

Extra vents are difficult to install, and require special tools to cut through lumber, concrete block, concrete, and brick. Don't go poking holes in your foundation on your own — call a carpenter or masonry contractor to do the work. They have the know-how, tools, and experience to do the job right.

Foundation ventilation

Foundation vents can be damaged in the same way as eave vents. In fact, because they are closer to the ground, there is greater potential for damage. Critters that can't get into your attic will settle for the area beneath the floor. Establish a no-holes policy. Maintain foundation vents in the same way that we have suggested for eave vents.

If your crawlspace has a dirt floor, you may be able to avoid adding vents by installing a plastic vapor barrier. See Chapter 3 to find out how to do this.

Chapter 15

Fireplaces

● ●

In This Chapter

▶ Preventing your home from being leveled by a chimney fire

▶ Burning the right fuel

▶ Getting a fire going, safely

▶ Repairing fireplace cracks

▶ Cleaning and adjusting glass doors and screens

▶ Getting soot off of your face — your fireplace face, that is

● ●

*(1*DG) - North Pole. Well-informed sources have it that Ol' St. Nick has been forced to replace his bright red uniform with a new one as a result of extensive soiling due to unusually dirty fireplaces last holiday season.

While we are sure that St. Nick's wardrobe concerns many, there are other more critical reasons to keep your fireplace and chimney clean and in good working order. A dirty chimney not only diminishes the effectiveness of a fireplace, but, with severe neglect, could be the cause of a chimney fire. And, chimney fires lead to house fires.

The U.S. Consumer Product Safety Commission reports that some 23,600 residential fires were related to solid-fuel appliances and equipment in 1996. An additional 5,500 fires were attributed to chimneys and chimney connectors serving heating systems burning liquid and other fuels. As a result of these fires, 130 people died, 2,300 people were injured, and total property losses were set at more than $184.4 million. These fires may have been prevented by burning the right fuel and by regular chimney inspection, cleaning, and repair.

Fundamental Fireplace Facts

Natural gas, electricity, and oil are the most prevalent fuel sources for modern home heating systems. However, before these modern resources were available, the fireplace or wood stove was the sole source of heat in a home. Although the fireplace can't compete with modern heating systems as an energy and cost-efficient source of heat, the fireplace remains one of the most popular features in a home.

There are two basic styles of fireplace construction: masonry and prefabricated metal (also called *zero clearance*). The former set the standard for fireplace construction until the late 1970s when the latter became a popular and affordable alternative for builders and home buyers. The different fireplace styles operate in essentially the same fashion. Both have a firebox, damper, flue, and spark arrestor. Both types of fireplaces are typically outfitted with a mesh screen and glass doors.

True to its name, a masonry fireplace is custom-built of brick and mortar. The firebox is constructed of firebricks, and the flue consists of brick or a clay or terra cotta liner (see Figure 15-1). Firebricks and the mortar that surrounds them are intended to withstand extreme temperatures.

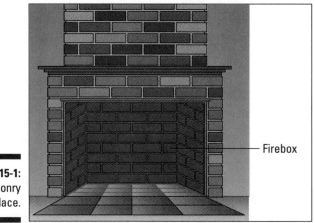

— Firebox

Figure 15-1:
A masonry
fireplace.

On the other hand, a prefabricated metal fireplace is installed and assembled on-site. The metal box contains firebrick panels (see Figure 15-2), called *refractory brick panels,* that line the sides, back, and bottom of the firebox. The flue for a prefabricated fireplace consists of a metal pipe that is concealed by a chimney constructed of plywood or another siding material.

In both cases, the hearth and fireplace face can be constructed of brick, stone, or another decorative finish.

Many people use a fireplace as a secondary source of heat during winter. For others, a crackling fire and the aroma that accompanies it can simply be the source of many pleasurable moments. In either case, a poorly maintained fireplace can spell disaster.

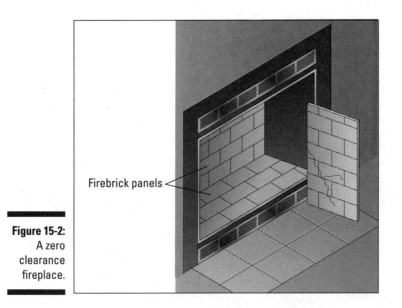

Firebrick panels

Figure 15-2:
A zero
clearance
fireplace.

Failing to maintain your fireplace properly can lead to a chimney fire. Chimney fires occur when combustible deposits on the inner walls of the chimney ignite. These explosive deposits, called *creosote,* are a natural byproduct of combustion. A fire hazard exists if ⅛ to ¼ inch of creosote (or more) coats the inner walls of the chimney, creating a time bomb waiting to go off. A chimney fire can literally level your house.

One thing stops creosote from becoming a problem: a fireplace inspection and sweeping by a professional chimney sweep at least once annually or after burning one cord of wood — whichever comes first. More frequent cleanings may be required, based on the type of wood burned, the type of appliance, and the frequency of use. In general, an older, uncertified wood stove, or any appliance that is used frequently, requires more than one cleaning per year.

Prefabricated metal fireplaces often need more frequent cleaning. They burn cooler, allowing a higher degree of condensation of combustion deposits on the interior surface of the fireplace flue.

According to the National Chimney Sweep Guild (www.ncsg.org), a national trade association comprised of chimney sweeps, a visual inspection is all that is normally required for most chimneys. In the case where a visual inspection is neither possible nor adequate, many chimney sweeps are equipped to do more elaborate inspections with a video camera and monitor referred to as a "chimscan." The chimscan is more costly than a visual inspection, but will reveal more and better information about the condition of a chimney. This is especially important when the integrity of the flue is in question due to age or damage from an earthquake or chimney fire.

Understanding combustion

As firewood burns, it goes through three phases: water, smoke, and charcoal.

Up to half the weight of a freshly cut log is water. After proper seasoning, only about 20 percent of its weight is water. As the wood is heated in the firebox, this water boils off, consuming heat energy in the process. The wetter the wood, the more heat energy is consumed. That's why wet wood hisses and sizzles while dry wood ignites and burns easily.

As the wood heats up above the boiling point of water, it begins to smoke. The hydrocarbon gases and tars that make up the smoke are combustible if the temperature is high enough and oxygen is present. When the smoke burns, it makes the bright flames that are characteristic of wood combustion. If the smoke doesn't burn in the firebox, it may condense in the chimney, forming creosote. (See "Fundamental Fireplace Facts" earlier in this chapter.)

As the fire progresses and most of the hydrocarbons vaporize, charcoal remains. Charcoal is almost 100 percent carbon, and it burns with very little flame or smoke. Charcoal is a good fuel that burns easily and cleanly when enough oxygen is present.

Of the total energy content of the wood you burn, about half is in the form of smoke and half is charcoal. The challenge in burning wood efficiently is to burn off the smoke before it leaves the firebox.

Treating Your Fireplace Well

The first step to having a healthy, well-maintained fireplace is to burn the right fuel. Being choosy about what you burn improves heating efficiency and helps the environment, too.

Your fireplace is not an incinerator! Don't burn garbage, treated or painted wood, plastic, rubber, or any other non-recommended material. In addition to causing an unfavorable buildup on the interior of the firebox and chimney, these materials also produce noxious fumes which pollute the air (inside and outside of the home). Thus, being careful about what you burn is the first line of defense against a catastrophic house-leveling chimney fire.

Even if you're careful about what you burn, you still need to be concerned about creosote buildup (see the previous section).

Buying fuel for the fire

Unlike modern heating fuels, which are almost always supplied to the heating appliance by a local utility or fuel company, fireplace fuel, wood, is something that most people shop for.

Some people are as picky about the wood that they burn in the fireplace as they are about what they put on in the morning. Others would just as soon burn whatever comes along, including household garbage. We assure you, there is a happy medium. You don't need to be a Boy Scout to have the perfect fire; however, you should know a few things about wood that make for a stronger, safer, and cleaner fire.

First, be mindful of log length; logs should be 16 to 22 inches long. Anything longer will likely not fit in your firebox.

With all the choices of firewood out there, what's best to burn? Osage orange wood, oak, hard maple, madrone, hickory, ash, walnut, locust, apple, cherry, peach, and plum are the top-burning hardwoods. Mixed hardwoods burn longer and cleaner with less creosote buildup in the chimney than softer woods such as willow, poplar, pine, and cedar. Fortunately, most dealers don't sell softwoods and recommend mixed hardwoods.

Seasoning is of equal importance when shopping for wood. We're not talking about the kind of seasoning that you sprinkle on chicken, fish, or beef. We're talking about aging.

Forty-four percent more heat can be generated from a seasoned log. A clean-burning fire is a hotter fire with good drafting conditions that produce cleaner combustion and less smoke from the chimney.

Unseasoned (green) wood won't burn well due to its high moisture content. A sure sign of an unseasoned log is when it is extremely heavy and sap is oozing out of it. With seasoned wood, the sap has dried up and the logs are lighter. Green or improperly seasoned wood is free of checking and cracks on the ends, feels heavier, and may even feel moist to the touch. Often it also gives off more odor than dry wood. When it burns, it often sizzles and pops and gives off steam.

To tell if wood is seasoned, knock two logs together. Well-seasoned logs makes a sharp ringing sound. Also, a piece of dry, seasoned firewood has large cracks or checks in the end grain. Look for these when judging the quality of firewood.

If your wood is not properly seasoned when you buy it, you can do it yourself at home. To properly season wood, split the logs as soon as possible and stack them in a dry spot for 6 to 18 months. Pile the wood loosely, allowing air to circulate through the split logs. Hardwoods take longer to dry than softwoods; humidity and temperature levels also impact drying time.

Dry, seasoned wood ignites and burns much easier and causes fewer problems with condensation and creosote. There's that nasty word again.

If most of your fires consist of manufactured firelogs, you'll be pleased to know that independent tests have proven that manufactured firelogs burn much cleaner than firewood.

The manufactured firelog is an example of how recycling can work. It was created in the 1960s when companies were seeking a productive way to dispose of waste sawdust. Manufactured firelogs combine two industrial byproducts, sawdust and petroleum wax, which are mixed and extruded into familiar log-like shapes.

Manufactured firelogs are generally individually wrapped with paper and require no kindling or starting material. This convenient manufactured fireplace fuel product provides a safe, environmentally responsible alternative to firewood and natural gas logs.

Many areas of the country are enacting local wood burning control ordinances and implementing "no-burn" days. However, independent research shows that manufactured firelogs provide home owners with an alternative to help reduce emissions from residential fireplace use.

A recent study conducted by Science Application International Corporation/OMNI (SAIC/OMNI), and the Oregon Department of Energy indicates that firelogs are a cleaner source of fireplace fuel than natural cord wood. These tests found that firelogs produced 69 percent less particulate matter, 88 percent less carbon monoxide, and 50 percent less opacity (visible smoke).

Many local air quality officials now recommend manufactured firelogs as a clean burning alternative fuel for residential fireplace use.

Storing firewood

Well-seasoned firewood brings the promise of crackling fires on a cold winter's eve. Unfortunately, firewood can also bring some unwanted household pests, termites, along. Don't store firewood in the garage, under a carport, or against the house. This is an open invitation to pests to make your home their home. These pests don't just want to visit — they want to take a piece of your home with them.

Store firewood at least 10 feet from the house and no less than 6 inches off of the ground to avoid infestation. We recommend that you create a platform for your wood using concrete blocks and boards.

Lay the concrete blocks on their sides in a row and place fence boards on top of the blocks from end to end. Be sure to leave gaps between the boards to promote airflow. Stack the wood loosely, alternating each row perpendicular to the next. If the logs are split, store them with the bark side up to help shed rain.

Starting or rekindling the fire safely

Starting a fire the right way helps keep your fireplace healthy by preventing smoking and a buildup of particulate matter in the flue. A poorly lit fire can allow the chimney to backdraft and fill your house with smoke.

The key to starting a fire is to use plenty of crumpled newspaper and kindling. With the damper open, fill the firebox completely with loosely crumpled newspaper and hold it down with at least ten pieces of finely split, dry kindling. Softwoods make the best kindling because they ignite easily and burn rapidly — producing minimal heat. This is just the opposite of what you want your firewood to do.

Another method of starting a fire is to preheat the flue. Make a torch out of several pieces of newspaper, open the damper, light one end, and stick it up the flue to warm the flue. When a draft is established, light the kindling. Once the kindling is burning, add pieces of larger wood. Be careful not to smother the fire with pieces of wood that are too large.

Don't overload the firebox and never use flammable liquids to start a fire.

To improve combustion in the firebox, install a layer of firebrick at the base of the firebox. The bricks needn't be mortared in. This process elevates the fire and diminishes the size of the firebox, which can contribute to a better burning fire.

Staying on Top of Fireplace Cracks

In a masonry fireplace, firebrick is used to construct the firebox (the place where you burn the wood). Refractory brick panels line the firebox of a prefabricated metal fireplace. In both cases, the bricks and fireclay mortar are designed to withstand extreme temperatures. However, over time, the brick, mortar, or panels can crack and crumble, creating a serious fire hazard.

If a brick in a brick fireplace cracks, follow the steps outlined in the section "A Few "Pointers" on Brick and Block Foundations" in Chapter 3 to patch the brick.

If the brick is crumbling, it should be replaced with a new firebrick embedded in refractory mortar.

Crumbling mortar joints in a firebox should be chiseled out and replaced with new refractory mortar (see Chapter 3). (Refractory mortar is specially designed to withstand high temperatures.) This process, known as *tuckpointing,* is the same as replacing or repairing mortar joints in any brick structure. The only difference is that in a firebox, the mortar must withstand extreme temperatures.

If the integrity of the majority of the firebrick and mortar in the firebox is in question, a qualified chimney sweep or masonry contractor should inspect it. If replacement is in order, this is a job that is best left to a pro.

Repairing minor cracks and mortar joints in prefabricated metal fireplaces is essentially the same as with a brick firebox with one exception. If a panel develops extensive cracks or is beginning to crumble, it should be replaced with a new panel.

To make the job of finding a replacement easy, you need to jot down the fireplace make and model number. It can be found on a metal plate just inside the opening of the firebox. Give this information to the manufacturer or an installing dealer. Although replacement panels are often a stock item, a special order may be required. This can take from a few days to a couple of weeks. Don't use the fireplace until a full and final repair has been made.

This is a job that most do-it-yourselfers can handle. Remove the old panel by unscrewing the screws that hold it in place. The new panel should fit snugly against the adjoining panels. When replacing a rear panel, the side panels must first be removed. Refractory mortar is not generally needed as the corners are designed to fit snugly against one another.

Dealing with the Damper

The damper is a steel or cast-iron door that opens or closes the throat of the firebox into the flue. It regulates draft and prevents the loss of heat up the chimney.

The fireplace damper must be in the full open position in order to start a fire. Once the fire has started, the damper should be closed down as far as possible without causing smoke to back up into the room. Doing so allows the chimney to exhaust all the smoke that is created by the fire, but not the heat.

Often, a damper becomes difficult to operate or sticks in one position. One of the most pervasive causes of a stuck damper is rust, often caused when rainwater enters the chimney through a faulty or non-existent chimney cap (see "Arresting sparks and other hazards" later in this chapter).

A dirty or rusty damper can best be cleaned using a wire brush along with lots of elbow grease. But, be advised that you're not going to like it. Wearing safety goggles, work gloves, a hat and old clothing; armed with a wire brush in one hand and a flashlight in the other, use the wire brush to remove soot and rust buildup (see Figure 15-3).

If after cleaning the damper, it still sticks, it's time for a little horsepower in the form of a pipe and small sledgehammer. Slide a short length of pipe — about 20 to 24 inches — over the damper handle. This extends the damper handle and allows you to beat on the pipe with the sledgehammer to break the damper loose. If the damper still refuses to budge, use cutting oil to help dissolve the rust.

Once the damper is operational, work it back and forth while applying a high-temperature lubricant at all of the joints and moving parts. Once clean and in good operating order, spray paint the damper with a black high-temperature paint to prevent future rusting.

Fireplaces without dampers or with faulty dampers can be retrofitted with a new damper. Unlike the style of damper located immediately above the fire-box, a retrofit model is mounted at the top of the chimney and is operated by a long chain that hangs down the chimney.

Caring for the Outside of Your Chimney

While it's important to care for the inside of your fireplace, chimney, and damper, don't forget the outside as well.

A chimney can be either an exposed pipe, a framed enclosure that is covered with siding ("a sided chase") that houses the flue pipe, or a masonry chimney. In all cases, the chimney travels from the inside of the home to the outside either through an attic and roof or out a wall. The point where the chimney exits the structure is a primary source of leaks. Thus, the flashing that surrounds this location should be water-tested (as should all other flashing) using a garden hose to make sure that it is in good condition and leak-free.

If your chimney is "in the buff," the metal pipe can be attacked by rust and the joints can become loose. Use a wire brush to remove the rust. Prime and paint the rusted area with high-temperature paint. Use a screwdriver to tighten screws at all connections. Install new self-tapping sheetmetal screws at locations where screws were previously installed and worked loose. Remove an existing screw and use it as an example when purchasing replacement screws.

Masonry fireplaces have a unique flashing detail called a *masonry counter flashing.* This secondary piece of flashing covers the primary flashing that is immediately adjacent to the roofing. The counter flashing has a slight lip that is inserted into a mortar joint and then either mortared or caulked into place. The caulking or mortar should be water-tested annually and should be repaired or replaced as needed.

A coat of paint helps to hide otherwise unattractive flashing and prevents it from deteriorating quite as rapidly.

Sealing the deal

In areas where the climate gets unusually cold, we've actually seen unsealed brick on chimneys shatter. Water enters the pores of the brick, freezes, and then expands, causing the brick to literally explode.

Water seepage and the damage to brick and mortar caused by freeze and thaw cycles can be prevented by applying a coat of top-quality masonry sealer to all the brick or stone surrounding the fireplace and chimney. The sealer can be applied with a pump garden sprayer, roller, or brush. Chimney sweeps usually keep masonry sealers in stock.

Arresting sparks and other hazards

A *spark arrestor* is a cage-like device with a solid cap, which is secured to the top of the chimney (see Figure 15-4). It prevents sparks and ash from escaping and causing a fire on the roof or other potentially flammable substances. It also keeps squirrels, birds, and raccoons from nesting in the chimney. Nesting materials can cause a serious safety hazard. Their droppings pose health risks because diseases may be transmitted through fecal materials.

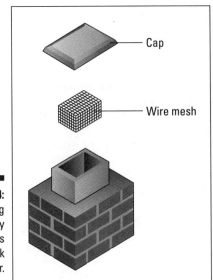

Figure 15-4:
Arresting
chimney
problems
with a spark
arrestor.

Cap

Wire mesh

The solid cap — usually metal — prevents rainwater from entering the chimney. Rainwater can cause significant damage to the interior of a chimney. It can combine with the creosote to produce an acid that breaks down the flue lining and mortar. Rainwater also causes the damper to rust.

If your chimney doesn't have a spark arrestor, install one. If it does, make sure that it is in good condition and is securely fastened to the top of the chimney. Check to make sure that there are no holes in the wire mesh and that the cap is not rusting or deteriorated. If you find holes in the mesh screen of your spark arrestor or if you should accidentally make a hole or two while attempting to remove rust with a wire brush, try patching the holes before replacing the entire unit. The method used to patch the spark arrestor screen is similar to the process used when patching a window screen. However, don't use window screen material to make the patch. Use galvanized wire mesh to match what exists. (See "Repairing Window Screens" in Chapter 5 for more information.)

A rusting chimney cap can be patched using a small piece of galvanized sheet metal that is slightly larger than the damaged area. Attach the patch using pop rivets. You'll need pop rivets, a pop rivet gun, and an electric drill with a bit that corresponds to the size of the pop rivets.

If rust is a problem, see Chapter 9 for tips on how to remove rust.

Once clean and repaired, the spark arrestor should be painted to prevent future rust and slow deterioration.

Cleaning a Soot-Covered Brick Fireplace Face

Oils and soot make an otherwise handsome brick fireplace face look tired and tattered. To reduce the effect of oils and soot, regularly vacuum a brick face and hearth and periodically wipe them down with a damp sponge. Also, you can prevent smoke from staining your fireplace face by elevating the fire; simply add a layer or two of firebrick at the bottom of the firebox.

If the hearth is soiled to the extent where you can no longer determine what material it is constructed from, then it's time for a more serious cleaning.

All you need is a 10-percent solution of muriatic acid. (That's 1 part muriatic acid to 9 parts water. Add the acid to the water.) Use a bristle brush to clean the affected area and rinse with fresh water. More than one application may be required for extra dirty areas.

Working with acid is dangerous. Be sure to wear rubber gloves, safety goggles, and have plenty of ventilation.

Making the Most out of Glass Doors and Screens

A fireplace exhausts smoke in a sort of siphon action. Once heat begins to rise through the stack, the siphon continues to draw air from within the house. Isn't it interesting that a heat-generating devise can actually remove warm air from the home? To offset the problem, install glass doors and add outside air ducts to the inside of the firebox.

Glass doors act as dampers when the fireplace is not being used and reduce the amount of warm air that is drawn out of the home and into the fireplace when a fire has been reduced to embers.

Outside air ducts (also known as *combustion air ducts*) are required in the construction of all new fireplaces and can be retrofitted into existing ones. Fires burn oxygen, and in a tightly sealed home, a fireplace drains a home of oxygen in no time. Combustion air ducts provide air from the exterior of the home, leaving oxygen in the home for you to breathe. Naturally, if the fireplace draws air from ducts it won't need to draw warm air from within the home. Periodically check these ducts to make sure that they are clean and free of spider webs and other debris.

A major fireplace-cleaning Advanage

We were once hired to enlarge a family room for a customer in a nearby community. During one of our regular visits to the project, we noticed that our customer had replaced her brick fireplace face. We were kind of hurt that she hadn't asked us to bid the work and asked her if we had done something to offend her. She smiled and told us that she was very satisfied with the work that we were doing and that all she had done was clean the brick. It hadn't been replaced. We were relieved to discover that we hadn't lost our customer's confidence, but we were even more amazed at how clean and new the brick fireplace face looked.

We asked what she had done to get it so clean. She said that she didn't know the name of the cleaning product, but that the bottle was under her sink. She said that a door-to-door salesman had sold it to her. The product was called Advanage (Advantage without the "t"). We were in such awe that we immediately contacted the Chicago-based manufacturer, Austin Diversified Products. We proposed that they send us 100 sample bottles of the product so that we could do a consumer test, and we did. We wanted to see if our customer's fireplace cleaning was a fluke. The results were amazing.

Ninety-nine out of the hundred raved about the concentrated cleaning product and its unique cleaning ability. The one lady who said that she couldn't get the soot off of her fireplace indicated that is was probably because she had varnished over it the year before. You can get information on this great product by visiting the company's Web site at www.advanage.com or telephoning 1-800-323-6444.

Cleaning glass fireplace doors

Here is a neat trick that keeps glass fireplace doors clean and neat year round. Once the doors have cooled, spray them with glass or window cleaner or your own mixture of vinegar and water. Then spray a clean soft cloth until a wet spot is created. Dip the wet spot into the fine gray ash left by your last fire and rub the ash onto the dirty surface. The ash fills the microscopic pores of the glass, thus reducing the surface tension, making it clean easier than ever before. After the ash has dried to a haze, the glass can be buffed clear with a clean, dry cloth.

Oven cleaner also works well for cleaning smoke-covered glass doors. Make sure to wear rubber gloves, eye protection, have plenty of ventilation, and follow manufacturer's directions.

Giving sluggish glass doors a pickup

If your fireplace doors are operating less than smoothly, some cleaning, a little lubrication, or a slight adjustment usually fixes these problems.

Most doors can be raised and lowered or adjusted from side to side using a screwdriver or a small open-end wrench. Make a small adjustment and open and close the door until it operates smoothly (see Figure 15-5). Hinges and other moving parts should be lightly lubricated with a high-temperature lubricant available from most fireplace dealers.

Since not all doors are alike (some are swinging, others are bifold), your best bet is to refer to the owners manual for specific information on how to adjust the doors. If you're unable to find the manual, visit a local fireplace shop.

Figure 15-5:
Adjusting a glass fire-place door.

Screening out difficulties

Fireplace screens have been around a lot longer than glass doors. However, even with glass doors, a fireplace screen is essential for safe fire. The mesh screen prevents sparks from flying onto the carpet or flooring in front of the fireplace and causing a fire.

Keep in mind that glass doors are designed for energy efficiency and not to prevent sparks from flying onto the carpet. Consequently, doors are left open when a fire is burning. There is an exception to this rule. Glass doors can be used as an added layer of protection when you need to leave the house while hot embers remain in the fireplace.

Some screens are freestanding, others are bolted to the fireplace face, and still others are an integral part of the glass door system. Although the free-standing models can be decorative, they offer the least amount of protection, thus, we suggest replacing or augmenting a freestanding screen with one of the other alternatives available.

Most screens include a metal rod. As the screen and rod become dirty, the screen becomes increasingly difficult to operate. Therefore, the top of the screen and rod should be periodically vacuumed using an upholstery attachment. Wiping with a damp sponge followed by a touch of high-temperature lubricant keeps the screen gliding.

Just as with every other surface near the fireplace, the screen can develop a buildup of soot and oils from combustion. Rust can also be a problem. Although many cleaning products can cut the grease, some screens are just too dirty to be cleaned this way. If yours happens to be the latter, there are a couple of effective alternatives — oven cleaner or ammonia.

In both of the following cases, we suggest that the screen be removed and that the cleaning task be performed in a bathtub or outdoors.

If the screen is affected by rust, use a wire brush to remove as much of the rust as possible. (Make sure to wear eye protection and work gloves.) Next, apply a light coat of oven cleaner to the entire surface of the screen. In addition to the eye protection and gloves, you need lots of ventilation when using oven cleaner — not a problem if performing this task outdoors. Allow the oven cleaner to do its thing and then rinse thoroughly with fresh water.

Once the screen has dried, it should be painted with a heat-resistant matte black spray paint. Doing this every few years keeps your fireplace screen looking like new.

Ammonia is a great alternative to oven cleaner. Remove the screens from the fireplace and place them in a large plastic trash bag. Pour in 1 cup of ammonia, seal the bag, and allow it to sit overnight. The ammonia takes all of the elbow grease out of cleaning the screens. Remove the screens, rinse, and paint.

Removing paint on a brick fireplace face

Peel Away is a non-solvent, biodegradable, paint and varnish remover manufactured by Dumond Chemicals, Inc. A green paste, Peel Away is applied with a brush or roller. The paste is then covered with a fibrous laminated cloth that controls evaporation and is left on until the paint dissolves. The fabric along with multiple layers of paint is removed in one fell swoop. For further information on the Peel Away Paint Removal System, contact the folks at Dumond at (212) 869-6350.

Chapter 16

Walls and Ceilings

● ●

In This Chapter

▶ Keeping walls and ceilings looking great

▶ Patching cracks in walls and plaster

▶ Painting for the uninitiated

▶ Maintaining wallpaper and paneling

● ●

*I*t doesn't take much to mess up a wall or ceiling. And as they say, stuff happens: A missing door bumper lets the knob punch a nice round hole. A shift in the foundation results in a 5-foot hairline crack. A heavy dresser leaves dozens of dents as it's carried down the hallway. A little kid's crayon makes unpaintable purple squiggles. An area of plaster ceiling loses its grip and sags. A flailing hockey stick rips the wallpaper. Careless movers use the couch to make a 3-foot gouge. An oily hand permanently dirties the basement stairway wall.

We thought we might mention that drywall and paint repairs are purely cosmetic. However, they can have a great deal to do with how people perceive your home. There really isn't any difference between a worn-out coat of paint, a gouged chunk of wallboard, and a broken window. When they are in good repair, they look great and so does your home — and that means happy occupants and top resale value.

Life is hard on walls and ceilings. Luckily, most maintenance to these surfaces is well within your reach.

Don't Let Cracks Crack up Your Drywall

Chances are the walls and ceilings of your home are made of drywall (also referred to as *wallboard, gypsum board,* or *Sheetrock*). Drywall is both easy to damage and easy to repair.

Drywall gets two kinds of damage: gouges and hairline cracks. Gouges are usually caused by accident — by you, an angry spouse, a guest, or the previous owner. Hairline cracks are usually caused by movement in the foundation or framing of the house, which is nobody's fault. The frame of your house expands and contracts with the seasons, as temperature and humidity levels change. As we mentioned, both can be easily repaired.

Got a small crack? Fill it with a flexible silicone caulk. The silicone will flex as the crack widens and narrows with normal house movement. Filling a crack with drywall joint compound or spackle isn't such a good idea. Spackle's brittleness allows the crack to come back year after year, until you take a hammer and pound a dozen frustration holes in the wall. Or maybe that's just how we would handle it.

Caulking is easy — just follow these steps:

1. **Buy a fresh tube of silicone caulking (the paintable kind).**

   The old tube in the basement has probably dried out, making it useless.

2. **Use a caulking gun to spread a thin bead of the caulk into the crack.**

3. **Wipe the excess from around the crack with alcohol (rubbing alcohol is perfect).**

4. **Coat the repair with primer.**

   Don't skip this step or you'll end up with a permanently goofy-looking, non-matching area.

5. **Repaint, as necessary.**

Silicone caulking also works for little nail holes.

Bigger cracks require a different kind of maintenance. Here's what you need:

- 6-inch taping knife
- 10- or 12-inch taping knife
- 1 square piece of plywood or a plastic mud pan
- Drywall compound
- Drywall tape (paper or fiberglass)
- Fine-grit sandpaper and a sanding block

Here's how to stop that crack dead in its tracks:

1. **Clean out the crack so that there are no loose "crumbs."**

2. **Put a blob of compound on the plywood or mud pan.**

   This makes it easy to load compound onto the knife.

3. **Use the 6-inch taping knife to apply a light coating of compound to the crack and then immediately embed the tape in the compound.**

   Use the knife to wipe the tape into the compound and scrape away any compound that squishes out.

   If necessary, cut the tape in short lengths to follow the line of a really crooked crack.

   Fiberglass tape is self-stick, so you skip the embedding coat of compound under the tape. Otherwise, you do everything the same way. Be aware, though, that fiberglass tape is a little thicker than paper tape, so it is more difficult to make a completely invisible repair. We prefer the tried-and-true paper tape, and we think you'll get better results with it. But some people are rebels.

4. **Apply a thin coat of compound over the tape and smooth it with the taping knife, making sure to feather the edges.**

   Let the patch dry completely (usually overnight).

5. **Apply a second, smoothing coat using the wide knife, again making sure to feather the edges.**

   Let the second coat dry completely.

6. **Apply a third (and, with luck, final) coat.**

   Let third coat dry completely.

7. **Sand the patch until smooth.**

8. **Apply a coat of good-quality primer.**

9. **Paint to match.**

Putting the Stop on Nail Pops

Nail pops are those nail head bumps or crescent-shaped cracks in the wall or ceiling. They occur when nails work themselves loose, literally popping out above the surface of the drywall. Unfortunately, they happen for as long as you own your home. If you get one, you need to fix it.

In addition to the tools mentioned in the previous section you will need:

- Hammer
- Drill or driver

> ✔ Nail set (or large nail)
>
> ✔ 1⅝-inch drywall screws
>
> ✔ 1⅝-inch drywall nails

Here's how you do the repair:

1. **Drive new drywall screws into the wall stud or ceiling joist a couple of inches on either side of the popped fastener.**

   The screws should pull the drywall tight against the framing, and the screw heads should barely dimple into the drywall.

2. **Use the hammer and nail set to drive a new nail immediately adjacent to the existing one.**

   Try to nail the new nail into the same hole as the old one. Part of the head of the new nail will overlap the head of the old nail. Use the nail set to slightly recess the new nail (about a ⅟₁₆ of an inch). The head of the new nail will prevent the old nail from slipping out again.

3. **With the 6-inch taping knife, apply a smooth, flat coat of compound over the dimpled heads of the new fasteners and the hole left by the old nail.**

   Let the compound dry completely.

4. **Lightly sand the patch with the fine-grit sandpaper.**

5. **Apply a second coat of compound. Let the compound dry, and then lightly sand it again.**

6. **Prime and paint.**

You can find nail pops (and other defects) by shining bright light at a shallow angle to the wall. Set a floor lamp about a foot from the wall in question, put in a 100-watt bulb and remove the lampshade. Voilà! You'll be amazed at how the nail pops pop out at you.

How to Be a Class-A Hole-Filler

Joint compound alone is not enough to fill anything larger than a quarter. You've got to put something into the hole or onto it and then use compound to make it smooth and invisible.

Holes that are too large to fill with compound, but are no more than a 4 or 5 inches across, can be patched with a precut stick-on patch and some joint compound. Use a peel-and-stick patch. Made of stiff metal mesh, these patches can be placed over the hole and covered with two or three coats (or more) of compound. Here's how:

1. **Cover the hole with the stick-on patch.**

2. **Smear compound over the entire area, feathering the edges. Here, less is more.**

   A thin layer of compound at a time is the big secret. A thick layer is diffi-cult to sand and shows up on the wall as a bump. Let the compound dry completely.

3. **Sand lightly.**

4. **Smooth more compound over the patch.**

   Let the compound dry completely. A third and fourth coat can be applied by repeating this step.

5. **Sand, prime, and paint.**

Holes that are too big for a metal patch require a little different technique. A patch must be made with drywall. The easiest and most effective way to make such a repair is to use drywall clips. These little metal wonders strad-dle the edge of the hole and create a "shelf" along the back edge of the wall-board, giving you something into which you can screw a cut-to-fit patch. Here's how it's done:

1. **Cut a square or rectangular patch from a piece of scrap drywall. Make sure it will completely cover the hole.**

2. **Hold the patch over the hole and trace its outline with a pencil.**

3. **Use a utility knife or drywall saw to cut away everything inside the outline.**

   Watch out for wires and pipes!

4. **Install drywall clips on all sides of the hole (no more than 12 inches apart) and secure them using the screws provided with the clips.**

5. **Insert the patch into the hole and drive screws through the patch into the clips.**

6. **Snap off the temporary tabs of the clips (the ones that extend from the edge of the hole onto the face of the wall).**

To complete a large patch, simply follow the finishing process for a smaller patch in the preceding section. With larger patches the only difference is that the joint tape must be applied all four joints of the patch (top, bottom, and sides).

When we started in the business, we thought that the only way to fix really big holes was to cut away the damaged area to reveal the studs on either side, then install a new, cut-to-fit piece of drywall. Although almost nothing's

---

Re-creating texture

If your walls have a textured surface, you need to re-create that texture on the patched area. Does the surface look swirly, flattened-bumps, or just plain bumpy?

For the swirly finish, place blobs of compound evenly throughout the patched area, then swirl (what did you expect?) a damp sponge through the blobs until the area is evenly covered. Try to duplicate the swirls on the rest of the wall. Almost any implement can be used that will duplicate the original pattern (a drywall knife, a paintbrush, a roller).

For the flattened-bumps finish, use spray texture in a can. Simply spray the texture on, and then, using one of various size spray-tips, apply a light, medium, or heavy pattern. Wait a few minutes and use a drywall knife to slightly flatten the bumps. A portable pump also can be used for larger areas.

Don't be in a hurry. Wiping the bumps when they are too wet will completely flatten them, and you will have a mess.

For the bumpy finish, use the procedure in the preceding paragraph but omit the flattening step.

Practice your texturing technique on a scrap piece of cardboard, plywood or drywall. You only get one whack at the real thing.

---

changed — we have learned that there is another way to fix cantaloupe-sized cavities or water-damaged areas without cutting back to the studs. The steps are the same — patch, compound, sand, compound, sand, texture, prime, paint.

Instead of cutting back to the studs, we simply cut away the damage and install wood backing. You use the same principal as the clip method. A narrow strip of plywood is attached to the back of the wallboard at each side of the opening. Screws are driven through the drywall and into the wood strip. Half the plywood is held behind the drywall while the other half is exposed, acting as backing for our patch.

Plaster: More Trouble Than You May Want

Hey, here's a bonus! If your plaster walls are in good condition, you can fix cracks and holes using patching plaster. But if you've got walls or ceilings that are sagging and have big holes, you've got a big job ahead of you.

Older houses have plaster walls and ceilings with wood lath for a base. These thin strips of wood were installed on the wall framing with gaps between them, which the original plaster then filled, creating "keys" that hold the plaster in place. Unfortunately, as plaster ages, as leaks occur, and as the house shifts, the plaster sags.

It's easy to find sags. You can confirm your diagnosis by pressing against suspect areas with the flat of your hand. If the plaster feels spongy or "gives," you've lost your keys. And that's a problem: If a sagging area is not repaired, it can suddenly let go, with a huge potential for damage and personal injury. Don't wait for this to happen.

If the sagging is severe (more than 1 inch away from the lath), or if the sag covers a large area, the best solution is to pull down the old plaster and replaster, or cover it with drywall. Neither is an easy do-it-yourself project. If the sagging is only slight, or covering a small area, you can re-attach the plaster to the lath using long drywall screws fitted with plaster washers.

Plaster washers are thin metal disks through which drywall screws are threaded and then driven through the plaster into ceiling joists, wall studs, or lath. The screw/washer duo pulls the loose plaster tight against the framing, fixing the sag and stabilizing the area. The tricky thing is that you can't just wail away with the drill/driver. You've got to go slowly, tightening each screw/washer a little bit at a time, so the plaster is gradually and evenly pulled snugly to the framing.

If your plaster is sagging in one place, it'll probably sag in ten other spots sooner or later. Crumbling plaster tends to become a chronic problem. Why? Your plaster simply may have reached the end of its useful life. Or maybe the original plasterers were learning on the job (not good!). Maybe you've got hidden water damage or rot (trouble!). Maybe your foundation is unstable (big trouble!).

Whatever the underlying cause, sags and serious cracks are problems that probably are going to keep cropping up. You could keep repairing them, but plastering is a difficult job best done by highly skilled, expensive professionals. Instead, you probably need to think about proactively covering your slowly crumbling plaster with a fresh layer of drywall. If you elect to do that, however, it may take some time to get used to having nice straight walls, flat ceilings, and 90-degree corners.

Interior Painting: It Pays to Do the Job Right

Whether it's a drywall repair, a conglomeration of silly-looking crayon marks, or a tattered surface, there isn't anything that will freshen things up like a new coat of paint.

Preparing to paint

You've bought your paint, you've got new brushes and rollers, you've spread out the drop cloths, and you've opened up the stepladder. You're ready to paint. Whoa! Stop right there, Mr. or Ms. Inabighurry. You've forgotten the most important thing: surface preparation. The real secret to a beautiful, long-lasting paint job is making the walls and ceiling really clean and perfectly smooth.

The following tasks don't take that much time to do, but can make the difference between a long-lasting paint job and one that you have to redo way before you're ready:

- ✔ **Prepare the room.** Remove lamps, irreplaceable knick-knacks, and as much furniture as you can and then push whatever is left to the middle of the room. Remove anything attached to the walls, including pictures, window treatments, and switch and outlet plates. Loosen ceiling light fixtures and wrap them in plastic trash bags. Take off all the window and door hardware. Finally, cover every inch of everything — floor, furniture, and radiators — with canvas or heavy-plastic drop cloths.

- ✔ **Clean the surface.** See the section "Keeping Walls and Ceilings in Prime Condition" in this chapter for the details. If you have mildew on the bathroom wall, you need to kill it and cover the remaining stain with a *stain sealer* primer made to hide stains. See Chapter 13 for more information on killing mildew.

- ✔ **Prepare the surface.** Fill nail holes, cracks, and other imperfections with patching compound. Scrape any loose or flaking paint on windows, sills, and woodwork. Sand patches and any bare areas on windows, sills, and woodwork. Lightly sand or use a deglosser to knock down the shine on glossy trim. Lightly sand walls if they are uneven, brushmarked, or bumpy. Fill gaps between the trim and the walls (especially along the baseboards and door trim) with caulk.

- ✔ **Clean again.** Vacuum the room to remove sanding dust and paint flakes (don't forget to do the windowsills and trim). Then wipe down everything with a tack rag or barely damp cloth.

- ✔ **Prime.** Prime any bare wood, all patches, and any still-visible marks or stains.

- ✔ **Mask the windows.** Use wax paper, or a layer of thin plastic taped to the windows to prevent paint splatters on the glass.

Removing paint from woodwork

For most woodwork, a putty knife and sandpaper removes loose flakes. But if your woodwork has 37 layers on it, try a scraper. Use a scraper designed specifically for moldings. If that doesn't work well, or if you're a little low on elbow grease, try an electric heat gun or chemical stripper. Heat guns soften the paint so that it can be scraped away. Strippers also soften the paint for easier scraping. Don't even think about using a propane torch as you would outside.

Scraping, sanding, or using a heat gun is not an option if the paint contains lead. Be safe, not sorry. Your local hardware store or home center carries a special test kit that will tell you if lead exists. The test only takes moments.

Selecting a primer

Primer creates a stronger bond between the paint and the wall, helps resist moisture, fills small cracks, and smoothes and seals the surface so that finish coats are more uniform and lustrous and longer lasting.

When you patch a spot or scrape down to bare wood, you create a rough, porous area that absorbs more paint than the area around it, creating uneven gloss and an area that is a slightly different in color than the surrounding area. Primer seals the area so this doesn't happen.

A stain-killing primer also keeps mysterious dark marks, water stains, and crayon, marker, or pen from bleeding through to the final finish.

If you can, use the same brand of primer and paint. Manufacturers formulate their paints and primers so that they work well together. In general, oil-based primers are the best (you can apply latex paint over them). The label on the paint can also advise you on what primer to use. If you're still befuddled, ask one of the experts at the paint store to help you select a primer.

Selecting the paint

Don't let anyone tell you differently: Latex paints are the top choice for walls and ceilings. They dry quickly, are relatively odor-free (for paint), and clean up with soap and water.

Sure, they can dry so quickly that brushmarks and lapmarks are hard to avoid. And, yeah, they don't stand up to scrapes and clunks as well as oil-based paints. But the pluses far outweigh the minuses, particularly when you consider that latex paints contain no toxic solvents.

With that said, we believe oil-based paints are the best choice for doors and trim. They dry slowly, giving brushstrokes time to disappear. They also dry to a very hard, durable finish. They offer greater moisture resistance, which makes them perfect for the walls and ceilings of damp areas such as the kitchen, bathroom, and laundry room. However, cleanup requires solvents, and as oil-based paints dry, they release volatile organic compounds into the air.

Buy the highest-quality paint you can afford — unless you like to paint. Poor-quality paint means that you need to apply at least two coats, and, what's more, you get to paint again in just a few years. Why not do the job right the first time?

How much paint should you buy? You can measure the area (square feet) of your walls and ceiling, look on the can of paint to see how many square feet it can cover, and divide your room square footage by that amount. Then you need to do the same thing for the trim.

When buying paint, err on the high side. You can always use the extra for touchups. On the low side may bring you back to the store for the same color mixed on a different date. Can you spell mismatch?

Good painting tools are a smart investment

When buying a paint brush, consider the following:

- The handle should feel good in your hand — you're going to be holding it for a while.

- The metal piece that holds the bristles should be securely attached.

- The bristles should fan out, not separate, when you press them against your palm They should be smooth, straight, and have split ends. Finally, the bristles should stay attached when you tug lightly on the them.

- Ask a sales assistant to help you select a brush that's appropriate for the kind of paint and surface that you want to paint.

The kind of roller you need also depends on the paint and surface in question. Again, ask a sales assistant for help.

Don't even think about using a sprayer to paint indoors. The same goes for power rollers. You'll make a big mess.

Painting made easy

You've bought the right paint. You've got good brushes and rollers. The room is thoroughly prepped. Everything is covered up. It's time to actually paint.

Before you do anything, stir the paint thoroughly. Paint looks better and lasts longer if all its components are mixed well from the start. Three minutes is a good amount of time.

Always paint a room from top to bottom. The job will go faster — and turn out better — if you follow this sequence:

- ✔ **Paint the ceiling.** Use a trim brush to cut in the edges of the ceiling where it meets the walls. Paint a 2- to 4-inch-wide strip that feathers out toward the middle of the room. Then paint the rest of the ceiling immediately. Start in a corner and paint across the narrowest dimension of the room.

- ✔ **Paint the walls.** Start when the ceiling is dry. Do one wall at a time. Use a trim brush to cut in where the walls meet the ceiling, around doors and windows, and along the baseboards.

- ✔ **Paint the windows.** Use an angular sash brush, and, if you prefer, a smaller brush for the dividers.

- ✔ **Paint the doors.** Use a trim brush. Work quickly but carefully. Don't forget to paint all the edges. Don't paint the hinges.

- ✔ **Paint the door and window trim.** Use a sash brush. Paint the edges and then the face.

- ✔ **Paint the baseboards.** Use a sash brush. Protect the floor or carpet with painter's tape or a paint shield.

It's best to work with a partner. One of you can cut in the edges, and the other can follow along with the roller!

Use plenty of paint. Most do-it-yourselfers try to make a brushful or rollerful go too far. Hey, it ain't champagne! If you skimp on the paint, you'll end up with a room that looks yucky.

Cleaning up right, storing smart

Latex paint cleans up with water. Wash the brush under warm water, making sure to work any paint out of the base of the bristles and the ferrule. Shake or snap the brush to get the water out, and hang it up to dry, bristles down.

Oil-based paint cleans up with paint thinner. And it's a messy, stinky job. Luckily, you only need to clean your brushes once at the end of the job. Whenever you take a break or stop for the day, wrap the brushes in plastic wrap and store them in the fridge overnight, and they'll be ready to go (once warmed to room temperature) when you start again.

As for the paint itself, place a sheet of plastic wrap over the mouth of the can, then put on the lid. Tap the lid into place snugly (use a rubber mallet or a hammer and a small piece of wood). Store the can upside-down. Your paint will be usable for years, because you've created an airtight seal.

Keeping Walls and Ceilings in Prime Condition

You can wipe away fingerprints, crayon, pen marks, dirt, and dust from walls, trim, and doors with spray cleaner and a damp cloth.

If your house is relatively new, make a bucket of soapy water and wipe the walls and ceiling with a damp sponge. If your house is older, you need something that cuts through the accumulated crud: a synthetic TSP solution.

Short for trisodium phosphate, TSP removes greasy dirt like nothing else. Mix up a bucketful, wipe down the walls and ceiling, then rinse thoroughly with clean water. TSP etches paint. It will eventually dull a glossy finish. A TSP cleaning should be performed only when nothing else works.

If you are planning to paint your wall after cleaning with TSP, a leftover film of TSP prevents proper paint adhesion.

You may not realize it, but everything in your kitchen is covered with a thin coating of grease and gummy dust. And your bathroom walls have their own coating of gunk, including hairspray, cleaning products, and stuck-on dust.

Morris's wife Carol recommends a sponge mop for cleaning ceilings. She used this technique for years (before she got a housekeeper). The foam-rubber sponge holds up best. She says that head protection is a must. An old bath towel can be used to dry. Remember: Mildew loves a wet surface. Get it dry right away!

Making Paneling Look Like New

Most houses more than 25 years old have at least one room with paneling. Believe it or not, it was very chic at one time, and still has its place in Dad's den, the basement rec room, and rustic homes. There are three kinds of paneling — solid wood planks, plywood sheets, and faux-finished hardboard.

If you've got solid wood or plywood on the wall, there are a number of things you can do to make it look like new. Cleaning is the easiest and most effective way to brighten the finish. Furniture polish won't do the job — you need something stronger.

Mix equal parts of white vinegar, turpentine, and boiled linseed oil in a small container. Wearing rubber gloves, dip a soft, clean, colorless cloth into the solution, wipe it on, and rub it in. Scrub the cleaner and moisturizer into the surface and keep scrubbing until it starts to evaporate, then wipe off the excess with a dry cloth. You'll be amazed with the results.

If your wood walls are just dry, bring them back to life by wiping on lemon oil.

To patch a small hole or surface imperfection, use wood dough, not spackle, because the wood dough is easier to hide. You can camouflage the repair with a color-match touch-up stick or, if you're feeling arty, by applying a *faux* finish. Faux finishing is literally an art. Here, the appearance of the existing wood surface is exactly matched with paint. You can't tell the area of the repair from the surrounding texture, color, or grain pattern. Faux finishing is for experts. It's expensive. If the paneling is beautiful and isn't available anymore, a faux finish could be the least expensive repair alternative.

If you're tired of the dark, woody look paneling provides, but like the texture of real wood, you can paint it. First, wash the surface with a solution of TSP (see the section "Keeping Walls and Ceilings in Prime Condition" in this chapter). When dry, prime with an oil-based stain-killer primer. If you want to eliminate the grooves between the boards, fill them with vinyl spackling compound, sand, and prime. Finish the job with a good-quality latex paint.

Wondering about Wallpaper?

If your wallpaper is looking dingy, and it's the washable kind, sponge it down with a solution of mild soap and cold water. Wipe with clean water and then wipe dry.

Test the colorfastness of the wallpaper in some inconspicuous corner before you clean it.

Time is not kind to wallpaper: The edges peel up, the adhesive gets tired, bubbles develop, and the wear and tear of normal life starts to take a visible toll. But that doesn't mean you have to rip it down. If it's still looking good, you can fix these problems.

Got an edge that's coming unglued, a seam that's sticking up, or a clean tear? Here's how to fix it:

1. **Moisten the damaged area with warm water and lift the softened wallpaper (carefully!) away from the wall.**

2. **Apply a thin coating of lap-and-seam adhesive (available at any wallpaper store).**

3. **Press the wallpaper back in place — match it up exactly!**

4. **Roll the edge with a seam roller.**

5. **Sponge off any adhesive that squishes out with a barely damp sponge.**

Got a stain or a big, ugly rip in your beautiful wallpaper? If you can find a matching leftover scrap, you can fix it this way:

1. **Cut a square or rectangular replacement piece that is a little bit larger than the damaged area, making sure to match the pattern exactly.**

2. **Attach the patch to the wall with masking tape.**

3. **Cut through both the patch and the wallpaper using a utility knife and a metal straightedge.**

   Don't make straight cuts.

4. **Remove the patch from the wall and put it somewhere safe.**

5. **Use hot water-soaked rag to dampen the area to be patched, and scrape it out (and all remaining adhesive) with a putty knife.**

6. **Clean the patch area with a damp sponge and let dry.**

7. **Apply a thin coating of adhesive to the back of the dampened patch.**

8. **Position the patch so the pattern matches, then carefully smooth it down with a clean damp cloth or a seam roller.**

9. **Sponge off any adhesive that squishes out.**

Chapter 17

Appliances

• •

In This Chapter

▶ Using natural gas and electricity in the home

▶ Cleaning to extend the life span of your appliances

• •

*T*here's something warm and magical about a home's kitchen that inevitably and unquestionably seems to draw us to it. So much so that it is, for all intents and purposes, the entertainment hub of most homes. If you doubt this fact, just throw (or go to) a party — and watch where everyone congregates. The kitchen becomes a warm and cozy gathering place, and the nicer and more inviting the kitchen, the more crowded it is.

The wonderful appliances that you find in the kitchen certainly add to this attraction. In this chapter, we offer you specific tips and ideas for the safe operation, maintenance, and longevity of the incredible array of marvelous and ingenious life conveniences that make the kitchen the *heart* of the modern 21st-century home.

While most home appliances can be found in the kitchen, some can be found in other parts of a home. For example, a washer and dryer can be found in the laundry room, mud room, basement, porch, or garage. A secondary refrigerator or freezer can also be found in one of these locations. Thus, as we discuss appliances throughout this chapter, we invite you to use the information to care for your appliances wherever they may be — hopefully not in the repair shop.

For some parts of this chapter, we sought the sage advice of one of our all-time favorite appliance gurus, Otto "Butch" Gross of Middletown, Maryland, who often consults as the Carey Brothers' appliance expert in our newspaper columns. He also visits our radio broadcasts from time to time — and is thus nationally known — as the lovable, all-knowing "Appliance MD."

What's Cooking in the Kitchen? Gas and Electricity!

The most important thing to remember about appliances is from whence they cometh. Appliances are powered by either gas or electricity. In every case, you must respect and care for the basic energy source. Misuse of the energy source can waste needless energy dollars and even cause bodily harm.

Natural gas has no odor. A heavy smell is added to the gas for only one purpose: to make it easy to detect even the smallest of gas leaks. If you smell gas, move quickly: Open all the doors and windows and leave immediately. If the range shut-off valve isn't within easy reach, turn off the main shut-off valve at your gas meter. Don't use the phone or flip a light switch. Even the tiniest spark can ignite a massive explosion. From a neighbor's home, call the gas company and the fire department. See "Gas Line Safety Tips" in Chapter 20 for information on how to turn off the main shut-off valve at your gas meter.

With electricity, your major danger is electrical shocks and destructive corrosion caused by carelessness, excessive wear in protective insulating materials, and water or moisture.

Cleaning Is Job One

The life span of most major household appliances can be severely shortened by neglect — and often greatly prolonged with simple care and very basic preventive maintenance that mostly centers on, you guessed it, cleaning.

Cleaning your appliances doesn't have to be complicated or expensive. You don't need a cabinet full of the latest hi-tech cleaners and commercial products from your local supermarket. Rather, just a few simple household ingredients and a little elbow grease from time to time keeps your appliances sparkling, operating efficiently, and often one step ahead of the repairman.

If you've ever heard us on the radio — our syndicated *On The House* one-minute daily tips and weekly call-in talk show is broadcast on over 200 stations nationwide — then you know we often delve deep into the Carey Brothers' vault of valuable information to give listeners many of our secret family formulas for various easy-to-make, noncaustic, homegrown cleaning solutions.

Many of our favorite kitchen cleaning formulas have simple, recurring components. Here's what they are and what they do:

- ✔ **Baking soda:** This is soduim bicarbonate, an alkaline substance that is used in everything from fire extinguishers to sparkling water and antacids. It is produced naturally in mineral springs or made from another natural substance called sodium carbonate (from which also comes washing soda). Often found in the familiar yellow-and-orange box, its mild abrasive and foaming action is a gentle, but effective, favorite.

- ✔ **White vinegar:** It's been around since ancient times and used for everything imaginable. The acetic acid in vinegar gives it a tart taste — and great cleaning properties! When we say *vinegar* in the following sections, we mean distilled white household vinegar with a standard 5 percent acidity. For tough jobs, you can increase its acidity (and cleaning power) by boiling off some of the water content. Just remember: Higher acidity requires more careful handling.

- ✔ **Lemon juice:** Next to vinegar, lemons are the hands down favorite for all-round cleaning and freshening. The secret ingredient of this wonder fruit is *ascorbic acid* — more commonly known as Vitamin C. It's a little more acidic than vinegar and often is a good substitute or even better choice. By comparison, vinegar is inexpensive and has a sharp odor, while lemons cost a bit more and smell a whole heck of a lot better.

- ✔ **Common salt:** Believe it or not, there are almost 15,000 uses for this ancient natural food accent and preservative. Salt's mild abrasive and absorbent action makes it a Carey Brothers' natural.

Even though our homemade cleaning solutions are made with natural products, they still contain mild acids that can sting and burn both eyes and skin. Commercial products can be even more dangerous and highly volatile due to caustic components and chemical ingredients that can sting, burn, and give off vapors. Always wear rubber gloves, protect your eyes with goggles, and have plenty of ventilation when using *any* type of cleaner — whether store-bought or homemade.

In the following sections, we give the recipes for our favorite cleaning solutions. We refer to these recipes frequently in the pages that follow.

All-Purpose, Handy Dandy Cleaner

The following solution can be used to clean and freshen just about any surface. It works especially well for day-to-day cleaning of range tops and cooktops.

Just mix up the following ingredients:

- 1 teaspoon borax
- ½ teaspoon washing soda
- 2 teaspoons white vinegar
- ¼ teaspoon dishwashing liquid
- 2 cups hot water

You can replace the washing soda with baking soda and use lemon juice instead of white vinegar depending upon what you have lying around the house. Though, the former is a bit stronger than the latter.

The secret to most cleaning formulas is hot water. It helps the various ingredients become a solution.

D-I-Y Cleanser Scrub

This cleaning formula is especially suited for cleaning up baked-on spills on glass or porcelain ranges and cooktops when you would normally pull out the cleanser.

Start with the following ingredients:

- ¾ cup borax
- ¼ cup baking soda
- Dishwashing liquid to moisten

Combine the two powders and moisten them with just enough dishwashing liquid to create a gooey paste. You can use all borax or all baking soda if you wish, and for a more pleasing and lingering aroma, add ¼ teaspoon of lemon juice.

Dishwashing liquid versus detergents

Dishwashing detergent, whether liquid, gel, or powder, is for machine washing. It's far stronger than liquids designed for hand washing dishes. You can use dishwashing detergent for tougher cleaning jobs, but use it with caution — detergent can be caustic.

Never use dishwashing liquid soap in your dishwasher. It severely oversuds, foams up, and doesn't properly rinse, causing your machine to float a sea of bubbles out onto your kitchen floor. Lucy, from the TV show *I Love Lucy,* found this out the hard way.

Gentle Glass Cleaner

The following solution works well for cleaning the glass shelving in you refrigerator, glass cooktops, and the windows in range and oven doors.

You need the following materials:

- ✔ 2 tablespoons ammonia
- ✔ ¼ teaspoon dishwashing liquid
- ✔ ½ cup rubbing alcohol
- ✔ Hot water

Mix the ingredients and add enough hot water to make 1 quart of cleaner. If you prefer, you can avoid the smell of ammonia by using white vinegar or sweeter smelling lemon juice. However, this will make the formula less powerful.

For super-duper window cleaning — especially in cold weather — add 1 teaspoon of corn starch to the formula to boost your sparkle horsepower.

People-Friendly Oven Cleaner

Here's a safe alternative to those conventional caustic oven cleaners. In addition to your oven, it's great for cleaning barbecue grills and grungy pots and pans.

Start with the following:

- ✔ 2 teaspoons borax or baking soda
- ✔ 2 tablespoons dishwashing liquid
- ✔ 1¼ cups ammonia
- ✔ 1½ cups hot water

Mix the ingredients, apply generously to spills, and let the solution soak for 30 minutes or as long as overnight. Loosen tough spills with a nylon scrubber and then wipe up with a damp sponge.

Super-Duper Disinfectant Cleaner

This solution works well anywhere you would use a store-bought disinfectant, such as appliance pulls and handles, the inside face of the refrigerator where the gasket seats, the refrigerator drip pan, counters and cutting boards, and around the opening of your clothes washer. It works especially well on all surfaces of a trash compactor — inside and out.

Mix the following ingredients and then scrub:

- 1 tablespoon borax or baking soda
- ¼ cup powdered laundry detergent
- ¼ cup pine-oil based cleaner or pine oil
- ¾ cup hot water

For kitchen use, dilute with more hot water.

Easy Mildew Remover

Our mildew formula works great on painted or other washable surfaces. Remember to wear gloves and eye protection and to have plenty of ventilation when working with this solution:

- ⅓ cup powdered laundry detergent
- 1 quart household liquid chlorine bleach
- 3 quarts warm water

Apply the remover using a spray bottle, a sponge, or an old toothbrush. Allow the solution to sit for 5 to 10 minutes, but don't let it dry. You will know the solution is working when the black mildew stains turn white. Rinse all the surfaces very well with hot water when through and towel dry.

Lettin' your cleaner sit a spell

All cleaners, whether commercial or home-made, work best when left to sit for varying periods of time. Generally, the tougher the stain, the longer you let it sit to work.

With commercial cleaners and solvents, always read the label for manufacturer usage directions and special warnings (which can range from potential health hazards to potential discoloration and surface damage).

Roaming the Range Top

Use our All-Purpose, Handy Dandy Cleaner (see the section earlier in the chapter) for day-to-day surface cleaning and our D-I-Y Cleanser Scrub for tougher cooked-on spills. Let the cleaners sit for a longer time to soften really tough stains and hardened spills.

When food spills occur, immediately sprinkle them with table salt, which absorbs the moisture and makes them easy to clean up later when the stove top cools.

Cut and remove filmy grease with full-strength white vinegar or lemon juice.

When cleaning a range top, pull off both upper and lower control knobs and wash them separately in warm soapy water. Air dry the knobs thoroughly and completely before replacing them. Use a hair dryer to remove moisture from nooks and crannies, if necessary.

Electric range tops

Plug-in burners have a tendency to collect grease and moisture down at the tips where they go into the power source receptacle. This leads to minor arcing (electrical shorting) that slowly builds and eventually ruins the burners. When you replace a burner, you must also replace the plug-in receptacle to prevent the arcing problem. This is not exactly a cheap or convenient repair.

To prevent this problem, remove the plug-in burners and carefully clean the surfaces and tips with a damp rag or stiff nylon brush. A soapy steel wool pad can be used if plain water and a rag or nylon brush don't do the trick.

Never fully submerse plug-in burners in water. If you do, while the metal prongs may appear to be fully dry, trace amounts of moisture usually remain on the plug-in tips and electric receptacles. The tips and receptacles contain porcelain, which is extremely porous and absorbs water. The result: you've brought water and electricity together for a potential electric shock and serious zapping.

Most ranges have two 6-inch and two 8-inch interchangeable plug-in burners. When removing them for cleaning, always mark their origin so that they can be put back in *exactly* the same receptacle. If not, one burner that may be corroded or dirty and starting to burn out gets switched over to a nice, clean receptacle that is functioning okay. You cause cross contamination that can make both burners fail rather than just the one.

Another kind of electric burner, the fixed unit, is hard-wired and generally lifts up for cleaning. The advantage to this type is that the tips never corrode or burn out from dripping grease.

There are also Euro-style solid cast iron burners (also called *hobs*). They have a coating that wears off with use. To prevent rusting, manufacturers and dealers offer a special cleaner/sealer that you apply to a cold burner (it burns off when the burner heats). You can also use a light coat of mineral or cooking oil to prevent rusting, but oil smokes a bit when the burner heats. Turn on the vent fan to remove any light residual smoking or burning odor.

Round cast-iron tops that cover elements to create a neat Euro-burner look can distribute heat more evenly and prevent spills from dripping down to the drip pan and receptacle below — but also they often cause undo heat stress and can ultimately shorten the life of a burner. There's no real danger; it's a question of whether you want to trade off a longer lifespan for a slicker image and ease of cleaning.

Always keep light-weight inexpensive aluminum drip pans under the heating elements to prevent grease and oils from entering the works of the range. Clean the drip pans using baking soda, rather than soaps, to keep them shiny.

Never line your drip pans with aluminum foil. The heat reflected off a shiny foiled drip pan creates hot spots underneath a burner that can quickly end the useful life of an electric element. If you want long life out of your drip pan, use heavier gauge porcelain-coated metal drip pans that last longer, look better, and are far easier to clean. After many years of use, they'll still look like new.

Gas range tops

Removable gas burners should be taken out periodically and cleaned with a stiff nylon brush, using baking soda and hot water to keep the ports (gas jet holes) clean. Most burners are can be removed by simply lifting them out of the opening in the cooktop, without the need for any tools. If you aren't sure whether your burners are the removable type, refer to your owner's manual.

Between the burners is a connector tube (called a "flash tube") with an opening and a pilot light or electric spark igniter. This is where the gas is actually ignited and carried or drawn to each burner by what is called a *venturi* action. In most cases, this configuration is part of the burner assembly and can be cleaned as described above. This is important since the flash tube can become clogged with grease.

Clean nonremovable sealed gas burners with a small brush and a solution of baking soda and water. You will know for certain if you have a sealed gas burner — the drip pan that surrounds each burner is anchored securely to the cooktop and can't be removed. The only components that can be

---

Taking a look at your gas grill jets

Outdoor gas barbecues operate just like indoor gas ranges. Dripping food juices easily clog your grill's gas jet orifices, and nature's little critters (like spiders) like to deposit egg sacks in the jets for family breeding.

Before you fire-up your grill, and especially after it's been sitting all winter, be sure you carefully inspect each opening and the tubes leading to it for obstructions. Sometimes, one side lights, while the other spews unlit gas that quietly collects and ultimately goes *ka-boom* when it reaches the other side.

---

removed for cleaning are the burner grate (the part that rests above the flame, where you put the pots) and the burner cap, which evenly distributes the flame.

Use the all-purpose cleaner or the D-I-Y Cleanser Scrub listed above to clean these components.

Never use any kind of soap for cleaning the burners. The chemicals in soap trigger corrosion on burner housings, which are made of aluminum. Baking soda is *non*corrosive and not harmful to aluminum.

Make sure that the burner housings are wiped thoroughly clean, and remove all water from the gas jet port openings — first with a soft cloth, and then use a hair dryer to remove all moisture, if necessary.

If you notice that a flame jet shoots further out than the others, it indicates that the opening is partially blocked and needs cleaning. Generally, if the flame burns yellow, it needs attention of some sort because it's starved for air or blocked at some point. If it burns clear and blue, it's a proper gas flame.

Opening the Door and Rolling Up Your Sleeves: The Oven

And now for the heart of the matter — cleaning the inside of your range. Aside from saving you embarrassment when company comes calling, a clean range will operate more efficiently by providing more even heating. A dirty range can also prevent the door from sealing properly, which allows heat and smoke to escape.

You can clean oven interiors with commercial cleansers, steel wool soap pads, or our People-Friendly Oven Cleaner (see the section earlier in the chapter).

If a commercial cleaner says you must wear rubber gloves and avoid breathing fumes, it's probably very caustic and possibly toxic. It may even give off harmful gases even after the cleaning is complete and the oven is again heated for use. Thus, we suggest that you avoid using them whenever possible. If you must use a commercial cleaner, follow label directions to the letter.

To loosen up tough, baked-on spills, preheat the oven to 200 degrees, turn off the heat, and then put a bowl of ammonia in your oven overnight. This works well as long as you don't mind the smell of ammonia in your kitchen the next day.

Ammonia and commercial window cleaners containing ammonia are also great for cleaning browned and discolored oven window glass. You can also use mild abrasives and scouring pads for tough spots.

For wire oven racks that are severely caked with food spills, put them in a plastic trash bag, add some ammonia, and seal the bag well with a twist tie. Leave the bag outside overnight, and then either hose them off, hand wash them, or put the racks in your dishwasher (see Figure 17-1).

Speaking of spills, many people believe that they can simplify oven cleaning by lining the bottom of the oven with aluminum foil to catch spills. This is a no-no! A layer of foil will cause the oven to heat unevenly and will also shorten the life of the element by causing it to superheat in certain locations.

Figure 17-1:
Cleaning
wire oven
racks.

REMEMBER

Your oven door is not a step

Many stoves don't have a *tip device* to keep them upright when weight is placed on the door. Heavy weight can also bend the oven door hinges and affect the seal, causing heat loss and other problems.

Checking the oven temperature control

You don't need to be in the same culinary league as Chef Julia Child to know that the accuracy of an oven temperature control can make all the difference when it comes to producing the perfect meal. A poorly calibrated control can make it virtually impossible to conform to heating instructions on recipes. Thus, you end up with a dish that is either under- or overcooked. Yikes!

To check the accuracy of oven temperature control, put an oven thermometer on the middle rack. Set the thermometer for 350 degrees and heat the oven for 20 minutes. Write down the temperature. Check three more times at 10-minute intervals, noting the temperatures. The average temperature should be within 25 degrees of 350.

If you find that the temperature is off, recalibrate the temperature control dial by removing the oven temperature knob and doing one of the following:

- ✔ Loosen the screws and turn the movable disk on the backside. One notch represents 10 degrees.
- ✔ Turn the adjustment screw inside the hollow shaft clockwise to lower the temperature, counterclockwise to raise it. If it requires more than an eighth of a turn or is off by 50 degrees or more, install a new temperature control.

If the temperature in your gas oven fluctuates or bakes unevenly, chances are good that your thermostat is faulty. Your best bet is to leave the installation to a pro. The only tool you should pick up to make this repair is your phone.

Electric ovens

In electric ovens, you find two heating elements: one for broiling (above) and one for baking (below). If possible, buy a model that allows you to lift the bottom bake element for easier cleaning of the bottom of the oven.

Replacing the oven light

When the oven light burns out, turn off the power at the main circuit, remove the glass shield and, using gloves or a dry cloth, unscrew the old bulb. Only replace it with a special 40-watt appliance bulb that can stand extreme temperatures (or whatever the manufacturer recommends). If the light doesn't light, it could indicate a larger problem that needs professional attention. Occasionally you might want to clean and vacuum the back of your range and the area behind, to the sides and below it. The back of a range consists of a metal panel that can be removed for service or repair. It's okay to clean dust and grime that collects on this panel, but it should otherwise not be removed. To do this, the range will need to be pulled out of the opening.

If the range is electric, the cord should be long enough for you to move the appliance out and then unplug it. Gas models should have a flexible gas line that will allow you to pull the appliance out. Do not move a gas range that has a rigid gas pipe — call a service professional.

Be especially careful not to damage flooring in front of an appliance when moving it. An old piece of carpet turned upside down and placed under the appliance feet, an appliance dolly or an appliance skid pad (available from an appliance service company) simplify appliance moving and prevent torn vinyl, scratched hardwood or chipped tile.

Open the oven door 8 to 10 inches and try lifting. Most ovens have special hinges that allow the door to lift right off. You can then easily clean deep into the oven interior without stretching over the lowered open oven door. You can also comfortably clean the glass and inside surface of the door itself on a towel at countertop level.

Use our People-Friendly Oven Cleaner discussed earlier in this chapter to clean the interior of you oven.

Gas ovens

You can use our People-Friendly Oven Cleaner to make the inside of your gas oven sparkle. For baked-on spots, use our D-I-Y Cleanser Scrub. The recipes for both of these solutions can be found earlier in this chapter. If neither of these solutions does the trick, use a store-bought oven cleaner, being certain to follow the label directions to the letter. Rubber gloves, eye protection, and plenty of ventilation are essential.

Like most ovens, it is the bottom of the gas oven that is the object of most cleaning attention. The bottom panel of a gas oven can be removed simply by lifting it out or by removing a couple of screws that hold it in place. This will allow you to work on it in a deep sink or bathtub. Over time, the bottom panel of a gas oven can become corroded or broken. It can be replaced using the steps to remove and replace it for cleaning.

With the oven bottom out you will be able to inspect and clean the gas burner. Uneven heating, poor baking, or an odor of gas when the oven is on are telltale signs of a clogged burner. Your best bet to determine how the burner is working is to turn it on with the bottom panel off. If the flame is not continuous along both sides of the burner, some of its holes are likely clogged.

To set your burner free, turn off the oven control and insert a wire — such as a coat hanger — into the clogged holes. Works every time!

Once the gas burner is clean, check to make sure that it is burning efficiently — a steady blue 1-inch cone, with an inner cone of about ½ inch. Adjusting the air shutter will control the air mixture and, in turn, the color of the flame. Consult your owner's manual for specific information on how to adjust the burner flame in your gas oven.

Self-cleaning electric ovens

Never use commercial oven cleaners on a self-cleaning oven. They can pit, burn, and eat into the porcelain surface. The result? When you reach the normal 850- to 900-degree level for self-cleaning, you can actually pop chunks of porcelain off the oven walls as large as 6 inches across.

Instead, let the intended high heat action turn food spills into carbon, which all but disappears with complete combustion, and then wipe up any minor dust-like ash residue with a damp cloth, paper towel, or sponge when the oven cools.

Don't open the oven door if you notice a flame-up or smell something burning. The oven is just doing what it's supposed to do. If you're really worried, just shut the oven off. The lack of oxygen in the closed and sealed oven and diminishing heat level extinguishes any burning in a matter of moments.

You *can* clean the area surrounding the oven door gasket with any type of mild abrasive, such as our D-I-Y Cleanser Scrub or a commercial silver polish. Use a wide spatula or paint scraper to lift the gasket edge up to prevent rubbing up against it and possible fraying.

Many heavier-weight porcelain-coated drip pans can be put into the oven during self-cleaning, making the cleanup of drips and spills a snap. Manufacturers will recommend removing racks during the self-cleaning process to prevent the racks from turning brown. Instead, they should be cleaned using the process mentioned earlier in this chapter. We strongly recommend that you consult your owner's manual for specific information on how to use your self-cleaning oven.

Continuous cleaning ovens

These ovens have a special rough-texture porcelain interior. Spills gradually burn off as you use the oven. A speckled surface helps hide foods while they burn off, but these ovens may not always look clean in the process.

Combusted foods tend to remain on the oven walls. To avoid this as much as possible, always wipe up large spills as soon as the oven cools — especially sugary or starchy foods. These models works best on greasy spills.

Never use harsh abrasives, scouring pads, or commercial oven cleaners on continuous cleaning ovens. These cleaners damage the special lining. Gentle cleaning by hand with baking soda and warm water works best.

We believe that continuous cleaning models are the scourges of mankind. They rarely perform well. Thus, when oven shopping steer clear of the continuous cleaning models. You won't be sorry.

Hanging Out in the Range Hood

The range hood has an important job. It removes excess moisture and smoke that is produced when cooking. The most important aspect of range hood maintenance is cleaning.

Remove and clean the metal mesh filter(s) that keep grease from getting into the ductwork. Soak the filters in a sink full of hot water and liquid dish detergent. Then rinse them clean with very hot water.

Frequently inspect the filters for grease buildup once a month or more, depending on how much you cook and operate the vent and fan. Worn or damaged filter screens should be replaced with new ones, which can be obtained from an appliance repair shop or through the manufacturer.

If you put mesh filters in the bottom rack of your dishwasher (as many amateur tipsters advise), they may leave a greasy residue behind that is hard to remove and can ultimately clog lines and affect your machine's operation. It's okay to put them in the dishwasher one you've given them an initial once-over as outlined in the previous paragraph.

For nonvented hoods, remember to replace the disposable charcoal filter every year (or according to manufacturer's directions).

With filters moved, wash the range hood interior with our All-Purpose, Handy Dandy Cleaner (see the section earlier in this chapter) or warm water and liquid dish detergent.

Microwave Maintenance Mania

If your microwave oven is over 15 years old, it should be checked for output efficiency. For 600- to 1000-watt microwave ovens, place an 8-ounce cup of water in the oven and operate the unit on high for three minutes. The water should reach a rolling boil. If not, take the microwave to a service shop for inspection.

Older microwaves should also be tested for radiation leakage by a professional appliance repair technician. In addition, the pro can check other aspects of operation to determine if the microwave is safe and if it should be repaired or replaced.

 Never attempt to repair an ailing microwave oven yourself. Besides the inherent dangers (the unit's capacitor holds up to 4,000 volts of electricity), unauthorized repairs by anyone other than an authorized service tech almost always void the manufacturer's warranty.

Poor heating in your microwave can result from an overworked electrical circuit. Operating a microwave on a circuit that is serving other appliances not only diminishes the effectiveness of the microwave oven, but could ultimately result in an electrical fire. If lights dim when the microwave is used, an electrician should be consulted. Whenever possible, a separate electrical circuit should be provided for the microwave oven.

Always wipe up spills promptly after use. Keep the interior of the oven and the area surrounding the door clean, using a damp sponge to catch spills and splatters as they occur.

Food particles left over long periods of time eventually turn to carbon and cause arcing (electrical sparking), which in turn can etch interior surfaces and could even compromise the seal around the door. Use our all-purpose cleaning solution mentioned earlier in this chapter.

To help keep the microwave's interiors clean, always adequately vent airtight packaging, plastic bags, plastic-wrapped bowls, eggs, and all fruits and vegetables with skins (like potatoes) by puncturing them or cutting vent slits. Doing so avoids bursting from steam buildups that creates messy food splatters.

Never use a microwave oven for anything other than what it was designed for — cooking and heating. Using it to dry clothing, papers, or (gasp) pets yields devastating results.

Never run an empty microwave, and always be sure there is plenty of ventilation surrounding the unit to avoid overheating which could cause serious damage.

Appliance repair pros say the most common repair problem they find is a simple microwave fuse that gets metal fatigue after three or four years' use. At that point, even a minor power surge can cause the fuse to burn out. If your microwave quits, don't panic. It may just be an interior fuse that needs replacing by a pro.

Dishwashers

The single most important aspect to dishwasher maintenance is to keep the interior clean. Doing so keeps all the hoses and passages clear, which, in turn, lets the machine operate freely and ultimately washes your dishes better.

Most people use far too much soap when they run the dishwasher. Any more than 1 tablespoon is too much and will lead to a residue buildup that is hard to get rid of.

Never wash anything other than dishes in your dishwasher. Tools, clothes, sneakers, greasy range hood filters, and so on can leave harmful grease and residue that clog the machine's works and inhibit proper operation.

If you see interior staining or have soap residue buildup, it means your pump is working too hard to move water through the system. The best way to clean the interior is with citric acid. Use pure citric acid crystals, which you can find in grocery and drug stores. Fill your main soap cup and then run the dishwasher through a complete cycle. This is best done with the dishwasher empty. The crystals clean everything, including the unit's interior, racks, hoses, and water ports. Then, once a week, add 1 teaspoon of the acid crystals to your soap for general maintenance.

You can substitute *Tang* and lemonade mixes that contain Vitamin C (which is citric acid) for the crystals. They work well too, only with lesser amounts of citric acid per dose.

Dishwashers should be run at least once a week to keep all the seals moist and to prevent leaks and eventual failure from drying.

Periodically wipe the area around the seals to prevent soap scum buildup, which can cause a leak.

Refrigerators and Freezers

The most important thing for any refrigerator is to keep the condenser coils clean. Air passing over these coils is what cools the refrigerator, and if they are dirty, the unit has to work harder to do its job.

These coils are usually located at the bottom of the refrigerator behind a removable grille. On some older models, they may be located on the back.

To clean the coils, first unplug the refrigerator. Remove the grille by grabbing both ends and pulling gently. Use a vacuum cleaner with a brush or crevice attachment to get as far into and under the unit as possible (being careful not to force access, which can bend condenser tubing and the thin metal coil fins).

While the grille is off, also remove the refrigerator drain pan and wash it.

Use the power-saver switch (usually located inside your refrigerator). It controls small electric heaters that keep the outside of the cabinet from sweating. Only turn the switch on when it's humid and you see moisture beads. When both the weather and your refrigerator are dry, turn this function off to save energy costs. The power-saver switch also helps prevent rust and nasty mold buildups.

The chilly environment of a refrigerator is kept that way primarily by a gasket at the perimeter of the door. It helps maintain a good airtight seal. It is also a prime candidate for mold. To remove mold from around the gasket, clean it with a solution of liquid chlorine bleach and water (4 tablespoons in a quart of hot water), and scrub well with an old toothbrush (see Figure 17-2). Afterwards, wipe all residue off completely with warm water and a mild liquid dish detergent.

Figure 17-2: Removing mold from around the gasket.

Replace the rubber gasket's oils you've removed by applying a light coat of lemon oil, mineral oil, or any type of body lotion with lanolin in it to keep the gasket soft and supple (just like with your skin). Always wipe off any food or liquid spills, drips, and runs from around the door and gaskets. If you don't, they dry and become sticky, possibly ripping away the gasket when you open the door.

Temperaturewise, keep the food compartment set between 34 and 40 degrees, and the freezer compartment at about 0 degrees. Generally, refrigerator controls should always be set midway initially, and then only adjusted up or down as needed.

Most people know that an open box of baking soda will keep the refrigerator or freezer smelling fresh. Did you know that you can also use a small bowl with a few tablespoons of instant freeze-dried coffee crystals in it? And believe it or not, granulated cat litter also works. An added bonus: The litter eliminates food odors in ice cubes. Kill two birds with one stone by pouring the contents of a box of baking soda into the garbage disposal and filling the baking soda box with cat litter. The baking soda will freshen the garbage disposal while the box of cat litter will keep the fridge odor free.

To clean the interior, first turn off the refrigerator and remove all the food. Wash removable shelves and bins in the sink with liquid dish detergent and warm water. Wipe down the interior walls with our All-Purpose, Handy Dandy Cleaner or a solution of warm water and baking soda.

Defrosting the freezer

Defrost your freezer when ice begins to build up on the interior. Aside from diminishing usable freezer space, the ice can prevent the door from sealing properly. Most freezers need to be defrosted at least once and sometimes twice each year. Start by turning off the power to the freezer and removing all of the contents. You can allow the ice to melt on its own or you can speed things up by placing a pot of hot water in the freezer and closing the door. Clean the interior of the freezer using the same method described in the preceding paragraph.

Defrosting the freezer drain line

Defrost the freezer drain line leading to the drain pan at least once a year. Mold buildup starts retaining moisture, which, in turn, starts freezing and ultimately completely blocks the line.

First turn the freezer off (so that you can melt the ice in the drain line). Then clear the line by putting very hot water into a turkey baster and inserting it into the ½-inch drain hole located at the back of the freezer floor. Release hot water into the line until it runs free, then blast in more hot water to blow out any mold buildup. Finally, put 2 tablespoons of chlorine bleach in 1 cup of hot water and pour it down the drain to kill off any remaining mold spores.

Garbage Disposals

Clean your disposal by putting ice cubes and ¼ cup of white vinegar into the unit and operating it with no running water. As the blades grind up the ice, it removes food particles and gooey build-ups. When it sounds like the cubes are all gone, start a slow trickle of cold water. You will probably find that the disposal's drain openings are frozen and clogged with ice, and the water will start to back up — which is good — because the churning water also washes the sides before the ice melts, the drain clears, and everything drains away.

For a more thorough cleaning, sprinkle some baking soda on top of the ice cubes. To make the disposal smell fresh, add some citic acid crystals, *Tang* or a drink mix containing Vitamin C, or half a lemon.

You can also use vinegar ice cubes as an easy means of cleaning your disposal and sharpening its blades. Pour 1 cup of vinegar into an empty ice cube tray and fill the balance of the tray with water. Put the tray in the freezer until you have solid vinegar ice cubes. Periodically pour an entire tray of ice cubes into the disposal while it is running. Just be sure to mark the tray with the vinegar ice cubes. Otherwise your guests will have an unpleasant experience next time you serve them a cold beverage.

Trash Compactors

Only compact dry trash — not banana or potato peels or anything else that contains moisture. If you do, the compactor squish out juices that ride up on top of the wiper (the rubber flap that surrounds the ram) and get into the inner workings of the ram, which you can't get to for cleaning. The result: nasty odors and a big flashing neon sign that says *"Insects Welcome!"*

Always keep interior surfaces clean and use a specially made trash compactor deodorant spray to discourage ants, roaches, and other insects that are hard to eliminate once they set up shop.

Aside from keeping the contents of the trash compactor dry, the other single most important step in keeping it clean is using an approved compactor bag that is designed to fit your model. Compactor bags are made of paper or plastic and line the entire trash bin. The liner should be folded back over the collar of the bin and held securely in place by retaining clips. This will prevent the ram (the trash smasher) from dislocating the bag when on its way up.

Most trash compactors have a heavy plastic saddle between the trash bin and the compactor bag. This saddle has two handles that are used to pull a full bag of compacted garbage out of the bin without the weight of the contents ripping through the bottom of the bag. Over time and with frequent use, the saddle can become torn and should be replaced with a new one.

The saddle should periodically be taken outside and cleaned with our All-Purpose Cleaner and hosed off with fresh water. Vacuum the inside of the trash bin to remove any debris that may have made its way through a tear in the bag. Also, wipe down the inside of the bin with detergent and hot water or our All-Purpose Cleaner.

Washing Machines

Use the same citric acid cleaning procedures to clean tub interiors as outlined for dishwashers earlier in this chapter. Doing so removes mineral deposits, lime, and soap buildups that affect the pump operation.

If you have rust stains inside the tub, try a professionally installed plastic tub liner before considering replacement. Temporary patch-ups on small nicks in the porcelain where rusting occurs can be made with a dab or two of enamel paint or clear nail polish — but these are very temporary solutions, at best. A better solution is a porcelain repair kit made for bathtubs, available at your local hardware store. It lasts longer, but not forever.

If your water outlet hose drains into a laundry basin rather than a stand pipe, cover the end with an old nylon stocking. Doing so collects 95 percent of all lint that otherwise would go into your sink's drain line. The nylon stocking filter also reduces splashing when the washer empties into the sink. When the stocking fills with lint, remove and replace it.

If your cold water is running slowly, turn off the water inlet valves, remove water hoses, and clean the small screen filters, which are probably clogged with mineral buildup and small debris. The fine mesh filters are usually at either end of the hose or on the back of the washing machine's water inlet port. If debris gets past these screen filters, it can damage the pump and lead to a costly repair.

Also consider switching from rubber water inlet hoses to long-lasting braided stainless steel hoses. They cost a little more, but both are good insurance against flooding caused by hose failure.

Electric and Gas Clothes Dryers

Clean the lint screen thoroughly after every load. If it's filled and clogged with lint, the air won't circulate, the clothes won't dry, and the dryer runs far longer, which wears it out faster and wastes lots of energy dollars in the process.

If you have an electric dryer, never open the door mid-cycle without first turning the dial to the air-dry mode or advancing the timer to shut off the heater. Otherwise, if you stop in mid-cycle, the red-hot heaters allow heat to collect inside the unit until it triggers the thermal fuse. The fuse is a built-in safety mechanism that works only one time; after is goes off, a service technician has to fix it before your dryer will operate again. If you want to interrupt a drying cycle, always let the heater cool off before stopping. Otherwise you may wind up line drying your duds for a while.

Dryer lint is a big fire hazard. In addition, excess lint makes the dryer work extra hard and can take forever to dry a load of clothes. Therefore, the dryer duct should be cleaned at least twice each year. The easiest means of cleaning a short dryer duct is with a dryer duct cleaning brush. The brush looks like a mini version of what a chimney sweep might use. A stiff-bristle circular brush is attached to a flexible handle. The brush is moved back and forth inside the duct to dislodge. The brush along with a vacuum is a winning combination for cleaning almost any dryer duct.

If you have an excessively long (20-feet or more) dryer vent leading outside or to the roof, make a vent-cleaning tool by fishing a nylon line from outside to the vent hose mounting inside (after removing the big, plastic, accordion-type flexible dryer vent exhaust hose). Then tie a nylon brush (one that's big enough to brush the vent walls) to the line which can then be drawn up into the vent, leaving enough line on the other end to draw it back again. When finished, leave some line exposed outside and — pulling the inside line off to the side — reattach the accordion-type flexible vent hose and let the brush and excess line lay off to the side for the next vent-scrubbing episode.

A dryer duct should always terminate at the home's exterior — never in the attic, basement, or crawl space — to prevent damage due to excessive moisture. Most dryer ducts terminate at a hood mounted at an exterior wall. The hood contains a damper that is designed only to open when the dryer is blowing air through the duct. The damper prevents cold air and birds and rodents from nesting in the duct. However, crafty varmints often find a means of breaching the damper. If you have experienced such a problem, install a protective screen especially designed to solve this problem. If you already have such a device, make sure that any holes are patched so that it is doing a good job.

Regardless of exterior vent length, periodically remove the flexible accordion-type exhaust hose and clean it out by vacuuming. Lint buildup reduces efficiency, wastes energy dollars, and can cause a fire by not letting superheated air pass freely.

Better yet, replace any flexible accordion type exhaust hose (especially if it's vinyl) with sheet metal ducting. It does not clog nearly as easily and is a more efficient vent, making your clothes dry faster.

Excess lint in a clothes dryer exhaust system is an accident waiting to happen. Aside from the lint screen and the dryer duct, lint can accumulate at the bottom of the housing that contains the lint screen. An easy means of removing this lint is to construct a custom vacuum hose attachment using a short piece of rubber hose, the cap to an aerosol can and some duct tape.

The cap acts as an adapter that fits over the end of a wet/dry vacuum hose. Make a hole in the center of the cap the size of the outside diameter of the hose. Insert the hose snuggly into the hole and attach the two using duct tape. Attach the cap to the end of a wet/dry vacuum and insert the hose into the filter housing until it reaches the bottom (see Figure 17-3).

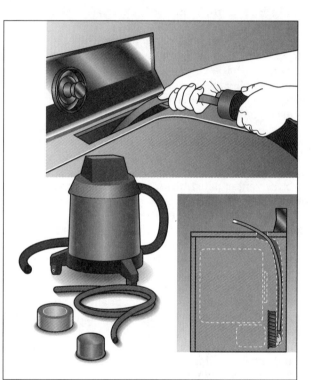

Figure 17-3: Removing lint from inside the machine.

The owner's manual: a friend indeed

The owner's manuals for your major appliances are filled with valuable information for day-to-day operation and preventative maintenance. If you can't locate a manual, contact the manufacturer and ask the customer service department to send you one. Some manufacturers allow you to download product manuals from their Web sites. After you assemble a full set of manuals for every major appliance in your home, keep them in a safe place for easy reference. They'll also be invaluable to someone else who may eventually purchase your home somewhere down the line.

Chapter 18

Cabinets and Countertops

In This Chapter

▶ Adding life to the finish of your cabinets

▶ Keeping cabinet parts on the move

▶ Giving countertops the love they need

*I*n this chapter, we look at two very different things — cabinets and countertops. They're made of different kinds of materials, and they require different kinds of care and repair. But you usually find them together in the home, and, to us, that's a great reason to lump them into one chapter.

Keeping Cabinets Looking Great

Kitchen cabinets are magnets for grease, food bits, spills, and moisture. And the slime and crud builds up, making them look dingy and dirty in no time. As the paint or varnish on the cabinet wears the wood beneath can become stained or even damaged.

If your cabinets are made of painted wood, metal laminate, or vinyl, clean them with a warm soap-and-water solution and a sponge. Remove soapy residue with a cloth and clean water and then dry with towels.

Wood cabinets

If your cabinets are made of solid wood (or high quality veneer over a solid base) and aren't terribly nicked up or scratched and have drawers and doors that still work well, all they may need is a little TLC. In fact, a good cleaning could be just the trick to make their surface look new again.

To give fine wood cabinets (or furniture) a super cleaning, mix up the following potion (our formula isn't made for painted surfaces):

- ✔ 3 tablespoons turpentine
- ✔ 3 tablespoons boiled linseed oil
- ✔ 1 quart boiling water

This mixture is moderately flammable. So, no smoking or open flames while you're working. For the same reason, don't try to reheat the mixture — mix up a new batch when it gets cold. Dispose of the leftover liquid by letting it evaporate outside (not down the drain). Even the rags can be flammable — let them completely air dry outside before disposing of them in trash. Do not keep these rags inside. They are subject to spontaneous combustion!

Here's how to do the job:

1. **Remove all the knobs and handles.**
2. **Cover countertops and floors with dropcloths.**
3. **Wearing rubber gloves, wet a soft rag in the mixture and ring it out well.**
4. **Thoroughly wipe all cabinet surfaces (inside and out), doing small sections at a time.**
5. **Wipe the surface dry with a clean rag.**
6. **Repeat wiping and drying until all old wax, sticky grease film, and grubby fingerprints are gone.**
7. **Replace the pulls and drawers and clean up the mess.**

Something old is something new

If cleaning doesn't do the trick, and your cabinets still look lousy, then it's time to cover up their flaws. In fact, a few minor surface repairs and a fresh coat of paint or varnish can make your old cabinets look new, make them easier to care for, and probably brighten up the room.

The cabinet finish not only looks good, it also protects the wood from moisture damage, a common commodity in places where cabinets rest.

Here's how to go about painting or varnishing your cabinets:

1. **Remove the cabinet doors and drawers.**

   You may have to move or remove the refrigerator, range, or vent hood to complete the job. Use removable stickers to label the drawers and doors so that you can get them back in the right place.

2. **Take the drawers and doors to your garage or basement workshop (to minimize disruption in the kitchen), and remove the drawer pulls, door handles and hinges.**

   While you do that, have your partner clean behind the refrigerator, under the stove, and up inside the range hood. (Why pass up this great opportunity for a thorough cleaning?)

3. **If you intend to reuse the pulls, handles, and hinges, soak them in a mild solution of soap and water.**

   Don't use ammonia. It can remove the plated finish.

4. **Wash all the drawer and door surfaces with a solution of TSP and wipe them dry.**

5. **Wash all cabinet surfaces to be painted or varnished with TSP and wipe them dry.**

6. **Lightly sand all surfaces to be painted with 200- or 120-grit sandpaper if you intend to paint, or 400- or 600-grit if you intend to varnish.**

   The goal is not to remove all the paint or varnish, but to create a uniform surface for the new finish. So don't go nuts — just get it smooth.

7. **If painting, fill all nicks and blemishes with vinyl spackling compound, and, when dry, sand the compound lightly. If varnishing, use colored putty, being careful to remove excess from around the gouge.**

   A second application of spackle or putty may be necessary if the first coat shrinks.

8. **Vacuum the cabinets, drawers, and doors using an upholstery brush and then wipe them down with a tack cloth or a soft cloth dampened with mineral spirits.**

9. **Cover everything with dropcloths.**

   Use canvas or heavy plastic, not the foodwrap kind. Use masking tape to protect the counters where they meet the cabinets and to create a paint/no-paint edge on the interiors.

10. **If painting, apply a coat of oil-based primer. (Skip this step if varnishing.)**

    If the cabinets are dark, use a heavily pigmented shellac-based primer to conceal the color and seal in the dark stain. If you're making a big change in color, have the primer tinted to closely (but not exactly) match the finished color.

11. **If painting, finish the cabinets with a high quality, oil-base, high gloss or semigloss enamel. If varnishing, apply a coat of high quality, glossy or satin finish, oil-base, polyurethane.**

   Use a natural bristle brush. You may want to enhance spreadability and reduce brushstrokes by thinning the paint or varnish with mineral spirits.

12. **Cover the drawer bodies with plastic and mask the edges of the drawer bodies where they meet the fronts.**

13. **Repeat Steps 10 and 11 for doors and drawers.**

14. **Install new hinges, pulls, and handles (or reinstall the now clean old ones).**

Ongoing cabinet maintenance

Maybe your cabinets look great and don't need cleaning or refinishing. There still are some things you'll need to do on a regular basis. Don't worry: None of them require any special tools or materials, and together they take no more than half an hour a year to do:

- **Tighten knobs and pulls.** Don't over-tighten them.

- **Lubricate and adjust hinges.** Don't go crazy — a lot of oil is not better than a little.

- **Lubricate and adjust drawer slides**. A little squirt of WD-40 works well on metal guides. Use beeswax or paraffin if your drawers have wooden guides.

- **Remove finger smudges.** Try spray cleaner first, then a vinegar-and-water solution, then, if all else fails, a little mineral spirits on a rag.

One small budget, one huge success

We have friends who had a terrible-looking set of kitchen cabinets and a terribly limited remodeling budget. The cabinets were real wood, however, and our friends had to admit that they still worked fine. They tried repainting them to see if they could avoid buying new ones. When they were done, the cabinets looked beautiful! Then they completed their cost-effective new look by replacing the countertop and installing a new vinyl floor. The total cost? Less than $2,500! The bottom line: Not every kitchen remodeling job has to cost $20,000 to $50,000. Sometimes the simplest things, like a coat of paint, can make a big difference.

Enduring Countertop Health

Countertops can be made of plastic laminate (a thin layer of plastic laminated onto a wood or hardboard base), solid-surface (solid plastic or solid acrylic), ceramic tile, stone (marble, granite and so on) and wood butcher block. Each requires different care and different cures for what ails them. Not withstanding maintaining their beauty, in many instances our cures will also protect these surfaces, and, therefore, their longevity.

Lovely, lasting laminate

It's easy to keep a laminate countertop nice and clean. All you need is water, a little soap, and a stiff nylon brush. Mix the water and the soap, and then scrub away with the brush. You'd be surprised at how dirty a "clean" countertop is.

Once your countertop is super clean, consider giving it a coat of car wax. A coat of wax will protect a counter in the same way that it protects the painted surface on a car. Just like waxing your car, it'll take a little oomph, but at least you won't scrape your hand on the edge of a license plate. If you're handy with a buffer, you can use it to get an extra glossy shine. But be very careful — too much high-speed buffing wrecks the plastic laminate surface.

Here are a few tips that will help you keep your laminate countertops looking lovely for a long time:

- Avoid using abrasive cleaners. That means no Ajax, no Comet, and no Soft Scrub.
- Don't let water stand, especially on seams and along the backsplash.
- Always use a cutting board (laminate is too soft to stand up to knives).
- Never place a hot pan directly on the surface.

Popping bubbles

Laminate countertops are made of a thin sheet of plastic bonded to a plywood or hardboard base with contact cement. Sometimes the contact cement loses its stickiness and the laminate forms a bump. Luckily, it's easy to stick the laminate back down (see Figure 18-1):

1. **Place a slightly damp towel over the bubble.**

2. **Apply low heat with a clothes iron for 10 seconds.**

   This softens the laminate and the adhesive "re-stickifies" the contact cement.

3. **Immediately place several heavy books on the repaired spot and leave them there for 12 hours.**

This keeps the laminate in contact with glue as it re-cures.

Figure 18-1:
Popping
bubbles on
a laminate
countertop.

A. Apply low heat for 10 seconds.　　**B.** Leave heavy books on repair for 12 hours.

Hiding chips, cuts, and scratches

Sooner or later, you're going to get a chip, cut, or scratch in your nice laminate countertop. Besides looking terrible, water can travel through the open area and damage the base.

When you get done strangling the person responsible, head out to the nearest home center for some SeamFil chip filler kit and a brand-new, well-polished putty knife. A SeamFil kit comes in 20 colors (mix them to match your countertop). It dries to a satin finish, and a gloss additive lets you match shiny surfaces. Just follow the directions on the package.

Neither SeamFil nor any other similar product can make a countertop gouge invisible; they just make them less noticeable. However, the repair does become water-resistant.

Supersolid surfaces

You probably know this beautiful, easy-to-care-for countertop material by one of its brand names — Corian, Avonite, and so on. Plain and simple, solid-surface countertops require little care and are virtually impossible to permanently damage.

Because they are made of a nonporous, plastic or plastic-like material, soap and water keeps them clean. Scratches, stains, and other imperfections are removed by sanding with 400-to 600-grit wet/dry sandpaper. A cigarette burn or pan scorch is not a disaster — it can be sanded out, too.

The manufacturer of your countertop probably offers a repair kit. If you need to undo some self-inflicted imperfection, read the instructions and do exactly what the manufacturer's instructions tell you to do.

Tough tile tops

A ceramic tile countertop offers a trade-off: It lasts forever, but it requires more maintenance than other types of tops. If you ask us, it's worth the extra work.

The tile itself is tough. It's the grout you have to worry about. Grout is the cement-like stuff that fills the gaps between tiles. For the record, grout readily absorbs moisture and stains.

Sealing out trouble

The best way to prevent grubby grout is to seal it after the tile is installed and before the first cup of coffee spills. You need to wait a few months or so for the grout to thoroughly cure.

Your local home center probably has several different brands of grout and tile sealer with handy sponge applicators. Silicone base sealer is best. Follow the manufacturer's directions.

The sealer goes a long way toward preventing stains and keeping your beautiful new countertop looking good. Actually, it couldn't hurt to seal it twice!

Cleaning grubby grout

To clean your grout, you need a bottle of vinegar, a bottle of hydrogen peroxide, water, and a small brass brush (a steel brush would leave rust marks in the grout and dark scratches in the tile). If you can't find a brass brush, grab a couple of brand-new hard toothbrushes.

Make a solution of 1 part water, 1 part vinegar in a big jar. Dip the brush in the solution and start scrubbing the grout (see Figure 18-2). Yes, it's going to take a while. And yes, it's going to be tedious. The vinegar, a weak acid, helps remove hard water deposits and other hard-to-remove chemical stains. Remove the sour-smelling solution by wiping the countertop thoroughly with a damp sponge.

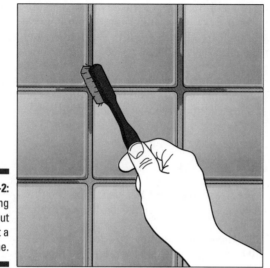

Figure 18-2:
Scrubbing
dirty grout
1 inch at a
time.

If the old sauerbraten treatment doesn't do the trick, grab the bottle of hydrogen peroxide (the stuff for disinfecting cuts) and do the same thing. The peroxide whitens the grout and helps dislodge stains caused by foods. Let it sit for a few minutes, then scrub like crazy. Work in a small area. After scrubbing, wipe down the surface with a damp sponge.

If neither vinegar nor hydrogen peroxide gets the grout nice and white, you have to scrub using a weak bleach solution — 2 tablespoons per quart. Open the windows, turn on the vent hood, and bring a box fan up from the base-ment. Wear old clothes, eye protection, and gloves. Scrub carefully. Rinse thoroughly and then rinse again.

This is one of those situations where more is not better. If you use more than the recommended amount of bleach, you'll give yourself one heck of a headache and a wheezy cough. Ask any doctor: It's not good to breath chlo-rine fumes. And, as always, never mix other chemicals or household cleaners with bleach.

If your grout is still grubby after this all-out chemical assault, the only solu-tion is replacement (which we get to later in the chapter) or the application of a grout stain.

Staining grubby grout

Grout stains are essentially paint. You can find them at any decent home center or tile store. Like it is for all paints, the grout to be stained must be really, really, really clean before application. Clean, rinse thoroughly, and allow the grout to dry overnight.

Read the directions on the container and apply it exactly the way the manufacturer tells you to. This is no time for freelancing. Something you should know: Although grout stain is a time- and energy-saving alternative to grout replacement, it doesn't last forever — you have to restain every year or two.

If you have just one spot that won't come clean, you can "stain" it white using white shoe polish on a cue-tip or a tiny artist's paint brush.

Replacing grout

Grout that leaks can allow water underneath where wood rot can occur. Replacing grout will make your counters look better and last longer. How often can you kill two birds with one stone?

There are two different kinds of grout: cement-based and epoxy-based. For a number of very good reasons (cost and ease-of-use, primarily), you want to use cement-based. For thin (⅛-inch) joints between tiles, use plain unsanded grout. For wide (¼-inch) joints, use sanded grout.

Grout comes in a rainbow of colors, and your choice has a big effect on the appearance of the finished countertop. Do what you want, but know that colored grout (even gray) shows dirt and stains less — and is easier to clean — than light or white grout.

Before you can do any actual grout application, you have to "saw" out old, cracked, and deteriorated grout from the joints between the tiles. You can use a grout saw to do the job, but for most people, a churchkey-style beer can opener does the job. The really sophisticated (lazy) do-it-yourselfer uses a Dremel tool with a tiny grinding bit. Be careful, and don't apply too much pressure — tools (especially power tools) and ceramic tile don't mix. When a tool slips out of the joint it can scratch or gouge the tile. When you've got all the loose grout out, vacuum the surface and wipe with a damp sponge to get up every bit of dust and debris. Then, it's time to get grouting!

You need:

- ✔ Grout (powdered or premixed)
- ✔ Rubber float or squeegee
- ✔ Big sponge
- ✔ Popsicle stick
- ✔ Rags or cheesecloth
- ✔ Vinegar
- ✔ Bucket
- ✔ Rubber gloves (grout is caustic)

Here's how you do it:

1. **If you bought powdered grout, mix it with water, according to the manufacturer's directions.**

   Make only as much as you think you can use in 30 minutes, which is not a lot. Be sure to use cold water. Using warm water can cause some colors to mottle when they dry.

2. **Wearing rubber gloves and working in a 3-foot square area, apply the grout to the surface of the tiles diagonally using the rubber float or squeegee held at a 45-degree angle to the surface.**

   Spread the grout liberally and force it into the joints. Use the Popsicle stick for corners and small, tough-to-reach spots. Remove excess grout as you go.

3. **Let the grout set for 20 minutes or however long the manufacturer suggests.**

4. **Wipe the entire surface with a damp sponge and keep wiping until all the grout lines are even and the joints are smooth.**

   Rinse the sponge frequently.

5. **Let the grout dry for another 20 minutes.**

6. **Polish the tiles with a rag or cheesecloth.**

   Use an old toothbrush to get into the corners and hard-to-reach areas.

7. **Mix fresh grout and move on to another area. Continue until entire tiled surface is grouted.**

8. **When all the freshly grouted areas are dry, remove any grout haze with soft rag and a 10-percent solution of vinegar and water.**

   You may have to wipe the haze off several times before the tile surface is completely clean.

9. **Caulk where the countertop meets walls and backsplash and around the edge of the sink. A few months or so after installation, seal all the joints with grout sealer.**

Replacing a broken tile

Got a loose tile? Dropped the big soup pot and cracked one? Worried about how it looks or that you might accidentally slash your wrist on the sharp edge? It's time for replacement!

If you're lucky enough to have a leftover tile stashed in your workbench, you're ready to go. But if you don't, you have to go on a tile hunt. Chip out a sample (see the following text for how) and take it to the biggest tile dealer you can find. If it's a standard, really common tile, they'll have an exact match for sure. Or they may have a tile that is very, very similar in color and texture. If your tile is not common, they probably have old partial boxes and piles of leftover discontinued tiles in the back for you to paw through. Good luck!

If you can't find an acceptable match consider replacing several tiles. By doing this you can randomly add tiles in a contrasting color or *decos* (decorator tiles with pictures).

With your perfectly matching replacement tile in hand (or some that don't match), grab the tools you need:

- ✔ Grout saw
- ✔ Glass cutter
- ✔ Hammer and a cold chisel (the kind that isn't for use on wood)
- ✔ Electric drill with a ¼-inch masonry bit
- ✔ Mastic (tile adhesive)
- ✔ Putty knife
- ✔ Block of wood bigger than the tile
- ✔ Masking tape

Here's how to do the job (take note of how often we use the word "carefully"):

1. **Carefully remove the grout from the joints around the damaged tile using the grout saw or a Dremel tool.**

2. **Use the drill to bore a hole in the center of the tile and use the glass cutter to scribe an 'X' in the tile (corner to corner).**

   Drilling a hole in the center and crosscutting the surface acts to relieve pressure when you begin to remove the tile with the hammer and chisel. Relieving pressure helps prevent damage to surrounding tiles.

3. **Use the hammer and chisel to carefully remove the tile and clean out the area behind it.**

   Remove all adhesive and grout. Try not to pry underneath adjacent tiles — you could loosen them.

4. **Test-fit the replacement tile to make sure it sits well with the other tiles.**

   You want it to be slightly recessed to leave room for adhesive.

5. **Carefully spread mastic on the back of the tile with a putty knife.**

   Keep it ¼ to ½ inch from the edges for squishing room.

6. Carefully place the tile in position, wiggle it a little to ensure good contact between the tile, the adhesive, and the base.

7. Place the block of wood over the tile and give it a couple gentle taps to make extra sure the tile is flush with its neighbors and to make super sure that the adhesive is stuck to everything.

8. Tape the wood over the repair to protect the repair.

9. Wait at least 24 hours and then apply grout (see the preceding section).

Marvelous marble

Whether in sheets or pieces marble is an elegant surface. Unfortunately, it is unbelievably soft. Many folks think that marble is a type of stone. It isn't. It's actually petrified calcium — old seashells. It can be easily damaged. A spill of orange juice, a few drops of hair spray or a splash of your favorite alcoholic beverage is all it takes. If you see a circle on the counter where the juice glass once was you can count on the fact that the spot has been permanently etched. There are companies that can be hired to polish out etched areas. Better yet is to keep alcohol and even the mildest acids away from marble. Silicone sealer can be applied, but prevention is the only safe method to preserve marble.

We have a neat trick that you can use to clean stained marble. You'll need half a lemon and a dish of table salt. All you have to do is dip the lemon into the salt and rub the marble. It really is amazing how well it works. If you can't get it clean with this trick, chances are you won't get it clean.

Amazing granite

Granite is stone — one of the hardest. In our opinion there is no surface that is as durable or easy to maintain. Ten years later it shines as beautifully as the day it was installed.

Warm water on a cloth or paper towel is all that it takes to remove coffee or tea stains from granite. Hot pots have no effect on it, and cold granite is an absolutely perfect baker's surface. To maintain your granite, simply keep it clean by wiping with a damp cloth. It will remain beautiful and — literally — last forever!

Wonderful wood

People who love to cook love an in-counter butcher block. Heck, anyone who ever chops an onion likes the convenience of a solid, stable cutting surface. Care of this surface is simple:

✔ Maintain a smooth surface by sanding out scratches and cuts.

✔ Prevent swelling, shrinking, and warping by not flooding the surface with water or letting water stand on the surface.

✔ Clean with a soapy damp cloth and then remove soapy residue with a clean damp cloth. We bleach for stains.

✔ Protect and preserve the surface by periodically applying mineral oil (not vegetable oil or olive oil) monthly.

✔ Mineral oil doesn't go rancid like vegetable-based oils do. Vegetable-based oils also mess up polyurethane or varnish. Mineral oil also helps prevent the wood from drying out and cracking or literally coming apart at the seams.

✔ Apply the oil with a soft cloth, rubbing with the grain. Allow the oil to soak in and then wipe off excess oil.

Chapter 19

Flooring

In This Chapter

▶ Cleaning tips for all types of flooring

▶ Keeping your hardwood floor looking like new

▶ Keeping your carpet clean and smelling fresh

*I*n this chapter, we take a close up look at what's underfoot. To get in the proper frame of mind, we suggest that you get out of your comfy chair and sit on the floor while you read. From that position, you can clearly see — and understand — what we're talking about.

Luckily for you, we move quickly and stick to the basics, focusing on the most important flooring maintenance and repair tasks.

Ceramic Tile a Go-Go

Got ceramic tile on the floor? Need to know how to care for it? Go to Chapter 18 and read about caring for tile countertops. Everything described there works well for the floor, too. If you want to install a new tile floor, you need a different book. (Try *Home Improvement For Dummies,* by Gene and Katie Hamilton, published by IDG Books Worldwide, Inc.)

If you want your ceramic tile floor to stay looking good, never, ever use an abrasive cleanser on it. It literally sands off the finish on the tiles. Check the labels of the products you use — you'll be surprised by how many contain abrasives.

Vanquishing Vinyl Trouble

The odds are good that you have resilient flooring — sheet vinyl or vinyl tile — somewhere in your house. After all, it's the most popular flooring material for kitchens, bathrooms, and laundry rooms. It's popular because it's easy to care for. And that's good for you.

This is not to say that a vinyl floor won't ever have problems. It is fair to say, however, that most serious vinyl flooring problems are not problems with the material itself. For example, if you have a series of ridges in your floor, you actually have an uneven or swollen underlayment. If your vinyl tile or sheet vinyl is coming up in places, you probably have moisture in the subfloor from a leaking pipe, spillage from the sink, or condensation from below.

As tempting as it may be, you can't just cover up problems — you have to fix their underlying cause. If you've got a sagging subfloor, see Chapter 3 for information on how to level it. Fortunately, this can be done without having to pull up the vinyl.

If the vinyl has black, brown, or purple stains that are visible just below the surface of the vinyl, there is no way to remove the stains without removing the vinyl. These stains are mildew and fungus that are being fed by moisture from the crawlspace, basement, or concrete slab or from water leaking beneath the vinyl. If you've got moisture under your floor covering, you've got to find the source and stop it. Check out Chapter 3 for information on how to solve a moisture problem in your crawlspace or basement and how to seal concrete. Check the various plumbing chapters on how to deal with pipe leaks.

Once you solve your moisture problem, you can then deal with the stained vinyl. If the damage is widespread, you unfortunately need to rip up the vinyl and underlayment (a layer of plywood or particleboard that is used as a smoothing layer on which the vinyl is laid).

This is an excellent opportunity to inspect the condition of the subfloor and refasten it to the floor joist using construction screws to eliminate current and future floor squeaks. See Chapter 3 for information on how to do this. If you do the easy fix instead of the right fix, you better like working on your hands and knees — you'll be fixing the floor again and again.

With that said, there are a few things that you can do to keep your vinyl flooring looking good on a day-to-day basis.

Scuff marks

Get an art gum eraser (one of those grayish-tan ones you used in high school) or borrow a Pink Pearl eraser from your kid's school supplies. Just rub the mark and — voilà! — the mark disappears.

For tougher scuffs, use a little paint thinner on a rag to rub the spot clean. Be careful not to go nuts with the thinner — you could remove the no-wax finish. Then stop wearing scuff-makers, like cheap plastic-soled shoes, hiking boots, and running shoes, in the house.

Persistent grubbiness

Before you know it, a vinyl floor can acquire a funky gray cast. This comes from infrequent or inadequate cleaning. Diligence is the key to avoiding this problem:

- ✔ Vacuum or sweep regularly to remove abrasive dirt and dust.
- ✔ Wipe up spills immediately.
- ✔ Mop regularly with a damp mop and 1 tablespoon of white vinegar in 1 gallon of warm water (no detergent!).

For the best results, work on a small section at a time and dry it before moving on to the next section. If the vinegar solution is left on for an extended period and allowed to air dry, it can dull the finish.

If regular cleaning doesn't keep the perma-dirt away, use a mop or sponge and a solution of warm water (not hot) and a few drops of liquid dish soap. Don't rub too hard. Rinse thoroughly with clean water.

If the problem is a yellow discoloration, you need to remove and reapply wax. However, don't remove the wax more than once a year — the chemicals in the remover are hard on the vinyl.

When reapplying the wax, be sure to choose a product rated for floors as opposed to a paste furniture wax. Floor wax provides maximum protection without becoming dangerously slippery.

No-wax vinyl floors require basically the same kind of care. Again, the secret to a long-lasting shine is keeping the floor clean. Stay on top of dirt and spills. And when you mop, use only a little white vinegar rinse and dry thoroughly.

Eventually, no matter how diligent you are about cleaning, your no-wax floor will lose its shine. Then, believe it or not, the best way to make it new-looking is to wax it. Use a water-based self-polishing wax. Whenever possible use a product recommended by the manufacturer. If you don't know who the manufacturer is, get a recommendation from a reputable flooring contractor in your area.

Curling vinyl tile

Curls in your hair may look great, but when they're in your vinyl flooring, they can lead to bigger problems. Curling vinyl occurs at seams and edges. The adhesive that is supposed to hold the vinyl flat is no longer doing its job and, thus, the vinyl curls up and away from the underlayment.

Aside from being unsightly, this condition presents a trip hazard. It is also a catchall for dirt and grime. In addition, it exposes the surface below to water damage and makes the area especially susceptible to tearing. What's worse, left unrepaired, the condition will only get worse, which may turn a mole hill into a mountain.

Use a warm iron over a towel to heat the vinyl and soften the adhesive. Make sure to warm the entire tile, including the edges and middle. Carefully peel the tile out using a thin scraper, then scrape out all the old adhesive. Apply vinyl tile adhesive (get it at your favorite home center or flooring store) all over the empty space. Use a notched trowel if you've got one, or apply a thin, even coat using your scraper.

In the case of vinyl floor adhesive, less is more. Too much adhesive can cause the tile to ripple.

Place the replacement tile (you set aside "spares," didn't you?) carefully into the hole and press on it with a block of wood to ensure good adhesion. Remove the glue that squeezes out around the edges with a solvent like lacquer thinner or whatever the glue label suggests and a soft white cloth.

Lay a sheet of waxed paper over the repair and then place a couple of books over the tile to weight it down until the glue fully dries (usually 24 hours). Apply a clear vinyl seam sealer (also available at a home center or flooring store) around the edges. Keep traffic out of the area for a day until the seam sealer has had a chance to set up.

Vinyl tile and sheet flooring manufactured prior to 1978 may contain asbestos. That's the year the U.S. Environmental Protection Agency banned its use in the manufacture of building products. When left alone, they pose virtually no risk of exposure. But when disturbed, they could release asbestos fibers into the air, which could be hazardous to your health. Therefore, be careful not to disturb old tile. If you opt for a new floor, it's almost always best to go over it, rather than expose yourself and your family to the risks associated with removal. If you're not sure whether your floor contains asbestos, you can have it tested by a licensed testing lab. For more information on this, pick up a copy of *Home Remodeling For Dummies,* by us, published by IDG Books Worldwide.

Gouged, cut, or scratched sheet vinyl

In contrast to vinyl tile that has gobs of seams, sheet vinyl has far fewer seams. There is an advantage to fewer seams because there are fewer seams to repair should something go wrong. On the other hand, when it comes to making a patch, it can be a little trickier than replacing a single tile. You'll need:

- Clothes iron
- Towel
- Utility knife and several new blades
- Metal straightedge
- Masking tape or double-sided tape
- Putty knife
- Vinyl adhesive
- Notched trowel
- Clean rags
- Adhesive solvent
- Clear vinyl seam sealer

The best patch is a piece of the original flooring material. You need a piece that is slightly larger than the area you want to patch. And it's best to have one that gives you a chance to make an unnoticeable repair: Look for squares or distinct patterns or lines you can use to hide your cuts.

If you or the previous homeowner didn't save a scrap, you can steal a patch from underneath an appliance or from a closet floor. Cut the patch carefully using a straightedge. Work slowly using a warm iron over a towel and a putty knife to peel up the patch. Try not to leave too much of the backing stuck to the floor. Replace the stolen patch with any old scrap of vinyl floor. (Who's going to see it?)

Another consideration: Older vinyl floors may have been waxed, and wax tends to yellow (especially in exposed locations). To make sure your patch matches the surrounding vinyl, remove all the wax from the entire floor using a commercial-strength wax remover (available at a janitorial supply house) and floor scrubber. It's a good idea to remove the builtup wax and re-wax every few years, anyway.

Assuming you can find a good piece of material to patch with, here's how you do the job:

1. **Place the patch over the damaged area, match up the pattern/lines** *exactly***, then tape in place.**

    Again, it's best to place your cuts in the lines that define squares in the pattern or something (anything!) other than "blank" areas.

2. **Use a utility knife and fresh blade to cut through both the patch and the damaged area.**

3. **Set the patch aside and make sure the cuts went all the way through the damaged vinyl.**

   Carefully deepen any cuts that are too shallow.

4. **Make two corner-to-corner diagonal cuts in the repair area.**

   Doing so makes it easier to remove the damaged section.

5. **Peel back the damaged section from the middle.**

   You might have to use the old iron-and-towel trick to loosen the glue. Work slowly and carefully. If you're using a pristine, never-been-glued patch, make sure to remove as much of the glue and stuck-down backing material as you can. If you're using a "borrowed" patch that has some of the backing torn off, it's okay if you leave some of the backing material stuck to the floor — it'll help even things out.

6. **Apply vinyl adhesive to the floor.**

   Tub-and-tile caulk works great, too.

7. **Carefully place the patch in the hole, but do not press it down.**

8. **Cover the patch with waxed paper, then place several heavy books on top.**

   The bottom book should be bigger than the patch to avoid pushing the patch below the level of the surrounding floor. Let the adhesive cure for 24 hours. Remove the books and use mineral spirits to clean excess adhesive.

9. **Apply clear vinyl seam sealer and let it set a day before allowing traffic in the area.**

   The key to applying seam sealer is to apply just enough to cover the seam. Again, less is more. The material is self-leveling, will bond with the vinyl, and is designed to disappear.

Sheet vinyl bubbles

No matter how good your vinyl flooring is, or how well it was installed, bubbles or blisters will appear occasionally. Fortunately, they're usually easy to fix.

Before you do anything, make a trip to the crawlspace or basement area below the floor in questions to see if moisture is rising from below and causing the bubble. If moisture is the culprit, stop here and turn to Chapter 3 for advice on how to dry out your basement or crawlspace.

If you've got water vapor migrating into the space between the floor and the vinyl, you've got big trouble. Believe us, soon a bubble will be the least of your problems soon. Here's how to fix the problem.

If your bubble seems to be spontaneous, repairs are simple.

Use a large sewing needle to perforate small bubbles (1 inch or so in diameter) at their center. Make sure you go all the way through — you're making the hole to allow trapped air to escape. Then get out the old iron, towel, and books. Lay the towel over the area and use the iron (not too hot!) to soften and flatten the vinyl. Place heavy books over the area to ensure good re-adhesion.

If that doesn't work, you'll have to get a little glue into the bubble. To do this you will need a glue syringe. Insert the tip of the syringe into the hole you made with the needle, and squirt a couple of drops of adhesive (no more!) into the bubble. Place a piece of waxed paper on the repair and stack the books on top. Why the waxed paper? Because you don't want to accidentally glue a book to the floor!

Loving Your Linoleum

Some older homes still have linoleum floors. We don't know why. Made of ground cork and linseed oil, it stains, dents, and scratches easily. If you have a linoleum floor, it's time to replace it with a better-looking, better-performing sheet vinyl floor. But if you like the 1940s retro look of linoleum, and want to keep it, care is not difficult: Damp mop using 1 tablespoon of white vinegar in 1 gallon of warm water, then rinse and dry.

Remember to clean a small area at a time as the vinegar left to air dry can dull the finish over time. Add 1 tablespoon of baby oil to the rinse water to replace the oils lost over time. Never use ammonia, strong cleaning chemicals, or abrasive cleaners. Wax occasionally.

Do not remove old wax from a linoleum floor with a commercial wax remover — it's way too harsh. To strip a linoleum floor, use a solution of 3 parts warm water and 1 part isopropyl (rubbing) alcohol. A more aggressive alternative is 1 cup ammonia in 1 gallon of hot water. Pour the solution onto the floor (a section at a time) and let is stand for about five minutes — don't let it dry, or the wax will set up and you'll have to start over again. Scrape the wax off using a Teflon spatula. Wear gloves, eye protection, and open the windows for ventilation.

Taking Care of Torginol

Many years ago, someone posed a question of us via our home-improvement newspaper column that we simply couldn't answer. He stated that he had recently purchased a home that had decorative seamless flooring in the kitchen, bath, laundry, and family room, and he wanted to know if we knew what it was and how to care for it. Stumped, we responded by asking our readers if they had heard of such a finish. The response that ensued to this day amazes us. We received hundreds of letters from people across the United States who had this type of flooring. We even heard from the manufacturer of the product. Boy did we luck out! Therefore, it is with great pleasure that we share the following information on one of America's best-kept flooring secrets.

The material is called Torginol Vinyl Chip seamless flooring. Colorful vinyl chips are embedded in liquid resins creating a custom-made coating. This unique texture enhances Torginol's outstanding qualities of durability, waxless beauty, and easy maintenance. Although it is used extensively in commercial environments such as schools, hospitals, restaurants, and other "high-traffic" public places, it was very popular in the '50s and '60s as an alternative to residential linoleum and vinyl. It is even used on the Truman Balcony at the White House!

Torginol floors don't require hard scrubbing because dirt releases from the surface quite readily with only damp mopping. If you need a tougher cleaner, use a mild or pH-neutral cleaner. Waxing is not recommended, as it attracts dirt, making the floor more difficult to keep clean.

TLC for Terrazzo

Made of white portland cement and tan and white marble chips (the old method), or epoxy and marble chips (the new method), and formed into large "tiles" or slabs, terrazzo is a long-lasting, stone-like material. It's not a terribly common residential flooring material, but a friend of ours grew up in a late-1950s house with it in the front hall. So we'll humor him (and others like him) by including a few tips here:

✔ Sweep and mop frequently to remove abrasive dirt, sand, and dust.

✔ Don't use household cleaners. Most detergents and floor-cleaning products contain alkalis, which will damage the finish. For best results, use a commercial cleaner made especially for terrazzo.

✔ Use a wet mop and change the rinse water frequently to keep it clean.

    ✔ Buff occasionally with an electric buffer.

    ✔ To remove tough soil, use an electric floor-scrubbing machine, then buff.

Cement-based terrazzo must be sealed occasionally with a penetrating sealer to reduce its porosity and prevent staining. Use a sealer especially made for terrazzo.

Never clean terrazzo with soaps and scrubbing powders containing detergents, water-soluble inorganic salts, or crystallizing salts. They can damage the finish.

Laminate Love?

It has been one of the most popular finishes for kitchen counters for nearly half a century. Now, plastic laminate is one of the hottest products to hit the flooring market in decades. Harder than vinyl, it has the ability to match virtually any wood flooring or even ceramic tile pattern with uncanny accuracy. The reason? The floor pattern is essentially a photograph — but it's coated with a protective layer that provides years of virtually maintenance-free use, provided that you're not too rough on it. Remember, it's like having your kitchen counters under foot; although it has a harder finish, it can still scratch and dent.

Maintenance is simple. The first thing to keep in mind with laminate (and many other types of flooring) is to avoid abrasives. This includes abrasive cleaners. It also means keeping your floor clean from dirt, one of Mother Nature's most natural abrasives. Door mats, gliders under chairs, and frequent vacuuming are the easiest ways to avoid wear and tear.

Next, damp mop the floor with clean water. As you mop, keep changing the water to avoid re-depositing dirt on the floor. Never use wax cleaners, polishes, or abrasives like steel wool or scouring powder.

Scratches and dents can be fixed using specially designed repair sticks or fillers prepared by the flooring manufacturers. If you need such a fix, contact the manufacturer to find out what's available. If an exact match can't be found, keep in mind that you can often mix two colors for a perfect blend. Just choose one that's slightly lighter and one that's slightly darker than the color of the spot you're trying to match.

If you've got a really big boo-boo and ruined an entire plank, keep in mind that the whole piece can be successfully cut out and replaced. This procedure, however, takes practice and is best left to a trained installer.

Keeping Wood Good

Properly finished wood floors are without a doubt the easiest of all floor surfaces to keep clean and looking good.

Keep grit off the floor. Use walk-off mats at all exterior doors to help prevent dirt, grit, and sand from getting on your wood. Throw-rugs or small sections of carpet just inside the entrances are also recommended.

In addition, we recommend the following for maintaining your wood floors:

- ✔ Vacuum frequently to keep abrasive dirt to a minimum.
- ✔ In kitchens, use area rugs at high-spill locations and at work stations such as the stove, sink, and refrigerator.
- ✔ Avoid ultraviolet light damage to finishes by installing window tinting or draping large windows.
- ✔ Put fabric glides on the legs of your furniture to prevent scratching and scuffing when the furniture is moved.
- ✔ Wipe up spills immediately and then wipe dry.
- ✔ Clean using a not-very-damp mop and an oil soap solution, then wipe the floor dry immediately.

If a floor is waxed, occasional buffing helps renew the shine and remove scuffmarks that may appear in the wax coating. If the shine can't be renewed in heavily used lanes, occasionally re-waxing these areas may be necessary. Intervals for completely re-waxing a floor may extend to a year or longer when attention has been paid to proper care.

For more information on how to care for or repair your wood floor, contact the National Oak Flooring Manufacturers Association in Memphis, Tennessee, at 901-526-5016, or visit its Web site at www.nofma.org.

Keeping Carpet Clean

Carpet cleaning professionals tell us that the most effective method of keeping carpeting clean — and making it last a long time — is to vacuum it regularly. In fact, they recommend vacuuming three or more times per week, and daily in high-traffic areas.

They also point out that the quality of your vacuum makes a difference. An upright vac does the best job of removing deep-down dirt. But a big canister vac with a beater-bar head is good, too. Whichever you prefer, the motor must be powerful enough to create enough suction to remove the dirt, sand,

and debris that is ground into the carpet. If the vac has a beater bar, its brushes should be free of lint, fuzz, and threads. The suction port and hose should be checked regularly for suction-robbing blockages, and the bag should be changed frequently to ease the flow of air through the vac.

Why all this emphasis on vacuuming? Because soil is your carpet's biggest enemy. Carpets wear out because foot traffic grinds embedded dirt into the carpet fiber. And vacuuming is the best way to reduce the dirt that works its way into the carpet.

Aside from regular vacuuming, the best way to keep your carpet clean and reduce wear is to place welcome mats outside every exterior door, and rugs on the inside to catch any leftover grit before it gets further into the house. Finally, it really pays to have everyone remove their shoes when they come into the house.

But what do you do when little Nina spills some sticky red juice in the living room? Give her a big hug. Tell her that you love her. Spot clean!

Spot cleaning

Most of today's carpets are made with a factory-applied stain guard. So usually, a small amount of water and a drop of vinegar (or club soda) will get out a stain. Use a clean, white dry cloth. Don't scrub. Blot.

Over time, especially after numerous carpet cleanings, the factory-applied stain guard provides little stain protection. Although there are a host of stain repellants on the market, your best bet is to have an after-market stain guard installed by a professional carpet cleaning and dying company.

If this simple, quick fix doesn't work, there are a million carpet-cleaning products you can use. Be sure to follow the label directions to the letter.

The most common mistakes people make when they try to spot-clean are overscrubbing and using too much water. Scrubbing destroys carpet fibers. Excess water gets below the carpet into the pad, which leads to mildew and a funky smell.

Carpet cleaning

Sooner or later, your carpet will need to be cleaned. Some people like to do the job themselves, while others would rather leave the job to a professional.

The pros use a variety of methods, including dry powder, foam, and steam (hot-water extraction). Most do-it-yourself carpet cleaning machines use the hot-water extraction method: A hot-water-and-detergent solution is sucked out of a reservoir and sprayed on the carpet and immediately extracted with a powerful vacuum. They aren't difficult to use, just loud.

Here are a few tips that will help you be a carpet-cleaning success:

- ✔ Before you head off to the hardware store to rent a machine, you need to know what your carpet is made of in order to select the right cleaning solution.

- ✔ Before you start, test the solution on an out-of-the-way spot to make sure it won't leave a stain of its own or bleach the color out.

- ✔ Read the instructions on the machine and on the detergent. Follow them exactly. This is no time to freelance.

- ✔ Don't make the mistake of using too much water or too much detergent. Excess water creates mildew, and excess detergent stays in the carpet and attracts dirt like a magnet.

- ✔ Open the windows (or turn on the air conditioning) and use a powerful fan to help speed the drying process. The quicker you get the moisture out of the carpet, the better. If you can find one, rent a carpet-drying fan from a local tool rental company. It is many times more powerful than the most powerful fan found around most homes.

Professional carpet cleaning costs less than you think. In fact, the cost of renting a machine and buying carpet-cleaning solution may not be much less. Make a few phone calls before you decide to do the job yourself. One more thing: The truck-mounted extraction machines the pros use are way more powerful than any you can rent, so they get more dirt out and leave less moisture in.

De-stinking smelly carpet

Time, home life (especially cooking), and pets can make carpets stinky. You may not notice anymore, but anyone who comes into the house probably does. If your carpet has picked up a funky smell, you can try a commercial carpet deodorizer or you can go to the pantry and arm yourself with a box of baking soda. Sprinkle it into the carpet, leave it for a few hours, and then vacuum it up.

For less money and a little extra work, you can try sprinkling grated potato (Yes, potato!) all over the carpet in question. Let it stand for several hours and then vacuum.

If neither of these methods works, stop trying to avoid the inevitable and call a carpet-cleaning company.

Part IV:
Safety, Security, and Shutdown

The 5th Wave   **By Rich Tennant**

"Oh, Dave is very handy around the house. He manually entered the phone numbers for the electrician, the carpenter, and the plumber on our speed dial."

In this part . . .

Of all the parts, we regard this one as the most important. That's because it deals with personal safety and security. What good is a home if you can't feel safe and secure? Thus, in this part we blow the whistle on smoke, fire, carbon monoxide, and a host of other potential home wreckers. We also give you tips on shutting down your home for an extended period, emergency preparedness, and other important stuff that could extend your mortality.

Chapter 20

Safety and Preparedness

● ●

In This Chapter

▶ Preventing household fires

▶ Smoke alarms and carbon monoxide detectors

▶ Fire extinguishers

▶ General emergency preparedness

▶ Gas line maintenance tips

▶ Tightening up security

▶ Garage door safety

▶ Electrical safety

● ●

*I*n the following pages, we offer time-honored, proven safety practices blended with a host of new innovations, contemporary Carey Brothers' concepts, and the very best of today's hi-tech, space-age electronic wizardry. When all used together, these measures ensure greater peace of mind for homeowners.

Fire Safety

Fire has been a number one household danger ever since the day, many eons ago, when our prehistoric ancestors got the idea of bringing fire indoors for cave heating and dinosaur cooking. Since then, accidents and total household destructions have occurred due to misunderstanding, miscalculations, and mis-use of this powerful force of nature.

The following points are worth noting with regard to residential fires:

✔ Careless smoking is the leading cause of residential fire deaths.

✔ 25 percent of fires with child fatalities are caused by children playing with fire.

✔ Household fire hazards include overloaded electrical circuits, faulty wiring, unsafe appliances, wood and coal burning stoves and furnaces, electric and kerosene space heaters, unattended fireplaces, and the careless use of lighters and matches, especially by children.

Preventing fires

So what is your best defense against this household killer? Your best defense is quite simple: good old *common sense*:

✔ Exercise great care with all flammable materials, including fabrics (like drapes and furniture) near high heat sources (like stoves, space heaters, and open fireplaces) and especially combustible liquids (like solvents, cleaners and fuels) — both when using and storing them.

✔ Don't overload electrical circuits or put too great a burden on individual outlets or lightweight extension cords. Overloading causes overheating, which leads to wire fatigue and a possible fire. Dimming or flickering lights, a power cord that is warm or hot to the touch, and fuses that repeatedly burn out or breakers in the electrical panel that frequently trip are sure signs of an overloaded circuit.

✔ Don't use bulbs with a higher wattage than a lamp or fixture is rated for, because the lamp can seriously overheat. Most modern light fixtures and lamps have a label on the fixture that rates the maximum recommended bulb wattage for that particular fixture. If the label can't be found, bring the lamp or information on the fixture to a lighting store for recommendations on the wattage of the bulb that should be used.

✔ Watch for faulty electronic equipment, malfunctioning appliances, frayed electrical cords, flickering lights, or fuses that blow and circuit breakers that trip repeatedly — they're all potential fire hazards.

✔ Never smoke cigarettes, cigars, or pipes in bed — or when you are tired or lying down.

Make sure any ashes have cooled before you throw them away. Many fires are started by the careless dumping of ashes that are not fully extinguished. This includes ashes from ashtrays, fireplaces, and barbeques. Hot embers can smolder undetected in the trash for hours before igniting.

✔ Keep spaceheaters at least 3 feet away from flammable items. Only buy units with tip-over shut-off switches, and *never* operate one while sleeping.

Smoke detectors and alarms

Smoke detectors (now referred to as smoke *alarms* by the safety industry) are considered to be one of the least expensive, most popular, and best forms of life protection insurance you can buy. A working smoke detector doubles a person's chance of surviving a fire by warning of a dangerous situation before it's too late.

For minimum coverage, have at least one smoke detector or alarm on every level of your home and in every sleeping area. Alarms can also be added to hallways outside every bedroom, the top and bottom of all stairways, and often forgotten places such as basements, attics, utility rooms, and garages.

Smoke detectors can be either:

- **Battery-operated:** These inexpensive units can easily be installed any-where. They require frequent inspection to determine the condition of the battery.

- **AC powered units:** Installed by an electrician (or those with a good work-ing knowledge of electricity), these units are much more dependable over the long haul due to their direct-wired power source. But they should also have an independent battery backup so they that continue to operate during a blackout or electric fire that temporarily interrupts power.

Some newer models also have a hush-button feature that silences a nuisance false alarm and desensitizes the unit for a few minutes, until the air clears, when it resets itself. Other high-end models also have safety lights that come on when the alarm is activated.

Testing alarms and detectors

All smoke detectors and alarms have a "test button," which, when pushed, causes the alarm to sound. Also, most detectors have either a blinking or solid light that glows to let you know that the alarm is getting power.

Once a month, get up on a chair, or use a broom handle for extra reach, and push the test button (see Figure 20-1). If you don't hear anything, then your battery is dead. If after changing the battery, the smoke detector is still not working, immediately replace it with a new one.

The button test ensures that the batteries are working. However, it doesn't tell you whether the detector is operating properly. To do this, put two or three lighted matches together (the wood kitchen type is best), then blow out the flame, holding the matches so that the smoke wafts up toward the unit.

While battery-operated units have a built-in device that "chirps" when batter-ies get low, signaling the need for replacement, common wisdom dictates not waiting until that point. Batteries should be replaced twice a year, once in the spring and once in the fall.

Figure 20-1:
Testing your
fire alarm
batteries.

Never remove a battery from your smoke alarm for use in another item — like a radio, toy, or TV remote. Many people do so with every intention of replacing them in short order, only to remember that they forgot while standing and watching their house burn down (if they were lucky enough to awake and escape in time).

While you're up there checking your battery every month, also brush or vacuum the alarm to keep dirt and dust out of the mechanism. Never use cleaning sprays or solvents that can enter the unit and contaminate sensors.

Replacing alarms and detectors

After a period of ten years, a smoke detector has endured more than 87,000 hours of continuous operation, during which time the internal sensors have probably become contaminated with dust, dirt, and air pollutant residues.

If your alarm or detector is more than ten years old, consider replacing it to maintain optimum detection capabilities of deadly smoke in your home.

Fire extinguishers

Most fires start out small. Often they can easily and quickly be put out if you have a working fire extinguisher readily at hand.

Dealing with fire emergencies

Once a smoke detector sounds — whether night or day — a quick response and pre-planned actions are the number one and two best life savers you'll ever have.

Before opening any doors, look for smoke seeping around edges and feel the surface with your hand. The door knob is another good indicator as to whether fire exists on the other side, as metal conducts heat faster and more efficiently than wood does.

If it feels safe, open the door slowly and be prepared to close it quickly if heat and smoke rush in. Don't stop to get dressed, find pets, or collect valuables. Extra wasted seconds can cost lives. Gather only family members and exit immediately.

If smoke is extremely dense, crawl on your knees and keep your mouth covered with a towel or cloth if at all possible.

Families should develop and rehearse a home escape plan, with two ways out of every room. Second floor bedrooms should have a fold-up fire escape ladder stored in each one. Also include plans for a preset designated meeting place where everyone should gather once safely outside. Once you are out, stay put until helps arrives, and never re-enter the house under any circumstances.

Rehearse your family escape plan regularly. Once everyone knows what to do, also perform run-throughs with your eyes closed — simulating darkness or smoke-filled passages — counting and memorizing the number of steps to each and every turn and ultimately to safety.

Manufacturers of home safety products recommend having one fire extinguisher for every 600 square feet of living area. The kitchen, garage, and basement should each have an extinguisher of its own. Keep one in the car as well.

Fire extinguishers are rated according to force and how much fire-fighting agent they contain — both of which determine how long it operates when it is used and discharged. With most home extinguishers, this duration is short — so quick action and a good aim are important factors in fully quenching flames while a fire is still in it's early stage. (See the sidebar "PASSing on a fire" for some tips on using fire extinguishers.)

Always purchase fire extinguishers with a pressure gauge. The pressure gauge should be checked at least once each month to ensure it is ready for use at all times. If the fire extinguisher pressure is low and it is a model that cannot be recharged, dispose of it and replace it with a new unit.

Aside from making sure that a fire extinguisher is properly charged and readily accessible, there is no other regular maintenance to speak of. Under no circumstances should you periodically test the extinguisher by pulling the pin and squeezing the trigger. This can result in a premature loss of pressure.

PASSing on a fire

If you ever need to use a fire extinguisher, use the **PASS** method:

✔ **P**ull the pin.

✔ **A**im at the base of the fire.

✔ **S**queeze the handle.

✔ **S**weep the base of the fire from side to side, starting with the closest edge and working away from yourself.

Carbon Monoxide Danger in the Home

Carbon Monoxide (CO) is the number one cause of poisoning deaths in America. CO is an invisible, odorless, poisonous gas produced by the incomplete combustion of any fuel — such as gasoline, kerosene, propane, natural gas, oil, and even wood fires. In concentrated form, CO can be fatal when inhaled — killing in minutes or hours, depending on the level of CO in the air. In smaller doses, CO produces a wide range of flu-like symptoms ranging from red eyes, dizziness, and headaches to nausea, fatigue, and upset stomach.

One tell-tale sign of mild CO poisoning is flu symptoms without a fever.

Typical sources of CO in homes are malfunctioning gas furnaces, gas stoves, water heaters, clothes dryers, and even improperly vented fireplaces. Other major dangers include using a generator in or too near one's home, using a barbeque unit indoors to cook or heat during a power outage, and letting a car run in a garage or car port where exhaust fumes can collect and enter the home.

Many of today's energy-efficient, "tight" homes minimize outside air exchange and cross ventilation, giving CO no chance to exit once it enters the home.

Just as with smoke detectors, there are CO detectors for the home. The Consumer Product Safety Commission (CPSC) recommends that every home with fuel-burning appliances of any kind be equipped with a least one CO detector.

If you have only one unit, place it in the hall outside the bedroom area of your home. Invisible, odorless, poisonous CO in concentrated form is even less likely to awaken a sleeper than thick toxic smoke.

While heat and smoke rise toward the ceiling, CO wafts through a room like perfume — only you can't smell or see it. CO detectors should be placed from 14 inches off the floor to face height on the wall and never where there is a draft, such as near a window, doorway, or stairwell.

As with smoke detectors, CO detectors can be battery operated, hard-wired-mounted directly onto an electrical wall outlet, or plugged into an electrical cord, allowing units to sit on a shelf or tabletop. Units that plug into a direct power source should also have an independent battery backup in the event of a power failure.

Your CO detector should have a digital display with memory that indicates and records a problem, even when it's too small to trigger the alarm. A normal low level of CO in a home is zero. Nada, zilch, zip. However, even a small reading — such as 25, 30, or 35 parts per million — indicates a problem that could escalate.

The care and maintenance of CO detectors is basically the same as for smoke detectors with regard to cleaning and frequent testing. (See the section "Smoke detectors and alarms" earlier in this chapter for more information.) However, unlike using kitchen matches to test a smoke alarm, a carbon monoxide detector can't be tested using an outside source. Therefore, it is imperative that the test buttons provided on the equipment be tested at least once each month.

Additionally, have your heating system, vents, chimney, and flue inspected (and cleaned if necessary) by a qualified technician. Always vent fuel-burning appliances. (See Chapter 14 for more information on heating and venting systems. Chapter 15 tells you all about chimney and flue inspections.)

Other maintenance procedures should include checking and correcting any signs that indicate potential CO problems, including:

✔ A noticeably decreasing hot water supply

✔ A furnace that runs constantly but doesn't heat your house

✔ Soot collecting on, under, and around any appliance

✔ An unfamiliar burning odor

✔ A loose or missing furnace panel or vent pipe

✔ Damaged brick, chimney discoloration, or a loose fitting chimney pipe

Guarding Your Home against Damage by Natural Disasters

Natural emergencies can befall the average home and typical family without warning — anywhere in America. Earthquakes, tornadoes, hurricanes, floods, mud slides, blizzards, tidal waves, lightning, squalls, gales, downpours, monsoons, typhoons, whirlwinds, and zephyrs can come out of nowhere and cause substantial damage to the home.

While you can't do anything about the weather, you can be prepared for such emergencies, which may save your life and avert damage to your home.

Shoring up your castle

The same things that you do to maintain your home everyday pull double duty because they also can prepare your home for a natural disaster. The best defense against becoming a victim of an earthquake, fire, flood, snow storm, tornado, or other natural disaster is a strong offense — keeping your home in tip-top shape.

For example, maintaining your roof can prevent shingles from being blown off and a roof leak from occurring. Well-sealed masonry can prevent freeze and thaw damage brought about by bone chilling cold. Plumbing pipe heaters can prevent hundreds or thousands of dollars in damage caused by a burst pipe due to freezing.

How strong is your offense?

When disaster is upon you

When your castle comes under siege from any of Mother Nature's natural marauders, three defensive maneuvers should take place in rapid succession:

- ✔ **Go to your safe place:** Have a safe place ready in the home, such as a windowless room in the basement, and stock it with emergency survival supplies, including first aid equipment, a radio, bottled water, and emergency food provisions (see Figure 20-2).

- ✔ **Stay in your safe place until you get the all clear:** That's why you need the radio with functioning batteries! A portable phone (with extra batteries) can also come in handy at this stage.

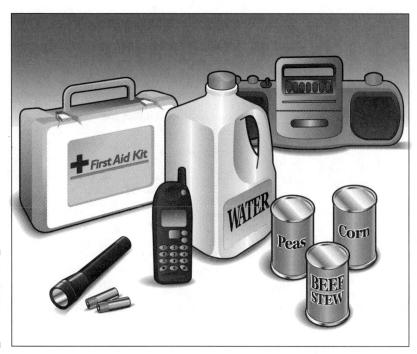

Figure 20-2:
Being
prepared for
life's little
disasters.

✔ **Check for damage:** Following any major disaster, first check the status and well-being of your family members and nearby neighbors. Then begin a thorough home inspection to ascertain any damage that may create larger problems.

Check especially for damaged power lines and dangerous gas leaks, which can cause fire and explosions. Next check for electrical system damage and downed power lines. If you see sparks, note exposed wiring, or smell overheated insulation on wiring, shut off the electricity at the main circuit breaker or fuse box. If water is present, be careful not to make contact if you suspect it may be electrically charged.

Also ascertain any damage to water pipes and sewer drain lines. If damaged, turn off the main water supply valve, avoid drinking any tap or well water, and don't flush toilets or drain water into tubs and sinks.

Well in advance of any natural emergency, you should know where your valves and circuit breakers are located. Make sure that you know how to turn off all major supply lines, and show your family members how to do this, too. Many hardware stores and home centers sell an inexpensive combination dual-emergency wrench designed specifically for quick gas and water shutoffs.

Additional emergency measures

When dealing with an emergency situation, once immediate dangers are dealt with and relatively under control, take photos to record all damage to your home and its contents for insurance purposes. All too often, this only comes to mind once cleanup and repairs are well underway.

Also keep emergency gear close at hand, including a pair of sturdy shoes (to prevent injuries from rubble and broken glass), heavy socks, heavy work gloves, and clothing for keeping warm and dry for an extended period of time, both day and night.

Emergency preparedness must also include putting together a full first aid kit with a manual instructing how to deal with most major situations and injuries step-by-step. Check this kit twice a year for expiration dates and freshness of the products it contains. Also watch for free first aid training classes in your area, often sponsored by local organizations, hospitals, or police and fire departments.

Immediately after a natural disaster, the power is often out. Thus, one's emergency preparedness should also include provisions for both portable and self-contained lighting, including flashlights, extra batteries, candles, a disposable butane lighter, and waterproof matches.

Putting things back together

Follow these general guidelines for getting back underway after an emergency:

- ✔ Deal cautiously with structural damage, watching for physical dangers, ranging from broken glass and nails to water and wet surfaces that may be electrically charged after power resumes. According to the American Red Cross, the number two flood killer after drowning is electrocution. Electrical current can travel through water. Report downed power lines to your utility company or emergency management office.

- ✔ Use a flashlight to inspect for damage. Don't smoke or use candles, lanterns, or open flames unless you know the gas has been turned off and the area has been aired out.

- ✔ Prevent deadly carbon monoxide poisoning by using a generator or other gasoline-powered machine outdoors. The same goes for camping stoves and charcoal grills.

- ✔ Some appliances, such as television sets, keep electrical charges even after they have been unplugged. Don't use appliances or motors that have gotten wet unless they have been taken apart, cleaned, and dried.

- ✔ Watch for snakes and wild animals that have been flooded out of their homes that may seek shelter in yours.

- ✔ Discard contaminated foods and kitchen and bath products.

✔ Boil drinking water until you are absolutely sure it is entirely safe.

✔ Pump out flooded areas in your home as soon as possible to avoid permanent damage to the house frame.

✔ Flooded basements should be pumped out slowly over the course of several days to prevent the basement walls from caving in due to the excessive amount of pressure being placed on the walls from water-logged soil on the opposite side.

✔ If hardwood floors get soaked, mop up excess water and debris immediately and dry the floors slowly to reduce warping. Don't use heat for drying. Open windows and doors and allow finishes to air dry. Rent a high volume fan such as those used by professional carpet cleaners to hasten the air drying process.

Drying finishes out too quickly can cause warping, buckling and cracking that can otherwise be avoided if finishes are allowed to air dry more slowly.

✔ If carpeting gets soaked, don't remove it while it's wet — that can cause tearing. Instead, pick up excess water with a wet/dry vac or carpet cleaning machine, slowly peel back wet carpet, and discard the padding. Then set up a box fan or two to completely dry the area. In most cases, carpets can be cleaned and reused; just the padding needs to be replaced.

✔ Have a pro check all plumbing and service your septic tank.

✔ Call your insurance agent to get the recovery process underway.

For more information on disaster preparedness and recovery, visit the official Web site of the American Red Cross at www.redcross.org.

Gas Line Safety Tips

Of all emergency preparedness efforts, gas lines deserve extra consideration — both in the event of natural disasters and for day-to-day living.

If not properly installed, monitored, and maintained, natural gas is without question the most potentially dangerous item in your home. Gas can cause instant flash fires and devastating explosions that can result from negligence and carelessness.

Don't pour concrete or put asphalt around the rigid gas delivery pipe leading to the meter. This pipe must remain in soft and pliable dirt to safely ride out any seismic activity.

An exposed gas meter is always susceptible to damage or being dislodged by contact. For protection from housework and gardening, and to keep gas meters near driveways and sidewalks from being hit, place two heavy metal pipes in concrete (much like you would set a fence post) in front of and on both sides of the gas meter.

To keep the gas line shutoff wrench handy and easily accessible in a gas emergency, attach it to the main line at the shutoff valve with a piece of chain and a hose clamp. If you ever have to close the main gas valve, only rotate the bar on the valve one-quarter turn so that it runs across the gas line (closed) rather than parallel to it (open).

Inspect all gas line connections in your home. Those leading to appliances, furnaces, and water heaters should only be a corrugated stainless steel or a new epoxy-coated *flexible* connector with a shut off valve where it meets the solid gas delivery line.

Always call before you dig. There are many types of underground lines serving your home — ranging from gas and electricity to water, telephone, and cable TV — and they are often only a few feet below the surface. So before you dig a ditch, sink a fence post, or plant a tree or bush, call your local utility companies for location information.

Maintaining Burglar Alarms

Not all household dangers are derived from natural forces. You also need to take measures to protect against those who would storm the castle, scale the proverbial stone walls, and plunder the family jewels.

Have properly installed solid and secure window and door locks strong enough to deter the average burglar. Then, be sure to use them. Sounds too mundane and simple, you say? Police report that 50 percent of all home burglaries are simply due to windows or doors being left unlocked.

One of the best ways of determining if your home is secure from a potential intruder is to lock yourself out and try to get in without using your house key. You'll either be surprised at how easy it is to gain entry or you'll feel relieved at how tough it is to get into your Fort Knox. During this exercise, be on the lookout for loose doorknobs and deadlocks and shaky windows and doors (including the garage door).

Many break-ins can be averted with the same techniques outlined in Chapter 22. A number of whole-house alarm systems are also available today, and — just as with smoke alarms and carbon monoxide detectors — these too need occasional testing, checking, and tuning up.

Most systems include a fail-safe battery backup, which needs checking and replacement at regular intervals — at least twice annually.

Many systems also have a fire-sensing capability that must be checked and maintained as outlined in "Smoke alarms and detectors" in this chapter.

Most systems also have a keypad for indicating system operation and points of intrusion, and a horn or siren installed indoors (in the attic) or outside under an overhang or eave. Follow the manufacturer's instructions for maintenance and checkup of these features at specified intervals — pay particular attention to all points that signal an intrusion when contact is broken.

Make sure sensitivity levels are properly set to avoid both frequent false alarms (that eventually go unheeded) and a system that doesn't respond properly when it should.

Before ordering and installing an alarm, check with local law enforcement agencies to see if there are any restrictions or special ordinances in your area. Most police departments now discourage homeowners from installing a dialer-type alarm system that automatically calls the police or sheriff's department when activated. They find that when a major disaster takes place, this type of alarm completely swamps incoming lines that are needed to field calls for specific individual emergency situations. A good alternative is to have your alarm monitored by a central reporting agency. Thus, if there is a false alarm, the police or sheriff won't be summoned, and you'll be off the hook for a false alarm fee and the embarrassment of having the cops show up at your home only to find you in your bathrobe collecting the morning paper. Oops!

Automatic Garage Door Openers

As with all mechanical components in a home, an automatic garage door opener requires periodic maintenance to ensure safe and efficient operation. In fact, because the garage door is often the heaviest and largest single piece of moving equipment around a home, frequent testing and maintenance are especially important.

One of the best resources for garage door maintenance is the opener owner's manual. Lubrication requirements and adjustment details are typically found in this manual. If you don't have an owner's manual, you can usually order a replacement copy by contacting an installing dealer or the manufacturer. Some manufacturers even make owner's manuals available on the Internet. All you'll need is the brand and model number.

A visual inspection of the garage door springs, cables, rollers, and other door hardware is a great place to begin. Look for signs of wear and frayed or broken parts. Most minor repairs, such as roller replacement, can be performed by a handy do-it-yourselfer, while more complicated tasks should be handled by a qualified garage-door service technician. The springs and related hardware are under high tension and can cause severe injury when handled improperly.

Rollers, springs, hinges, and tracks require periodic lubrication. Use spray silicone, lightweight household oil, or white lithium grease according to the instructions in your owner's manual.

Periodically test the balance of the door. Start with the door closed. Disconnect the automatic opener release mechanism so that the door can be operated by hand. The door should lift smoothly and with little resistance. It should stay open around 3 to 4 feet above the floor. If it doesn't, it is out of balance and should be adjusted by a professional.

In addition to extending its life, monthly inspection and testing of the automatic opener can prevent serious injuries and property damage. Careless operation and allowing children to play with or use garage door opener controls are dangerous situations that can lead to tragic results. A few simple precautions can protect your family and friends from potential harm.

Never stand or walk under a moving door. Don't let children play "beat the door." Keep transmitters and remote controls out of reach of children and teach them that they are not toys. The push-button wall control should be out of reach of children (at least 5 feet from the floor) and away from all moving parts. The button should always be mounted where you can clearly see the door in full operation.

Test the force setting of the opener by holding up the bottom of the door as it closes. If the door does not reverse readily, the force is excessive and needs adjusting. The owner's manual will explain how to adjust the force sensitivity.

To avoid entrapment, perform the 1-inch reversing test after any repairs or adjustments are made to the garage door or opener. Do this by simply placing a 2- by 4-inch block of wood flat on the floor in the door's path before activating the door. If the door fails to immediately stop and reverse when it strikes the wood, disconnect the opener and use the door manually until the system can be repaired or replaced.

Since April 1982, federal law has required that a closing garage door that is operated by an automatic opener must reverse off of a 2-inch block.

Even with the safety improvements resulting from the April 1982 legislation, injuries continue to occur, and safety is still an issue. Consequently, a new law as of January 1, 1993, requires that a garage door opener must be equipped with a monitored non-contact safety reversing device or safety edge that stops and reverses a closing garage door.

An example of such a safety device is an electronic beam sensor that is installed at either side of the door opening, which, when broken, causes the door to stop and reverse itself.

A second safety feature is a pressure-sensitive electronic rubber strip that attaches to the bottom of the door where it makes contact with the floor. Just as with the beam sensor, when engaged, this safety edge causes the door to stop and reverse itself, avoiding injury or damage to property.

Some of the most common garage door opener problems and their respective solutions are as follows:

- ✔ If an opener raises but won't close the door, the safety beam sensor may be faulty, misaligned, or unplugged.

- ✔ An opener that operates by remote control, but not by the wall switch, is the sign of a short in the wiring or a loose connection at the switch.

- ✔ A remote control that doesn't work may be something as simple as a weak or dead transmitter battery, an antenna wire on the opener that is not properly exposed, or a dead transmitter.

- ✔ If the opener is operating, but the door doesn't open, it may be due to a worn gear or chain drive sprocket, a broken chain, or the door has disengaged from the operator.

- ✔ An opener that operates by itself can be caused by a faulty transmitter, a short in the wall switch, a faulty circuit board, or a stray signal — the latter being very rare.

- ✔ If the remote control only operates the door when it is located a distance of 25 feet or less from the opener, the battery in the remote is usually weak or the signal is poor.

- ✔ A door that reverses while closing, or that doesn't completely open or close, is usually obstructed or binding. This condition can also be caused when the open limit or sensitivity is set wrong.

- ✔ A straining opener usually occurs when safety reversing is activated or the close limit is set improperly.

Electrical Safety

You should leave most electrical work to a qualified electrician. It's time to call the electrician when you see any of the following:

- Habitually flickering lights
- A breaker that repeatedly pops
- A fuse that repeatedly burns out

Any of these can signal a loose connection or a circuit that is overloaded, which can ultimately cause a house fire.

If you are plagued by flickering lights, blown fuses, and popped breakers, we suggest that you call in a pro. A professional electrician gives you the power you need to keep from blowing a fuse of your own.

Ground Fault Circuit Interrupters

The Ground Fault Circuit Interrupter (GFCI) was developed to help save people from getting shocked. The easiest way to think of a GFCI is to remember that a normal circuit breaker protects property, while a GFCI protects people.

When a short or ground fault occurs, the GFCI detects it. Any variation indicates some of the current is going where it's not supposed to go and is creating a shock hazard. When this occurs, the GFCI trips in one-fortieth of a second — a short enough period of time so that most healthy people aren't injured.

GFCIs should be installed at all receptacles within 4 feet of a sink, at all exterior and garage receptacles, and at all electric fixtures over showers and tubs.

All GFCI receptacles have test buttons. You should test each GFCI receptacle in your home at least once a month. If the test doesn't trip the breaker, replace the GFCI immediately.

Chapter 21

Shutting Down Your Home

. . . .

In This Chapter

▶ Reducing risk when you're away

▶ Improving everyday home security

▶ Shutting down your home for extended periods

▶ Keeping a home shutdown checklist

. . . .

*Y*our home is always most vulnerable, and at its greatest risk, when you are not there — whether for a few minutes, hours, days, weeks, or months at a time.

Vulnerable and at risk? From what you say? Everything, ranging from any conceivable type of normal household malfunction to breakins, burglaries, and various mishaps.

In this chapter, we tell you about some of the things you should do to minimize the risk of damage to your home when you're not there.

Water, Water, Everywhere

All those little hoses and lines — in the kitchen, bathroom, or utility room — that bring water to your sinks, toilet, and washing machine are also potential causes of floods in the rooms they serve. They create a messy problem if they break while you're at home. They spell disaster if you're out for the day and a catastrophe if you're gone for weeks — or months!

Turn off the water supply valves to each water-fueled fixture in the home. This provides iron-clad flood insurance (at least for these items) for as long as you intend to be away — up to and including a yearlong around-the-world cruise. Why not simply turn off the main water shutoff valve? Simple — because the water supply to most landscape irrigation systems is controlled by the same valve, you would return from your extending trip to find your garden transformed into desolate surroundings.

Checking your connections

Check the rubber hoses leading to your washing machine periodically and especially before leaving on a trip. If they feel brittle, it's time for replacement. Never thought about it, you say? We guarantee you will — one day, when they burst, and they surely will, sooner or later. Even when you're home, one should always keep these hoses fresh to prevent problems. You can reduce risk even further by upgrading hoses with an outer covering of braided stainless steel.

The same thinking goes for the small water leads to your kitchen and bathroom sinks and toilets. Over a period of time, these small lines (often only lightweight metals) can corrode due to natural electrolysis and may develop pinhole-sized leaks that can wet down a room in minutes. If this happens at your house, want to bet when that will be? We're guessing that it's while you're away in Hawaii for a few weeks.

Obviously, these water leads need frequent inspection to spot potential problems — and like their washing machine cousins, they too can be easily and inexpensively replaced or upgraded (again with stainless steel braid covered lines) for greater peace of mind.

Also, open a faucet and let it drip ever so slowly. This isn't the best suggestion when it comes to conserving water, but can save thousands of gallons in the long run by preventing a burst water line from freezing conditions.

Your Turn-Off Checklist

When you prepare to be away, go through the house and think about the following:

- ✔ If it uses water, turn off the supply. This includes valves located in cabinets below sinks that supply hot and cold water to faucets, the water supply to each toilet, the water supply to an automatic icemaker, and so on.

- ✔ If it uses electricity, unplug it. This includes all electronics and appliances such as a VCR, DVD, stereo, television, window air conditioner, washer, dryer, and so on. Resetting clocks is easier than replacement or a possible malfunction that results in a fire.

- ✔ If it uses energy, turn it down, turn it up, or turn it off. Think of the furnace or air conditioner or electric water heater.

- ✔ If it burns fuel, remove the ignition source, such as the water heater, a gas dryer, furnace, gas cooktop or range, or automatic ignition fireplace.

Preventing Break-Ins

Over 50 percent of all break-ins are simply crimes of opportunity. These are situations where intruders are virtually invited in by unlocked windows and doors.

Beyond issuing an open invitation to intruders by leaving things unlocked, some homeowners often make things even more inviting by providing shrubbery to conceal actions and the cover of darkness to work within. These homeowners should be listed as accomplices to the crimes that befall their homes since they do everything possible to assist in the crime.

In contrast, a few simple guidelines can make your home as tight as the proverbial bug in a rug, affording you greater safety while you're home and when you're away:

- Check all window and door locks to make sure that they are operating properly. Install backup or secondary security locks and latches at vulnerable locations. Then use these simple protections — always.

- Add a heavy-duty security storm door to outside doors and toughen up sliding patio doors with pin-locks and crossbars to deter forced opening.

- Trim back any thin shrubbery and bushes near windows and doors that might provide cover for a burglar's work-in-process.

- Add outdoor security lighting with a motion detector on/off control. (See *Home Improvement For Dummies,* by Hamilton and Hamilton, published by IDG Books Worldwide, Inc., for more information on installing a motion detector.)

- Add metal security bars over windows and doors in high-risk areas, such as basement windows. Make sure that these bars have quick-release safety latches for easy emergency escape for those inside.

- Never hide a house key in an obvious location. Even amateurs know most favorites, like under mats, in flower pots, and inside fake rocks.

- Close drapes and shades when you're out to prevent looky-loo's.

- Always watch for unusual activity and new faces near your home.

Making It Look Like You're at Home

Even first-time burglars-in-training know it's better to hit an empty house than to break in and possibly contend with a gun-toting, professional wrestler-sized, teamster-tough, angered homeowner.

'Tis the season for emergencies

During the holidays, thieves know that home-owners are busy with things other than security issues — and that their houses often contain extra goodies, like presents and lots of cash for holiday shopping. Don't leave large displays of gifts and presents in plain view when out. After the holidays, engrave all your new gifts with your driver's license number as soon as you can.

If your holiday involved decorating a tree, keep it well-watered for fire safety, and unplug all indoor decorative lighting before leaving the house.

Even greenhorn thieves know to look for tell-tale signs that the owners are away. They know the difference between your spending an evening at Jane's versus having left the country for a three-week African safari. What do they look for? First and foremost is a home that is dark, quiet, and appears to be unoccupied at the moment. In criminal jargon, it's known as "casing the joint."

The best way to fool them? Make it look like you're home! Use the following tips to scare off potential invaders:

- Use timers in different rooms to turn lights on and off.
- Have others turn the TV or radio on and off at normal hours as well.
- Leave a car parked in the driveway. It says: Somebody's home.
- Have a friend or neighbor pick up mail and newspapers until you return. As an alternative, stop all mail and newspaper deliveries until you return.
- Never, ever change the message on your answering machine to proudly announce something like "The Wilson's are off to Hawaii. See ya'll in three weeks! Aloha!" You may as well be there to help crooks load their truck with your belongings.
- Arrange to have the lawn mowed. In winter, keep snow on front porches, sidewalks, and driveways shoveled.

In addition, consider the following before leaving on an extended trip:

- Hide all valuables in unlikely places, like the freezer or empty boxes and cans in kitchen cabinets.
- Make sure a neighbor has your itinerary and phone numbers to contact you in the event of an emergency.

Long-Term Considerations

Being away for really long periods of time requires even more planning and efforts toward prevention.

After you take care of the basics (as outlined in the previous sections), think about what maintenance you might perform on an ongoing basis if you were to be home during that period of time. Do that maintenance before you leave, or arrange to have someone else do it.

Think about what will happen weather-wise while you're gone and do anything that will be needed in advance of leaving. This includes putting up storm windows, cleaning out gutters, and any other normal seasonal chores that would normally be necessary during the time period the home will be sitting unattended.

In winter months especially, when heating is discontinued for extended lengths of time, freezing pipes are a serious consideration. Your best defense against burst pipes and other damage is to turn off the main valve at the water meter, or turn off the pump (if you have a well), and open all faucets and valves to allow pipes to drain somewhat.

There will always be some residual water, especially in p-traps under sinks, in drain lines, and in toilets. Purchase a gallon or two of special non-toxic Propylene Glycol anti-freeze offered for RVs, boats, and lightly insulated cabins; that, when used full strength, protects from freezing down to 50 degrees below zero. It works extremely well, and only costs a few dollars per gallon. You can find it at most RV dealers and big automotive stores.

Propylene Glycol can also be poured into toilets and drains. In the spring, when you reestablish housekeeping, just flush well before using — and you'll be all set.

Never use automotive antifreeze to prevent a home's water pipes from freezing. It's toxic and poisonous. It also disrupts septic tanks and contaminates drinking water and the environment when flushed into sewers.

See the Annual Home Maintenance Schedule in this book for more tips on getting ready for winter.

Part V:
The Part of Tens

The 5th Wave   By Rich Tennant

"Hellfire or brimstone – which one's it gonna be? I can't hold these all day."

In this part . . .

If you think that David Letterman has the market cornered when it comes to top ten lists, you are in for one big surprise. Prepare yourself for the crème de la crème of maintenance tips, tasks, and hints that will save you money, bring you comfort, and perhaps even save your life. Bet you Letterman never came up with a list that good.

Chapter 22

Ten Important Preventive Maintenance Tasks

- ✔ **Caulking:** This stuff is pumped into a gap to make it airtight or water-tight. There are a million different types and colors. It sticks to just about anything.

- ✔ **Painting:** Painting provides a protective coating to a surface that pre-vents rot and deterioration and makes for easy cleaning.

- ✔ **Cleaning:** One of the least expensive and most important maintenance tasks. It is almost always the first step when performing a specific main-tenance task.

- ✔ **Replacing filters:** Good air quality in your home can make you feel better and prevent illness — especially if you have allergies. Replacing furnace filters often helps keep the air in your home clean. It's like taking out the garbage.

- ✔ **Lubricating:** A little lubrication can go a long way in helping parts move more easily. Lubrication puts less stress on a motor, which reduces its operating cost and extends its life.

- ✔ **Controlling infiltration:** A fancy name for getting rid of drafts around windows, doors, pipes, and electrical switches and outlets. This is done with insulation, caulking, weather-stripping, expandable foam, and foam gaskets. Controlling infiltration makes you more comfortable, lowers your utility bill, and saves energy.

- ✔ **Testing:** If it has a "test" button, test it! Smoke detectors, water heater pressure and temperature relief valves, and carbon monoxide detectors are a few examples. Many a life has been lost due to a faulty smoke detector.

- ✔ **Keeping up with heating, ventilating, and air conditioning systems:** These systems contain motors, fan belts, refrigerant, tanks, burners, flues, filters, dampers, ducts, and a host of other elements. Clean, adjust, and lubricate them often for maximum efficiency.

- ✔ **Caring for drains:** Few things are more irritating than a backed-up sink, an overflowing toilet, or a slow-draining tub. Keeping your drains running freely can help prevent nasty accidents from occurring and eliminate foul odors.

✔ **Looking after water shed:** Water is without a doubt one of a home's biggest threats. Be it from rain, snow, or irrigation, water can turn your crawlspace or basement into a pond, pool, or steam bath. Gutters, downspouts, drainage systems, and grading are your best defense.

✔ **Sweeping out the chimney:** Nothing is as romantic as a crackling fire. Nothing can level your house faster than the explosion and raging fire from a creosote-laden chimney. Save the fireworks for the fairgrounds on the 4th of July — clean your chimney at least once a season.

Chapter 23

Ten Tasks to Address Every Month

● ●

✔ Check the furnace and air-conditioner filters.

✔ Check water filters and softeners.

✔ Clean the dryer duct and filter.

✔ Clean and freshen sink drains.

✔ Test smoke detectors.

✔ Test CO detectors.

✔ Check the PTR valve on the water heater.

✔ Flush the water heater.

✔ Clean and/or lubricate at least one major appliance.

✔ Test the GFCI receptacles.

Chapter 24

Ten Hints for Your Maintenance Checklist

- ✔ Never lubricate hinges, window frames, or other metals with oil or water-based products. Use graphite, bee's wax, or waterless silicone.
- ✔ Rub a latch key with the tip of a pencil to lubricate locks.
- ✔ Cleaning refrigerator coils allows the refrigerator to operate more efficiently.
- ✔ Wood and water don't mix. Most canned polishes are mostly water. Use equal parts of turpentine, boiled linseed oil, and white vinegar.
- ✔ When you change your clock for Daylight Saving Time, change the batteries on safety devices, such as smoke detectors and CO detectors.
- ✔ Never use a bulb size that exceeds the fixture rating.
- ✔ Never use a penny to bypass a fuse in the fuse box. Doing so could create an electrical fire.
- ✔ Cleaning your water heater and regularly changing the cathodic anode makes the heater last longer.
- ✔ Never paint over mildew — it will only return.
- ✔ Don't attempt a task that's better left to a pro.

Part VI:
The Home Maintenance Schedule

The 5th Wave   By Rich Tennant

"First of all, the stupid elves never return my phone calls, and now I find out they put the roof on without the nougat sealer."

In this part . . .

Any one you talk to will tell you that a contractor is never on schedule and rarely in budget. So, we figured that since, as contractors, we constantly have our backs up against the scheduling wall, that we would afford you the same courtesy. Actually, it isn't quite that bad. This isn't a performance schedule — it's a home maintenance schedule that suggests what you should do and when you should do it. Consider the content a gentle reminder or two, or three . . .

The Home Maintenance Schedule

Timing is everything. This certainly holds true when it comes to home maintenance. Maintenance performed regularly and "on schedule" provides optimum longevity and helps prevent potential breakdowns or malfunctions.

The other popular saying that holds true for home maintenance is "Better safe than sorry." Beyond maintenance procedures for operational sake, the primary (and most important) reason for checking, inspecting, and constantly tuning up your home is to ensure maximum safety for you, your family, and friends.

Together, these two concepts — faithfully and consistently employed — will help you turn frequent frustration and constant chaos into a better life. One filled with the joy that modern conveniences are intended to bring.

We have designed the following checklists so that you can pick and choose what's right for you, your home, and your family. Whether you live in a typical suburban house, a condominium, a high-rise apartment, or a palatial country estate, you're sure to find many items that pertain to you and your home.

Seasonal Maintenance Checklist

Spring

✔ Check gutters and downspouts for debris; touch up paint (Chapter 3).

✔ Check for efflorescence, fungus, and mold in the crawlspace or basement (Chapter 3).

✔ Pressure wash and repair exterior siding (Chapter 4).

✔ Inspect exterior walls and roof for winter and seasonal storm damage (Chapter 4).

✔ Inspect the attic for signs of roof leaks (Chapter 4).

✔ Clean the roof and oil wood shingles (Chapter 4).

✔ Caulk and patch all exterior cracks and openings (Chapter 5).

✔ Caulk window trim and door frames (Chapter 5).

✔ Repair holes and tears in window and door screens and wash them (Chapter 5).

✔ Adjust sticking doors (Chapter 5).

✔ Tighten and lubricate door knobs, locks, and latches (Chapter 5).

✔ Clean and preserve (or paint) your wood deck (Chapter 6).

✔ Replace batteries in irrigation controller (Chapter 8).

✔ Clean adjust, lubricate, and tighten sprinkler heads (Chapter 8).

✔ Check for damaged sprinkler head risers (Chapter 8).

✔ Inspect railing and ornamental iron for rust and touch up paint (Chapter 9).

✔ Clean and degrease exterior concrete surfaces (Chapter 10).

✔ Spring clean stained plumbing fixtures (Chapter 12).

✔ Clean faucet aerators (Chapter 12).

✔ Test furnace, clean burners, and lubricate (Chapter 14).

✔ Have your air conditioning serviced (Chapter 14).

✔ Clean lint from dryer duct and from the interior of dryer housing (Chapter 17).

✔ Inspect washing machine water supply hoses and clean filters (Chapter 17).

✔ Lubricate door hinges and drawer glides (Chapter 18).

Fall

- ✔ Check gutters and downspouts for debris; touch up paint (Chapter 3).
- ✔ Repair (tuckpoint) mortar joints around masonry surfaces (Chapter 3).
- ✔ Check for efflorescence, fungus, and mold in the crawlspace or basement (Chapter 3).
- ✔ Prepare for and prevent roof ice dams (Chapter 4).
- ✔ Look for loose shingles, siding, trim or anything else that could become airborne in a winter storm (Chapter 4).
- ✔ Caulk and patch all exterior cracks and openings (Chapter 5).
- ✔ Caulk window trim and door frames (Chapter 5).
- ✔ Check the condition of heat duct and water pipe insulation (Chapter 5).
- ✔ Check roof decks for deterioration, damaged flashing, and waterproof integrity (Chapter 6).
- ✔ Clean and degrease exterior concrete surfaces (Chapter 10).
- ✔ Seal and protect all concrete and masonry surfaces (Chapter 10).
- ✔ Reverse motor or install ceiling fans (Chapter 14).
- ✔ Test furnace, clean burners, and lubricate (Chapter 14).
- ✔ Open and adjust damper (Chapter 15).
- ✔ Clean and adjust fireplace screen and doors (Chapter 15).
- ✔ Check condition of chimney spark arrestor (Chapter 15).
- ✔ Clean lint from dryer duct and from the interior of dryer housing (Chapter 17).
- ✔ Inspect washing machine water supply hoses and clean filters (Chapter 17).
- ✔ Lubricate door hinges and drawer glides (Chapter 18).

Things to Do Annually

- ✔ Check for and repair bouncy or squeaky floors (Chapter 3).
- ✔ Repair insulation, weatherstripping, and air leaks (Chapter 5).
- ✔ Pressure wash and oil or repaint wood fencing and check for rot (Chapter 6).
- ✔ Install or check termite flashing at decks- and fence-to-house connections (Chapter 6).
- ✔ Inspect and test landscape irrigation system (Chapter 8).

✔ Clean and check irrigation anti-siphon valves and backflow prevention devices (Chapter 8).

✔ Check the water heater anode and the condition of the dip tube (Chapter 11).

✔ Check and clean water heater burners, tank, and flue (Chapter 11).

✔ Clean or replace electric water heater elements (Chapter 11).

✔ Clean toilet siphon jets (Chapter 12).

✔ Ensure that tub overflow is secure to avoid flood at tub (Chapter 13).

✔ Bleed air-logged radiators (Chapter 14).

✔ Professionally inspect and clean fireplace and chimney (Chapter 15).

✔ Fill cracks, gauges, and nail pops in wallboard (Chapter 16).

✔ Repair sagging plaster at ceilings (Chapter 16).

✔ Scrub and touch-up-paint walls, ceilings, and painted cabinets (Chapters 16 and 18).

✔ Check and adjust the oven temperature (Chapter 17).

✔ Check and replace appliance lights (Chapter 17).

✔ Clean refrigerator door gaskets and lubricate hinges (Chapter 17).

✔ Vacuum refrigerator condenser coils (Chapter 17).

✔ Seal and protect tile and grout (Chapter 18).

✔ Update your emergency preparedness kit and provisions (Chapter 20).

✔ Vacuum dust off smoke alarms and carbon monoxide detectors (Chapter 20).

✔ Check flexible gas line connections at appliances (Chapter 20).

Things To Do Monthly

✔ Check water purification and water softener filters (Chapter 11).

✔ Test the pressure and temperature relief valve for proper operation (Chapter 11).

✔ Clean and freshen your drains (Chapter 13).

✔ Degrease and freshen your disposal using vinegar ice cubes (Chapter 13).

✔ Clean and replace furnace and air conditioner filters (Chapter 14).

✔ Check the steam system safety valve and steam gauge (Chapter 14).

✔ Check the water level of your steam system (Chapter 14).

✔ Clean the filter on the interior of wall mount heat pumps (Chapter 14).

✔ Check air intakes for insect blockages and debris (Chapter 14).

✔ Clean range hood filter (Chapters 17).

✔ Appliance cleaning using All Purpose, Handy-Dandy Cleaner (Chapter 17).

✔ Remove and clean range burners (Chapter 17).

✔ Wash and rinse clothes-dryer lint-screen (Chapter 17).

✔ Inspect, clean, and lubricate at least one major appliance per manufacturer's instructions (Chapter 17).

✔ Deep clean laminate surfaces (Chapter 18).

✔ Clean and brighten tile and grout (Chapter 18).

✔ Deep clean all types of flooring (Chapter 19).

✔ Test fire extinguisher pressure gauges (Chapter 20).

✔ Test smoke detector sensors and alarms (Chapter 20).

✔ Test carbon monoxide detectors (Chapter 20).

✔ Test auto reverse safety feature on garage door openers (Chapter 20).

Shutting Down

Exterior

✔ Open outside faucets and wrap with towel or cloth.

✔ Disconnect all LP gas tanks and safely store them away from house.

✔ Wrap all LP regulator valves in plastic to prevent corrosion.

✔ Stop mail, newspaper, and magazine delivery.

✔ Arrange for neighbor to check property.

✔ Alert local police that you'll be gone.

✔ Arrange to have lawn mowed or snow shoveled.

Interior

✔ If electricity remains on, put lights and radio on timers.

✔ Remove valuables or place them out of sight.

✔ Draw drapes and blinds to prevent looky-loos.

HVAC and plumbing

✔ Turn off well pump or close water main valve (Chapter 13).

✔ Open all faucets — especially break a union near shut-off valve to allow maximum amount of water to drain out.

✔ Drain flexible spray hoses in sinks and hand-held showers.

✔ Turn off all water lead lines under sink, lavatories, and toilets (Chapter 12).

✔ Use a plunger to push water out of all p-traps (in sinks, tubs, toilets, and so on) (Chapter 12).

✔ Turn off or drain water heater (Chapter 14).

Appliances

✔ Turn off washing machine inlet hoses; remove and drain.

✔ Clear water valve by setting timer for fill cycle. Press "warm water" setting and run a few seconds.

✔ Remove dishwasher inlet and outlet hoses. Operate pump to clear valve. Remove drain hose.

✔ Unplug all electric appliances and electronics big and small.

Winterizing

✔ Insulate water lines to prevent freezing (Chapter 5).

✔ Winterize your pool or spa (Chapter 7).

✔ Turn off and drain your sprinkler system (Chapter 8).

✔ Drain, insulate, or remove irrigation backflow prevention devices (Chapter 8).

✔ Install storm windows.

✔ Clean, oil, and store all garden tools for winter.

✔ Clean, wrap, and store all garden furniture for winter.

✔ Thin major trees and shrubs prior to winter to allow sunshine through during the cold months.

Extra Special Maintenance Tasks

- ✔ If your refrigerator is more than 10 years old, defrost and clean every two months (Chapter 17).

- ✔ Inspect electrical plug-in tips for grease or corrosion weekly if stovetop range is used often (Chapter 17).

- ✔ Clean removable gas burners weekly (if stovetop range is used often) using baking soda and water with a stiff brush (Chapter 17).

- ✔ Run dishwasher at least once a week to keep seals moist and to prevent leaks and eventual failure caused by seals drying (Chapter 17).

- ✔ Save manufacturers' instructions and product manuals for maintenance instructions and cleaning tips.

- ✔ Check and replace all exterior light bulbs.

- ✔ Use 1 teaspoon of Tang each week to keep the inside of your dishwasher clean (Chapter 17).

- ✔ Make sure that emergency shut off wrenches are present at gas and water locations (Chapter 20 and 11).

- ✔ Replace smoke detectors if they are over 10 years old or they have been operational for more than 87,000 continual hours (Chapter 20).

- ✔ Review shut-off procedures for electric, gas, and water mains (Chapter 13 and 20).

- ✔ Replace smoke alarm and carbon monoxide batteries at least semi-annually (Chapter 20).

- ✔ Test back-up battery at burglar alarm at least twice annually (Chapter 20).

- ✔ Have your home inspected for termites or other structural pests at least once annually.

- ✔ Have a professional check your septic tank at least once annually and drain as necessary.

Journal

January: _____
_____
_____
_____

February: _____
_____
_____
_____

March: _____
_____
_____
_____

April: _____
_____
_____
_____

May: _____
_____
_____
_____

June: _____
_____
_____
_____

Journal

July: _____

_____

_____

_____

August: _____

_____

_____

_____

September: _____

_____

_____

_____

October: _____

_____

_____

_____

November: _____

_____

_____

_____

December: _____

_____

_____

_____

Index

• *D* •

• *E* •

• J •

• K •

• L •

Notes

Notes

Notes

IDG BOOKS WORLDWIDE
BOOK REGISTRATION

Register This Book and Win!

We want to hear from you!

Visit **http://my2cents.dummies.com** to register this book and tell us how you liked it!

- ✔ Get entered in our monthly prize giveaway.

- ✔ Give us feedback about this book — tell us what you like best, what you like least, or maybe what you'd like to ask the author and us to change!

- ✔ Let us know any other *For Dummies®* topics that interest you.

Your feedback helps us determine what books to publish, tells us what coverage to add as we revise our books, and lets us know whether we're meeting your needs as a *For Dummies* reader. You're our most valuable resource, and what you have to say is important to us!

Not on the Web yet? It's easy to get started with *Dummies 101®: The Internet For Windows® 98* or *The Internet For Dummies®* at local retailers everywhere.

Or let us know what you think by sending us a letter at the following address:

For Dummies Book Registration
Dummies Press
10475 Crosspoint Blvd.
Indianapolis, IN 46256

™

...FOR DUMMIES

BESTSELLING
BOOK SERIES